Web Pages the Smart Way

Web Pages the Smart Way

A Painless Guide to Creating and Posting Your Own Website

Joseph T. Sinclair

AMACOM

American Management Association
New York • Atlanta • Boston • Chicago • Kansas City • San Francisco • Washington, D.C.
Brussels • Mexico City • Tokyo • Toronto

Special discounts on bulk quantities of AMACOM books are available to corporations, professional associations, and other organizations. For details, contact Special Sales Department, AMACOM, a division of American Management Association, 1601 Broadway, New York, NY 10019.
Tel.: 212-903-8316. Fax: 212-903-8083.
Web Site: www.amacombooks.org

This publication is designed to provide accurate and authoritative information in regard to the subject matter covered. It is sold with the understanding that the publisher is not engaged in rendering legal, accounting, or other professional service. If legal advice or other expert assistance is required, the services of a competent professional person should be sought.

Library of Congress Cataloging-in-Publication Data

Sinclair, Joseph T.
    Web Pages the Smart Way : a painless guide to creating and posting your own website / Joseph T. Sinclair
        p. cm.
        ISBN 0-8144-7102-1
        1. Web sites--Design. 2. Web publishing. I. Title
    TK5105.S88.S592000
    005.7'2--dc21   00-059414

Printing number
10   9   8   7   6   5   4   3   2   1

To my mother, Miriam Christian Hoener Sinclair, who has always been supportive in everything I've done throughout my life.

Contents

Introduction xxvii

I. Web Page Basics 1

1. Making a Web Page 3

Getting Started 4
    Creating a Working Folder 4
    Text for Tutorials 5
    Using Netscape Composer 6
    Entering Text in Composer 6
    Using FrontPage Express 9
    Entering Text in FrontPage Express 9
Entering Text with Copy & Paste 12
Summary 12

2. Getting Organized 15

Authoring Software 16
   Authoring 16
   Netscape Composer 17
   Microsoft FrontPage Express 18
Downloading the Authoring Software 20
   Looking for Downloads 20
   Download Procedures 20
      Specific Downloads 21
      Download Folder 21
      Zip Files 21
      Automatic Installation 21
A Few Words about the Authoring Programs 22
   How Far? 22
   Word Processor 23
   And Vice Versa 24
Image Editing Software 25
   On-Your-Disk-Ware 25
   Freeware 25
Downloading FTP Software 26
Other Software 27
Summary 27

3. Testing Your Work 29

Testing Procedures 30
   Using Your Programs 30
      Working on the Web Page 30
      Saving the Web Page 31
      Browser 31
      Refreshing the Web Page 32
   Different Resolutions 32
   Not a Separate Process 32
Advanced Testing Procedures 32

What Is a Web Page Anyway? 34

  Where Is It? 35

  What's a Website? 36

  How Does It All Work? 37

    Test 37

    Upload 37

    Host Computer 37

    Web Surfers 38

    Request 38

    Receive and View 38

  Summary 39

4. Making the Text Look Better **41**

Making a Table with Composer 45

  Adjusting the Table 47

  Placing the Text in the Table 47

  Typeset the Headings 49

  Changing the Type Size 49

Making a Table with FrontPage Express 51

  Adjusting the New Table 53

  Placing the Text in the New Table 53

  Typeset the Headings 55

  Changing the Font Size 55

The HTML 57

Summary 59

5. Adding Pictures **61**

Getting Ready 63

Embedding Pictures with Composer 63

Embedding Pictures with FrontPage Express 67

Refinements for Embedding Pictures 71

  Composer 71

  FrontPage Express 72

Correct Pixel Dimensions 73

Summary 75

6. Adding Links 77

Creating a Link with Composer 79

Creating a Link with FrontPage Express 81

Image Tricks 82

Image Link 83

Linked Image 83

Learning about URLs 84

Absolute Reference 84

Relative References 85

Advance 85

Retreat 86

Retreat and Advance 86

Test Immediately 86

Good Practice 87

File Names 87

Anchors 88

Composer 88

FrontPage Express 89

Creating an Email Link 90

Summary 91

7. Fill-in-the-Blank Web Pages 93

Fill-in-the-Blank Web Host 94

PageWizard 95

Page Builder 96

Multiple Web Pages 99

Templates 99

Composer and FrontPage Express 100

Composer 100

FrontPage Express 100

HTML 101
Summary 102

II. Web Page Skills 103

8. Making Text Look Good 105

Communicating with Text 106
What Visitors Have 106
Layout 107
   Steal That Web Page 109
   Search for Templates 109
Typesetting 110
   Not Typewriting 110
   Follow the Traditional Guidelines 110
      Italic 110
      Bold 111
      Bold Italic 111
      All Caps 111
      Superscripts and Subscripts 111
      Bullets 111
      Numbers 111
      Border 112
      Type Size 112
      Rules 112
      Underlines 112
Add an Image 113
Advanced Web Typesetting 113
Text for Tutorials 114
Using Composer 115
   Bold and Italic 115
   Change Type Size 116
   Change Typeface (Font) 116
   Headings 116

Centering 117
Bulleted Lists 117
Rules (Horizontal Lines) 117
Numbered Lists 118
Unnumbered Text 119
        Lists 119
        Sidebars 121
Using FrontPage Express 121
Bold and Italic 121
Change Type Size 121
Change Typeface (Font) 122
Headings 122
Centering 122
Bulleted Lists 122
Rules (Horizontal Lines) 123
Numbered Lists 123
Unnumbered Text 124
        Lists 125
        Sidebars 125
The Future of Text 126
Summary 127

9. Adding Color **129**
Color Basics 130
Color Combinations 130
The Great White Problem 132
Web Color 132
        RGB 132
        Hex 133
Why Color Designations? 134
Composer Colors 135
FrontPage Express Color 136
Background Pictures 136

Design Elements 137

Summary 138

10. Getting Digital Photographs 139

Digitizing Photographs 140

Ordinary Scanner 140

Film Scanner 140

Professional Scanner 140

Kodak Picture CD 140

Kodak Photo CD 141

Digital Cameras 141

Consumer Digital Cameras 141

Professional Digital Cameras 142

Camcorders 143

Image Files 143

Stock Photos 143

Quality 144

Resolution 144

Devices 145

The Aesthetic Factor 145

Summary 145

11. Preparing Pictures 147

Web Image Files 148

GIF 148

JPEG 148

PNG 149

Choosing an Image Editor 149

Using an Image Editor 151

Where? 151

Saving Images 152

Contrast 152

Brightness 153

Cropping 154

Resizing 155

Sharpen 156

Making Text Images 157

Making Design Elements 160

Changing Colors 160

Making Transparent GIFs 161

Planning 162

Summary 163

12. Adding Navigation Menus 165

Using Tables for Menus 166

Multi-Row, One Column 166

Composer 166

FrontPage Express 169

Multi-Row, Multi-Column 171

Using Composer 171

Using FrontPage Express 173

A Line Menu 174

Using Pictures in Menus 174

Imagemaps 175

Summary 175

13. Using Tables for Layout 177

Multiple Columns with Composer 178

Text and Menu 178

A Table 179

Multiple Columns with FrontPage Express 181

Text and Menu 181

A Table 183

More Columns 185

Text Plus Two 185

Broken Text Column 188

Summary 189

III. Posting Web Pages 191

14. What Is a Web Host? 193

What Is a Server? 194

Where Is the Web Server? 195

Internet Service Provider (ISP) 195

Dial-Up Connections 195

Web Hosting 196

Network Server Computer (Intranet) 197

Co-Location Computer 198

Direct Connection Computer 198

Other Web Hosting Considerations 199

The 7 x 24 Grind 199

More than Web Pages 199

Media Server 200

Database Server 200

Applications Server 200

Summary 201

15. Choosing a Web Host 203

Criteria for Choosing 204

Minimum Criteria 204

Special Criteria 206

Pricing 207

The Norm 207

The Smorgasbord 208

The Multiple Host Approach 208

Traffic Charges 209

Hometown Web Hosting? 209

Host Yourself 210

National Online Services 210

Summary 210

16. Uploading Your Web Pages 211

Using WS_FTP Lite 212

Connecting 213

Uploading 215

Other Functions 215

Other Software 216

Other Chores 217

Authoring Uploads 217

Composer 217

FrontPage Express 218

Download-Upload 218

Summary 219

17. Registering a Web Address 221

What You Get with Your ISP 222

On Your Own 223

Choosing a Name 223

Conforming to Your Business Name 223

Choosing a New Name 224

Nonbusiness Names 225

Choosing a Registrar 225

Before You Register 226

Making the Registration 226

Expenses 226

Purchasing a Domain Name 227

What You Can Do 227

Summary 228

IV. Website Skills 229

18. Storing and Linking Web Pages 231

Folders 232

Storage by Media 233
Storage by Sections 233
Storage by Media and Sections 234
Links 234
Absolute Links 235
Relative Links 235
Multiple Domain Websites 235
Two Domains 236
Website Visitor Confusion? 236
Website Structure 238
Summary 238

19. Organizing Web Pages 239
Interactivity 240
A Web of Links 242
Usability 244
Links 248
Navigational Links 248
Common Links 249
Convenience Links 249
Gratuitous Links 250
The Metaphor 251
Planning 252
Summary 252

V. Advanced Skills 253

20. Adding Dancing Digital Doodads 255
Animated GIFs 256
Templates Everywhere 256
JavaScripts 257
Dynamic HTML 261
SMIL 261

Other Technologies 262
Summary 262

21. Adding Special Software 263

CGI Scripts 264
JavaScript 265
Java 266
    Servlets 266
    Applets 266
    Example Applet 267
    Another Example 268
The Template Approach 270
Plug-ins 271
    Installing 271
    What's the Point? 271
Summary 272

22. Adding Sound and Video 273

Streaming Media Player 275
    RealPlayer 275
    QuickTime Player 276
    What Plays? 276
Encoding 276
Embedding 279
Delivery 280
    HTTP 280
    RealServer 281
Both 281
Summary 282

VI. Using Your Website 283

23. Sharing a Website with Others 285

Security 286

    Planning 286

    Limit Access 287

Asset Security 287

    Backup Tape 287

    Parallel Website 288

Business Website 288

Summary 289

24. Family Fun 291

    Share Photographs 292

    Share Privacy 292

    Family Forum 294

    Plain Old Website 294

    Family Voices 295

    Your Project 296

    Family History 297

    Vacation Communication 298

    Family Warehouse 298

    Family Investments 299

    Family Resumes 299

    Family Portal 299

Summary 300

25. Group Activities 301

    Schedule 302

    Sales 302

        eCommerce 303

        Fund-Raising 303

        Memberships.. 304

    Newsletter 304

    Web-Based Training 305

    Archives 306

    Directory 307

Forums 307
Special Information 308
Publicity 308
Vendors 309
Self-Promotion 309
Summary 309

26. Publishing 311

Opportunity 312
Guidelines 313
Usability 314
Readability 314
Print on Demand 315
Editing 315
Templates 315
The Other Half of the Story 316
Summary 317

VII. Using Your Website for Business 319

27. Determining a Business Purpose 321

General Purposes 322
Common Purposes 324
Brochure 324
Customer Service 325
Sales 326
Summary 326

28. Understanding eCommerce 327

Retail Transaction Procedures 328
Software 328
Catalog 330
Shopping Cart 330
Checkout 330

Shipping 330

Sales Tax 331

Payment Input 331

Notification 331

Order Processing 332

Merchant Account 332

Authorization Processing 332

What Does It Cost? 333

ISP Hosting 334

eCommerce Software 334

Credit Card Merchant Account 335

Credit Card Authorization Processing 335

Check Verification Processing 336

Package Deals 336

Marketing on the Web 337

Create Some Content 337

Court the Search Engines 338

Trade Links 338

Create Affiliates 339

Hang Out 339

Run eBay Auctions 340

Other Techniques 341

Avoid Cybermalls 341

Summary 341

29. Intranet **343**

Website 344

Personnel Publications 345

Maintenance Manuals 345

Policies and Procedures 345

Data Access 346

Records 346

Inspiration for the Troops 346

Ordering 346

Directory 347
WBT 347
Recoginition 347
Forums 348
Collaboration 348
Scheduling 348
Summary 349

Appendix I 7 Steps **351**

Obtain and Install Authoring Software 351
Open Composer or FrontPage Express 352
Type a Few Paragraphs 352
Put Headings before the Paragraphs 352
Typeset the Headings 352
Add an Image 352
Test Your Work 353

Appendix II HTML Tutorial **355**

Defining a Web Page 357
<html></html> 357
<head></head> 357
<title></title> 357
<body></body> 358
Typical Web Page Setup 358
Markups Alphabetically 359
<b></b> 360
<blockquote></blockquote> 360

 363
<dl></dl> 363
<dt> 366
<dd> 366
<div></div> 366
<font></font> 367
<h1></h1> 368

<hr> 369
<i></i> 370
<img scr=" "> 370
<ol></ol> 370
<li> 372
<p></p> 372
<sub></sub> 373
<sup></sup> 373
<table></table> 374
<tr></tr> 378
<td></td> 378
<ul></ul> 379
 380
<!-- --> 381
Anchors & Hyperlinks 382
<a name=" "></a> 382
<a href=" "></a> 382
Example Web Page 383
Viewing the Web Page Source 384
Summary 385

Appendix III Useful Skills **387**
Using the File Directory 388
Navigating the Folder Tree............................ 389
Transferring Files 390
Creating New Folders 390
Saving to Folders 391
Copy & Paste 393
Cut & Paste 395
Saving Browsed Web Pages 395
Saving Images 395
Zip Files and Automatic Installation 395
Summary 396

Appendix IV Media Tips **397**

    Production 397

        Sound 398

        Video 398

        Creativity 399

    Digitizing 399

        Sound 399

        Video 400

    Editing 400

        Sound 401

        Video 401

Appendix V Top 14 Reasons **403**

    To Establish Your Own Personal Website

Appendix VI Top 12 Reasons **409**

    To Establish a Website at Your K-12 School

Acknowledgments

The stimulus to write this book came from three places. First, it came from the students and teachers at Mare Island Technology Academy charter middle school in Vallejo, California, who needed a quick and easy way to learn how to create Web pages for posting on the Web and on their intranet website. Second, it came from friends and colleagues working in corporations who wanted a quick and easy way to learn to publish on their intranet websites. Third, it came from Jacqueline Flynn my editor at AMACOM who perceived that even the most basic Web development books already published were not simple enough to encourage many of those who want to take part in the new world of the Web. She specifically had in mind family members who desire to post Web pages for family use. As a result, I have written a book intended to be a simple and direct means for anyone to quickly master basic Web-page-making skills. These diverse sources of personal aspiration reflect that the desire to learn how to create Web pages today is on its way to becoming almost universal.

My thanks to Tim Berners-Lee who invented the Web. When one writes about advanced Web topics, it is easy to lose sight of how simple and ingenious the Web is. When one writes about the basics, the genius of the Web is hard to overlook.

My hat's off to the Netscape (Mozilla) and Microsoft programmers who have given us such easy-to-use Web authoring programs in Composer and FrontPage Express. Thanks also to my agent Carole McClendon, Waterside Productions, and to Jacqueline Flynn, Michael Sivilli, Lydia Lewis, and the other folks at AMACOM who contributed to the book. And finally, thanks to my spouse Lani and daughter Brook who were, as always, supportive.

Introduction

This book gets you off to a quick start and builds your confidence. It shows you some Web tricks. It leaves out some of the glitz, but it aims to provide you with the basics painlessly. It includes much of the fun, such as color photographs. But in the end, if you want to be a Web developer, you'll have to move on to another book. This is not a thorough bible about Web authoring. It's an introductory book.

Most people don't find making Web pages difficult, and this book convinces you of that by helping you make a Web page in the first chapter. If you don't want to be a Web developer but you would like to make some Web pages, this book will help. If you want to be a Web developer but you don't want to learn too fast, this book sets a modest pace and covers basic Web development techniques.

The book requires that you feel comfortable using a PC, a Web browser, and a word processor. If you don't, you might want to learn some PC basics first before you start making Web pages.

With Apologies

This book uses the PC and Windows and is still a long book. To add step-by-step instruction for the Mac goes beyond my experience and would make the organization and length of the book a little too intimidating. So, if Mac users find the book useful, that's nice. But if you're a Mac user, it's not something you should count on. Sorry.

This book doesn't require expensive software. The book features Netscape Composer and Microsoft FrontPage Express, both free Web authoring programs and both powerful yet easy to use. In addition, the book features the popular freeware IrfanView image editor, also powerful and easy to use. Finally, the book illustrates WS_FTP Lite, a freeware program you can use to upload Web pages to a website. This book, of course, mentions software you can buy, but these free programs will take you a long way.

Beta

Netscape had not yet released Netscape Comunicator 6.0 before this book went to press. Hence, I used the beta version for the book, and there may be some differences between the beta verson and the final release. Such differences, if any, will affect primarily the step-by-step instruction.

Few software activities give a nonprogrammer the equivalent thrill of making his or her first Web page. The amazement comes not so much from the creation of the actual page—similar to creating a page with a word processor or desktop publisher—but from its immediate publication in an international medium that hundreds of millions of people can now see. You will never forget the first page you publish on the Web. And I hope to help you to do that with this book.

My First Web Page

In October 1994 I launched the Fine Food Emporium, the first gourmet food store on the Web. My next-door neighbors were in the food business and had lined up about two-dozen gourmet products to sell online. The first HTML book was not yet published, and I was self-taught from documents published by the Web Consortium (a tough way to learn). I worked diligently to create a catalog with scanned images from gourmet food brochures. The final website was attractive, because the images from the brochures were quite pleasing. I was so thrilled, I sent an email to Tim O'Reilly, publisher, O'Reilly & Associates, announcing the event.

Somehow I had exchanged an email or two with Tim prior to this significant event. He was one of the early pioneers of the commercial Web. At that time I was not an author and did not know Tim. He had just launched the first portal (megawebsite) on the Internet, the Global Network Navigator, a huge undertaking. In retrospect, my email to him asking him to take a look at my tiny website seems humorous. But in those days the Web was a small place, and I didn't know anyone else who might appreciate my good work. (I don't recall whether I heard back from Tim or whether he appreciated my website.)

Subsequently, my neighbors lost interest in their Web business when it didn't make a fortune immediately, and the Fine Food Emporium didn't even last a year. I went on to create numerous websites and write eight books about the Web. But nothing since has equaled the thrill of publishing those first Web pages.

As I see it, my job is to lead you straight to the Web with a minimum of distractions so you can have the thrill of putting up your first Web page and then go on to bigger and better things. No lectures on the history of the Internet. No instructions on setting up a modem or choosing dial-up Internet service. No cheerleading on the wonders of the Web. No pontificating on the psychology of Web surfers. You probably know all that already, or you wouldn't be reading this book. The book takes a more direct approach. Just do it!

Considering that many novices will read this book, I have included in Appendix III some useful instructions on doing a few things that will come in handy and are a necessity for using this book. If you're a novice, you might take a look at Appendix III, but this book will make reference to it in the appropriate chapters.

Appendix II presents a Hypertext Markup Language (HTML) tutorial for ambitious readers. You don't need to know HTML to make Web pages, but it never hurts to learn the basics. Appendix II will get you off to a good start with HTML. For further instruction you need to read a basic HTML book.

Appendix I is a list of steps that will lead you through the making of your first Web pages. Use it as a preview and a reminder.

Every author must decide what to include in a book and what to leave out. I have given you what you need to make attractive Web pages. If I were to cover more, I would have to start providing instruction on specialized techniques that most people will never use. To avoid confusion, many techniques about which you might hear people talk have been left out, not only because they have limited use but because, in many cases, their use is ill-advised. Although this book is simple, it will take you further than you think.

Let Me Know

*Let me know (*jt@sinclair.com*) what you think of my approach to the subject matter of this book written for beginners. And stop by* http://bookcenter.com *for more information on making Web pages.*

In the end, just doing it is the best way to learn how to create Web pages. It amazes me that many introductory books try to cover everything. They try to be reference books. Who wants to learn from an encyclopedia of Web techniques? A moderate and deliberate pace of hands-on instruction that covers the basics seems best for making Web pages the smart way.

I

Web Page Basics

1

Making a Web Page

With no muss, no fuss, you can make your first Web page within minutes by reading this chapter. You need the right tools, however, and if you don't have them yet, Chapter 2 explains how to get them. You need only a copy of Netscape Composer 6.0 or Microsoft FrontPage Express 2.0. Composer comes free with the free Netscape 6.0 browser (Netscape Communicator package). FrontPage Express comes free with the free Microsoft 5.0 or 5.5 browser (Internet Explorer package). If you have Composer or

FrontPage Express installed now, you're ready to roll. No need to get held up by Chapter 2, which is there to help you get the appropriate software. But if you don't have one of these Web page authoring programs installed, proceed to Chapter 2 to get one installed; then return to this chapter and start.

This chapter and many of the following chapters provide duplicate instruction for Composer and FrontPage Express. You will need only to read the instructions for the program you use.

Getting Started

This chapter assumes that you can use computers, know how to create folders, can save a file to a folder, and can use a word processor. The chapter covers some of these skills, so you don't really have to know them all, but you'll have an easier time if you already have some familiarity with them.

Creating a Working Folder

The first task is an essential one to make things as easy as they can be. You need to create one folder where you can store all your Web work. By using only one folder, there should never be any doubt where your work is located. All you have to do is remember to always save your Web page files to your Web work folder.

Thus, you need to create the folder *1webwork* on the *C:* drive. Because the *1* is in the front of the folder name, this folder will always be at the top of the directory (folder tree) under the *C:* drive in Windows Explorer, a handy place to look for it.

Windows Explorer is the folder management software that's a part of Windows. If you don't know how to create the *1webwork* folder, consult Appendix III. Once you have established the folder for your Web work, you're ready to move on.

Text for Tutorials

Use the following text for the Composer and FrontPage Express tutorials that follow in later sections:

The Start

We started the trek at the restaurant by the river in Mexican Hat with a hamburger and a coke at lunch, a pleasant commencement ritual. Then we drove northwest on Hwy 261 and headed off (south of the Kane Ranger Station at Grand Gulch) across Cedar and Polly mesas dirt roads. The further you go on the dirt roads, the worse they get. You may have trouble in a vehicle without high clearance. In wet weather, a 4WD vehicle is required. Check with the BLM office in Monticello for information on current conditions. We started our trek at the northernmost fork of Slickhorn Canyon at a place some call the "first fork."

The Group

The four of us had trekked in the canyons before, although Mike Campos and Topper Craft had not hiked together. Charlie Craft and I were the common denominators on all of our canyon trips. We had two 4WD vehicles. The clear warm weather held for the entire trip and could not have been more pleasant. It's a great time of year to hike these canyons with one caveat: water can be scarce.

The Trailhead

We had started out of Mexican Hat about 3:30 PM. By the time we started down the trail off the mesa, it was about 6:00 in the evening. The shuttle for vehicles between the trailheads at Slickhorn Canyon and East Slickhorn Canyon is about four or five miles, and you can make good time driving it in good weather. We carried ten gallons of water in each vehicle (five in each of two containers). We took one five-gallon container out of the vehicle at each trailhead and stowed it in the bushes. This is an arid area. If your car is stolen at the trailhead, you don't want to come out of the canyon to find no water.

Now you don't really have to use this text. You can substitute your own. If you substitute your own, use three paragraphs with three headings. Then we'll be working with the same raw material.

Using Netscape Composer

Open the Netscape Navigator 6.0 browser. At the left-hand bottom corner reside four icons. Click on the one that looks like a pen.

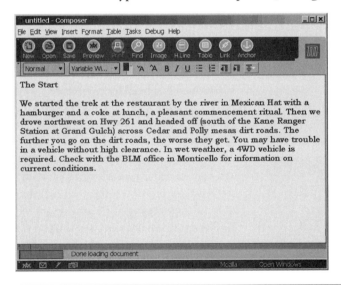

This opens Composer with a fresh new Web page ready to go.

Entering Text in Composer

Your first task will be to type the text in Composer (see Figure 1.1).

Figure 1.1   Typing text into Composer.

It doesn't get any easier than this. When you finish typing the provided text, you have completed your first Web page (see Figure 1.2).

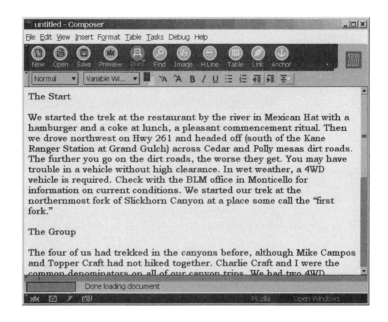

Figure 1.2   Your first Web page.

Pick Something You Want to Publish

Perhaps for this celebratory moment you might want to go back and substitute your text for mine if you haven't done so already. Pick something you want to publish on the Web and make your progress through this book a compelling project. I would rather your first Web page be about your subject matter (content) than about mine.

I'm sorry to report that it's as simple as this to create a Web page. Who needs a book? But this book has a few more tricks to offer, so stick with it.

Next you'll learn how to test your new Web page. You'll see that it's really a Web page (Chapter 3). Then you'll learn how to make it look a little better (Chapter 4). But for now simply save your new Web page with the file name myfirst.html (see Figure 1.3).

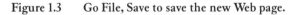

Figure 1.3   **Go File, Save to save the new Web page.**

Note that Composer is a WYSIWYG (*what you see is what you get -* pronounced "wizzywig") program. It shows the text and images pretty much as you will see them in a Web browser.

Using FrontPage Express

Using FrontPage Express is surprisingly similar to using Composer. But the details remain important, so this book in many cases provides additional separate instructions for FrontPage Express.

Don't Read

If you use Composer, you won't want to read the FrontPage Express sections. They're mostly the same. Likewise, if you use FrontPage Express, you won't want to read the Composer sections.

Open FrontPage Express 2.0 by clicking on the application icon.

You can find this icon at *C:/Program Files/Microsoft FrontPage Express/bin* (*fpxpress.exe*). (Make sure that Windows Explorer is set to Large Icons. See Appendix III if you don't know how to set the view in Windows Explorer.) This opens FrontPage Express with a new Web page ready to use. You should see the cursor in the upper left-hand corner.

Icon on the Desktop

You can move the FrontPage Express icon onto the desktop for more convenient access to the program. See Appendix III for details.

Entering Text in FrontPage Express

Your first task will be to enter text on the blank Web page you're looking at in FrontPage Express. Use the text provided in the earlier section. As you type the text in FrontPage Express, it appears as in Figure 1.4.

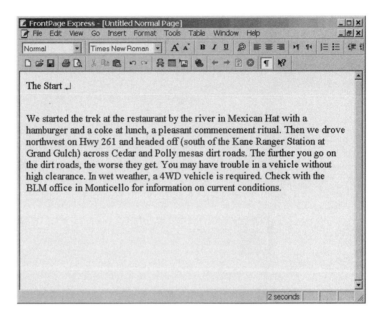

Figure 1.4   Typing text into FrontPage Express.

It doesn't get much easier than this. When you finish typing the provided text, you have created your first Web page (see Figure 1.5).

Pick What You Want to Publish

Perhaps for this celebratory moment you might want to go back and substitute your text for mine if you haven't done so already. Pick something you want to publish on the Web and make your progress through this book a compelling project. I would rather your first Web page be about your subject matter (content) than about mine.

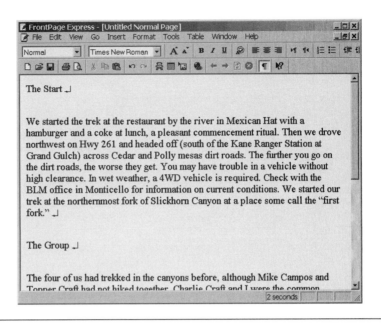

Figure 1.5   Your first Web page.

Sorry to report that it's as simple as this to create a Web page. Who needs a book? But this book has a few more tricks to offer, so stick with it.

Next you'll learn how to test your new Web page. You'll see that it's really a Web page (Chapter 3). Then you'll learn how to make it look a little better (Chapter 4). But for now simply save your new Web page with the file name *myfirst.html* (see Figures 1.6).

Note that FrontPage Express is a WYSIWYG (*what you see is what you get* - pronounced "wizzywig") program. It shows the text and images pretty much as you will see them in a Web browser. However, a browser is better, and Chapter 3 will show you how to test your Web pages in a browser.

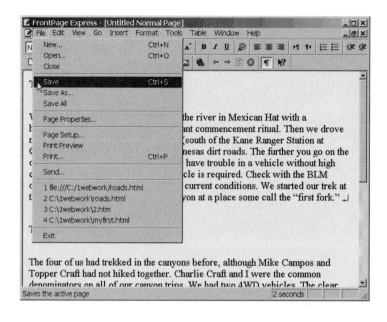

Figure 1.6   Go File, Save to save the new Web page.

Entering Text with Copy & Paste

When you work with existing text (text in digital form), you don't necessarily need to type the text into the Web page. You can copy and paste (or cut and paste) it directly into the Web page in Composer (or FrontPage Express) from another source like a word processor file. See Appendix III for instructions.

Summary

Just like a word processor, you can open either Composer or FrontPage Express and start typing. Quit typing and save your work. Voila! You've created your first Web page. Chapter 3 shows you how to look at it.

You need to read Chapter 2, even if you have Composer or FrontPage Express already installed. Chapter 2 has additional information beyond downloading and installing Composer and FrontPage Express, and it explains how to get a free image editor and a free FTP program, both of which you will need for later chapters.

2

Getting Organized

Getting the appropriate software and installing it is your first step in making a Web page. The question is, what should you use?

You could use a plain text editor (e.g., Windows Notepad) and Hypertext Markup Language (HTML). This is the most direct way to create Web pages, but it requires familiarity with HTML. You can learn HTML using the HTML tutorial in Appendix II. But there's an easier way: you can use Web page authoring software. If you do, you don't have to learn HTML.

Fortunately, both Netscape and Microsoft provide free authoring software with their free Web browsers. This chapter helps you get this free software. The book uses Netscape Composer 6.0 and Microsoft FrontPage Express 2.0, the latest versions available when the book went to press. These authoring programs are similar, and it doesn't matter much which program you use.

The Smart Way

Keep in mind that if you don't want to learn HTML, using a Web authoring program is the smart way to create Web pages.

Authoring Software

What is authoring software? It's software that enables you to create *content*. And what is content? Content is the text, images, sound, video, or embedded programming in your Web presentation. For instance, the content of a book might be a story or a nonfiction narrative.

Authoring

One way to understand authoring is to think of a word processor as a text authoring program for printed presentations. You type sentences, arrange sentences into paragraphs, add headings, and choose the typeface you want to use. You can manipulate the text by moving paragraphs around and replacing words. When you're done, you print your creation using a printer.

Multimedia authoring is similar to word processing (text authoring). It has added capabilities for handling additional media such as images, sound, video, and embedded programming but works much the same way. You add your content, and then you manipulate it. You move the various media elements around and replace different elements until you are satisfied with what you have created. If you've never done it, it sounds exotic, but it's as mundane as word processing.

The Web is a multimedia medium. A Web page can include both text and color images, a combination that has made the Web an exciting new medium. It can also contain sound, video, and embedded programming. And it's online. This means you can create rich content and *publish* it easily, conveniently, and inexpensively.

Of course, Web development can get complicated, but it's simple to get started making Web pages. This book covers only the basics and makes no attempt to turn you into a polished Web developer. Nonetheless, it's amazing what you can do with just the basics. And the way to get off to a good start with the least amount of effort is to use a Web authoring program.

Netscape Composer

Netscape Composer is the star of this book for several reasons. First, it's easy to use. It's no more difficult than a word processor. In fact, it's similar to a word processor. Second, it's free. When you download Netscape Communicator (free), Composer comes with it. Finally, even though it's free software, it's packed with features that help you do the things you need to do.

This book features Netscape Composer 6.0, the latest version. Netscape had a substantial facelift with version 6.0, and the browser works a little differently than prior versions. But Composer works much the same as prior versions, even though it looks different. If you have an earlier version of Netscape Communicator such as 3.0 or 4.0, you will find that Composer operates in a similar manner to version 6.0. (There is no version 5.) Nonetheless, you will want to download, install, and use Composer 6.0; after all, it's free.

Beta

Unfortunately, I finished writing this book well before Composer 6.0 was released. I used the beta version, Milestone 16. Therefore, the steps illustrated in this book may be slightly different than what the released version requires.

In talking with the Netscape people, they assured me that they were trying to keep Composer 6.0 similar to version 4.0. I consider this a wise approach. Composer 4.0 is excellent software.

Microsoft FrontPage Express

Microsoft FrontPage Express is the other star of this book. Actually, it's similar to Composer and works much the same way. You can obtain FrontPage Express free by downloading it with the Microsoft browser.

FrontPage

Don't confuse FrontPage Express with FrontPage. FrontPage is Microsoft's website building program and is not free. It is included with certain versions of Microsoft Office (Microsoft's office software suite), or you can purchase it separately.

The version of FrontPage Express available free with the Microsoft browser is similar not only to prior versions of FrontPage Express but also to FrontPage Editor, the Web authoring program that's a part of FrontPage (see Figures 2.1 and 2.2).

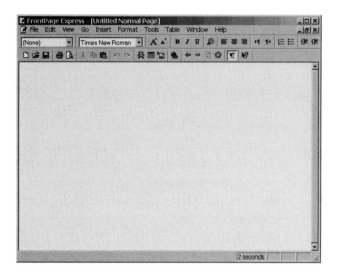

Figure 2.1   FrontPage Express, the Web authoring program.

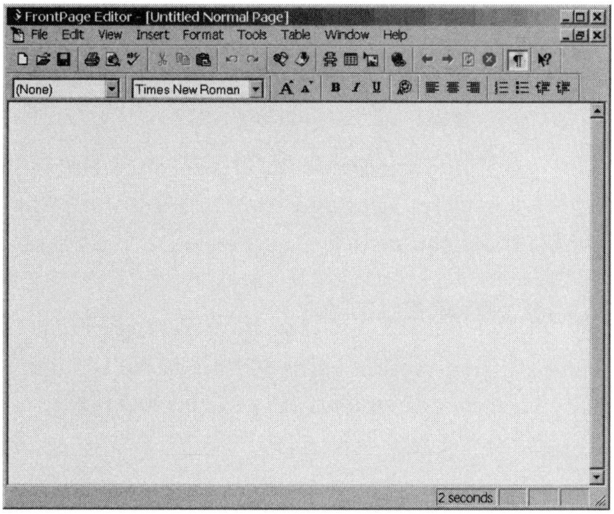

Figure 2.2   FrontPage Editor (from the website building program).

Consequently, if you happen to have a copy of FrontPage (e.g., because it came with your version of Microsoft Office), you can probably comfortably use FrontPage Editor in place of FrontPage Express for the purposes of this book.

Downloading the Authoring Software

The bad news is that a step-by-step tutorial on downloading the browser packages is not practical. Both the Netscape and Microsoft websites change so often that step-by-step instruction would almost certainly be obsolete by the time you read this chapter. The good news is that both Composer and FrontPage Express are free. It's worth a little investigation to find one of them and download it.

Looking for Downloads

You need to download either the Netscape or Microsoft browser. Go to either the Netscape and Microsoft website:

http://www.netscape.com

http://www.microsoft.com

Look for *downloads*. That's often the word used to identify free software, although sometimes finding the right place takes a few trials and errors.

Download Procedures

When you find the download Web page, follow the instructions. Do not download only the browser by itself. Elect to download the browser *package*.

Specific Downloads

Netscape calls its browser package Netscape Communicator. The browser by itself is Netscape Navigator. The Communicator package contains Navigator and Composer as well as other useful Internet software.

Microsoft presents a variety of choices, and it's not so easy to determine what you need. Currently, if you choose the browser, it comes with a package of other software that does not include FrontPage Express. However, when you get to the point where you have a choice of downloading the typical package or the *custom* package, choose *custom*. You will find FrontPage Express in the custom list of free software, and you can elect to download it together with the browser.

Download Folder

Create a *download* folder on your *C:* drive using Windows Explorer (see Appendix III for instructions). By using only one folder for downloads, you should never have any doubt where your downloads are located. All you have to do is remember to always save your downloaded files to your *download* folder.

Zip Files

Be ready to handle the Zip files (*.zip*) you happen to download. If you're not sure how, consult Appendix III. After you unzip the Zip file, install the downloaded software.

Automatic Installation

Netscape has available an automatic installation procedure. If you happen to use this, the automatic process will unzip the files and install Netscape Communicator for you. Once it has been installed, the most likely place to find the Netscape browser package is *C:/Program Files/Netscape/Communicator/Program* (*netscape.exe*). Create a shortcut icon on your desktop to conveniently open the Netscape browser.

Microsoft also offers an automatic installation procedure. If you happen to use this, the process will unzip the files and install Internet Explorer for you. Once it has been installed, the most likely place to find the Microsoft browser is *C:/Program Files/Microsoft FrontPage Express/bin* (*fpxpress.exe*). Create a shortcut icon on your desktop to conveniently open FrontPage Express.

Preloaded

Your computer or operating system (Windows) undoubtedly came with the Microsoft browser preloaded. If your browser is version 5.0, you may not have to download and install FrontPage Express. If you have a prior version, you may need to upgrade.

A Few Words about the Authoring Programs

Composer and FrontPage Express deserve a few final words before you commit yourself to using one or the other for the duration of this book.

How Far?

You might ask yourself, how far can this free software take me? After all, you're serious about doing this Web authoring stuff and willing to spend some money on software. Should you buy other authoring software instead of using Composer or FrontPage Express?

Many professional Web developers prefer to use HTML editors rather than Web authoring programs because they can fine-tune Web pages more easily with such software. But you have to know HTML well to use HTML editors. Some of the leading HTML editors are: Allaire's Homesite (*http://www.allaire.com*), Soft Quad's Hot Metal Pro (*http://www.sq.com*), and Sausage Software's Hot Dog (*http://www.sausage.com*).

Other professional Web developers use sophisticated website building programs, but you may find such programs more difficult to learn than the ones featured in this book. Some of the leading website development programs are: Macromedia's Dreamweaver (*http://www.macromedia.com*), Adobe's GoLive (*http://www.adobe.com*), NetObject's Fusion (*http://www.netobjects.com*), and Microsoft's FrontPage (*http://www.microsoft.com*).

The leading Web software packages are generally serviceable and practical. Once most people learn to use a particular Web development program, they often like it. Happily, that's likely to be exactly how you will feel about Composer or FrontPage Express after you use one or the other for a while. These are two useful, powerful, and practical programs. They will take you a long way. If a poll were taken of what professional Web developers use, Composer and FrontPage Express would show a significant market share. They are free and they are handy. Consider them to be professional software. You won't need anything else for a long time.

Word Processor

What are the strengths of Composer and FrontPage Express? They both resemble the word processor. This is a logical approach to Web development. Although the glitz draws one into the Web, it's the content that makes the Web worthwhile and brings people back. Most of that content is text. A word processor approach makes things easy. You just open the Web authoring program and start typing!

But what's the difference between a word processor and Composer and FrontPage Express? Very little. Think of a word processor as a print page authoring program. You make a nice document, and as the final step, you print the document on a printer. With Composer and FrontPage Express, the final step is to post the document on the Web rather than to print it.

And Vice Versa

Can you print a Composer or FrontPage Express Web page? Sure. Not only can you print it, but it will look great. The only thing over which you have little control is where the pages break. Naturally, a word processor gives you much more control over your documents for the purposes of printing. And that thought brings us to a final question: What about using a word processor for Web page authoring? Today the leading word processors all have the capability to convert documents into Web pages. Why not just use a word processor as Web authoring software? Interestingly, that's a reasonable approach if your purpose is to post a lot of text-only Web pages on the Web. If your objective is to integrate other media into your documents and create interactivity, either Composer or FrontPage Express makes a better choice. Each gives you more handy control than a word processor over the nontext elements in Web pages.

With XML

Extensible Markup Language (XML) is the Web language of the future, and the current versions of the browsers have robust XML capabilities. This is not something to be overly concerned about, but it's relevant to mention while discussing word processors. With XML, future word processors will have the power-

> *ful new capability to publish great looking documents on the Web, with finely-tuned layout and typesetting, documents that are flexible as well as attractive.*

Image Editing Software

For Chapters 5 and 11 you will need an image editor. If you don't have one, download and install one now to save yourself the inconvenience later.

On-Your-Disk-Ware

Most people have an image editor on their hard drives somewhere. Image editors come bundled with new computers, other hardware, and even other software. If you can find an image editor on your hard drive that can do the following, you can use it for this book:

1. Change the contrast as you move a slider.

2. Change the brightness as you move a slider.

3. Crop a smaller image out of the existing image.

4. Resize an existing image.

5. Add text to an image.

6. Convert to and from a wide range of graphic file formats, including GIF and JPEG.

Freeware

IrfanView is a freeware image editor that does almost everything needed for this book and more. It became popular because people find it easy to use yet powerful. And it's free for personal use and only $10 for commercial use. You can download it at *http://members.home.com/rsimmons/irfanview/*. Once you download it, just click on the file in Windows Explorer. The file will unzip and take you through the installation procedure. This book will feature this program in the later chapters covering images.

If you have confidence in your image editing abilities, however, use the image editor of your choice. Most image editors operate in a similar manner. Although IrfanView can do a lot, unlike Composer and FrontPage Express, you should not consider it to be a professional program. You will undoubtedly choose to use a more robust image editor as you gain some experience. In the meanwhile, IrfanView will get you through this book, and it's free.

Downloading FTP Software

This book features WS_FTP Lite, a File Transfer Protocol (FTP) shareware program that you can use for free, if you qualify; if not, you can have a 30-day trial. It has been one of the leading FTP programs for years. You can download WS_FTP Lite from almost anyplace that offers shareware. Go to CNET (*http://www.cnet.com*) to download it. Look on CNET for free downloads. You will find WS_FTP Lite under Internet, FTP most likely. You need to read the download and installation instructions carefully.

Download Folder

If you always download to the same folder (e.g., download), you are less likely to "lose" the WS_FTP Lite file when you download it.

You will use WS_FTP Lite in Chapter 16, which covers uploading your Web pages to your website.

Other Software

Is there other appropriate software available? Sure. I believe I have picked from the best of what's available for free. But if you want to spend money, you'll find no shortage of high quality Web authoring programs, HTML editors, image editors, and FTP programs.

Summary

This is the chapter that provides some hints on how to download the programs you will need for the book: Composer or FrontPage Express (Web authoring programs), IrfanView (image editor), and WS_FTP Lite (Internet upload program). Do it all now and save yourself the interuption later.

3

Testing Your Work

Looking at your Web pages in Composer or FrontPage Express gives you a pretty good idea of how they display in a browser, but it's not exact. Only a Web browser tells the whole story. Therefore, you need to test your Web pages in a Web browser periodically as you work. You do this by switching back and forth between your Web authoring program and your browser.

Fortunately, you can test Web pages without a Web server. A browser will display an individual Web page just by opening the

29

Web page file itself (on your hard disk). You do not have to be on the Web.

Testing Procedures

The testing procedure is simple. You simply take the following steps:

1. Open your authoring program.

2. Open the Web page in your authoring program.

3. Open your browser.

4. Open the Web page in your browser.

5. Work on the Web page in your authoring program and save it.

6. Refresh the Web page in your browser and look at it.

Using Your Programs

The Web work process and the testing process are straightforward. You simply open your authoring program (Composer or FrontPage Express) and a browser and start working.

Working on the Web Page

Open your authoring program. Open the Web page you are working on or start a new Web page. Work on the Web page as long as necessary. You will probably find making Web pages more satisfying than making word processor pages to be printed. You have more flexibility in the way you present information on the Web, and you can publish instantly.

Saving the Web Page

Like other computer work, you will want to save your work periodically by going File, Save in your authoring program or clicking on the save button.

If you don't do this, should your computer become temporarily disabled or crash, you might lose your work. I try to remember to save Web pages at least every 15 minutes.

The other reason for saving is to test with a browser. The browser cannot display your work until you have saved it (saved it in your authoring program). Sometimes when I am trying to fine-tune a Web page, I change it, save it, and test it at as little as 30-second intervals until I get it exactly the way I want it.

Browser

Open your browser.

Open the Web page you are working on. Go File, Open File (Composer) or File, Open, Browse (FrontPage Express). The browser will display the Web page as it was the last time it was saved. This is a good point to remember. A Web page in a browser doesn't change just because you've changed the original Web page. There are steps to be taken.

Refreshing the Web Page

How do you test your latest work? First, you save it in your authoring program as explained earlier. Second, you refresh the Web page in your browser by clicking on the refresh button.

The browser displays the latest saved version of your Web page for you to view. Seeing your latest work is the test.

Different Resolutions

Test at different resolutions. Chapter 4 covers the various resolutions at which people view the Web. After reading Chapter 4, you will need to adapt your testing procedures to take into account different resolutions. You will work at one resolution in which you will do 95 percent of your testing. But occasionally you will want to test at other resolutions too.

Not a Separate Process

Testing is not a separate process from Web page authoring. You cannot create Web pages efficiently without constant testing. With your authoring program and your browser opened at the same time, you can quickly test your Web work as often as you need to.

Advanced Testing Procedures

"Advanced testing procedures" sounds complicated. Still, you can easily do such testing. It's more tedious than it is complicated. You simply test your Web pages in each version of each browser that you expect your website visitors to use. Here are some choices.

Netscape Navigator versions 2, 3, 4, and 6.

Microsoft Internet Explorer versions 2, 3, 4, 5, and 5.5.

Other browsers are mostly irrelevant because such small numbers of Web users use them. If you test browser versions 4 and up, you will cover most of the Web users. Few people use old browsers. Why should they? The newest versions are free.

If you use Netscape versions 4 and 6 and Microsoft versions 4, 5, and 5.5, that's five browsers for testing your Web pages. That's a lot of work and may not be necessary for the Web work that you do with this book. Just keeping all those browser versions installed on your computer can get complicated.

What's the alternative? Use only basic HTML markups. The browsers render basic HTML in about the same way. It's for the more exotic markups that they display differences.

Exotic Markups

This book covers few exotic markups, so you don't have to worry much about browser differences. Many exotic markups enable highly specialized functions you may never need or use. The results of some exotic markups can be duplicated by using basic markups in an offbeat way, which is usually preferable to worrying about browser differences. The more you stick with basic HTML markups, the less you will have to test with multiple browser versions.

I usually use the latest version of the Netscape browser to do all my testing. As a final gesture before I post the Web pages on the Web, I test the pages in the latest Microsoft browser to make sure they work well.

It seems to take about two years for the latest version of a Web browser to saturate the market. Thus, for Microsoft version 5 released in December 1998, you can expect it to replace most prior Microsoft versions by December 2000.

What Is a Web Page Anyway?

A Web page is a plain text file otherwise known as an ASCII (American Standard Code for Information Interchange) file. Hypertext Markup Language (HTML) markups make it different than a plain text file. The markups (using plain text characters) instruct the browser how to display the text and the images as well as enable links. Angle brackets (< >) enclose the markups, making them easy to spot and read (see the text immediately below).

```
<table width="540"
align="center"><tr><td>

<div align="center"><h2>Slickhorn -
East Slickhorn Loop, Utah</h2>

<b>by Joseph T. Sinclair</b></div>

<p>September 25 - October 1, 1999</p>

<p>These two canyons which run into
the San Juan River are located in
southeast Utah near Mexican Hat. They
are wilderness canyons with access
from trailheads reached via dirt roads
on Polly Mesa or accessed from the San
Juan River via raft.</p>

</td></tr></table>
```

Were you to view the Web page above in a plain text editor (e.g., Windows Notepad) or an HTML editor, it would look as it does above. When the browser displays it, however, it looks as it does in Figure 3.1.

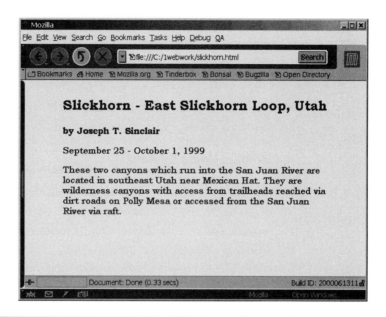

Figure 3.1   Web page as displayed by browser.

As you can see, the World Wide Web is a simple system. Add some markups to plain text, and voila, you have a nicely typeset Web page in the browser. Should you wish to learn more, Appendix II provides an HTML tutorial.

Where Is It?

Where is that Web page? The Web page resides on the hard drive in the computer that runs the Web server. The Web server is software that handles Web pages and delivers them to whoever requests them over the network (i.e, one requests Web pages using his or her browser). Consequently, if your Web pages are in a website somewhere, they are on the hard drive of a computer operated by the Internet Service Provider (ISP) that hosts the website. Inside a company on an intranet, the Web files reside on the hard drive of the network server computer that runs the Web server and the company network.

Thus, Web files are just like any other files. You can find them on a hard drive. Specifically, you find them via the Internet on a hard drive in the computer that runs the Web server. The Web server delivers the Web pages at a particular website.

Domain Name System

The domain name system enables Web surfers via their browsers to easily find Web pages and read them wherever they're located. For instance, if you want to see the Web pages on the Disney website, you use the domain name disney.com. Where is the Disney website? Who knows? You don't need to know. The Disney domain name will get you to the Disney server computer (and the Web server that delivers the Disney website Web pages).

What's a Website?

A website is a collection of Web pages organized into a coherent presentation available at a domain name address. In other words, a website is just a collection of Web files in one place that anyone can access (request) with a Web browser via the Internet. Web pages at a website are organized by the links between them.

In fact, technical definitions don't matter much. A website really defines itself by its cultural or intellectual content. The technical part is often transparent. But this book deals with technical concepts, and later chapters will elaborate on the technical aspects of a website.

How Does It All Work?

How does the Web system work? It's as simple as can be, and it works with plain text files.

Test

First, you create and test your Web pages on your own computer. With Chapter 1 and this chapter, you're well on your way to becoming a Web page maker.

Upload

Next, you upload your Web page files to a host computer. The host computer typically belongs to an ISP with which you have contracted to host your website. The ISP furnishes the connection to the Internet and provides a domain name for you to use (or sets up a domain name that you request). Chapters 14 and 15 explain hosting for you in greater detail, and Chapter 16 shows you how to upload your Web page files to the host computer.

Host Computer

The host computer has Web server *software* which serves Web page files to Web surfers faster and more efficiently than Web surfers (website visitors) can otherwise get them.

Need a Web Server?

Theoretically, you can have a website on the Web without a Web server. However, more than a handful of website visitors accessing the website at one time would cause a traffic jam, and the access would be slow in any event. A Web server provides fast and efficient delivery of Web pages to website visitors.

Website visitors find your website not by knowing where your host computer is located (it could be located anywhere) but via your domain name address.

Web Surfers

Website visitors use your domain name address to find your website and access your Web pages. Your domain name address is a *universal resource locator* (URL) and is unique. No one else has the same address. Where do people find your URL? Wherever you make it available: advertising, promotion, publicity, and via the search engines such as Yahoo!

Request

When a website visitor puts your URL into his or her browser (or clicks on a link that contains your URL), the browser sends a request for a particular Web page over the Internet to the specific Web address and thus to the Web server handling your website. The Web server answers the request by sending the requested Web page.

Receive and View

The website visitor's browser automatically downloads the requested Web page into the visitor's computer and controls it. Once the visitor's browser has downloaded a Web page, the browser displays it and keeps track of it. The browser also downloads images (or other multimedia elements) that make up a part of the Web page and displays these images in the Web page.

The remainder of this book will fill you in on many of the details you need to know regarding this process, but the overview of the process itself is straightforward.

Summary

Test your Web work with a browser. That's the final proof. The WYSIWYG Web authoring programs are great, but they don't render Web pages exactly. Only a browser does. Test often to save yourself a lot of wasted time.

4

Making the Text Look Better

The first thing you will notice about your text when you test your Web page is that it wraps inside the frame of the browser. If your browser covers your whole screen, the text goes from edge to edge making long lines. If your browser covers only one-quarter of your screen, the text goes edge to edge in shorter lines. The text adapts; that is, it "wraps."

When the browser is small, the text may seem natural and readable. When the browser is large, the body of text may seem huge and difficult to read due to the long lines (see Figures 4.1 and 4.2).

Figure 4.1   Browser with reduced window.

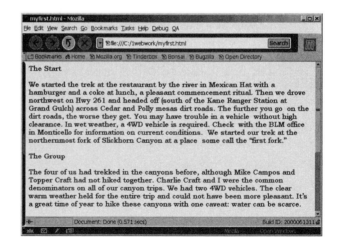

Figure 4.2   Browser with full window.

A 9-11 word count on a line of 12-point type (default size) is the proper column width for the most comfortable reading. How do you get from text wrapping to the ideal column? More on this later.

Another consideration is that most people use one of three resolutions (measured in pixels) on their computer monitors: 640 x 480, 800 x 600, and 1024 x 768. Most use 800 x 600 or larger, but some still use 640 x 480. If you want to make Web pages usable by everyone, you must keep the width down to 640 pixels wide, right? Actually, there's even another consideration. WebTV, used by over one million people, shows Web pages at a usable resolution of 544 pixels wide, because the users view Web pages on their televisions. Therefore, it seems reasonable to use a width of about 544 pixels for Web pages if you hope to make an effective presentation to everyone (see Figures 4.3-4.5).

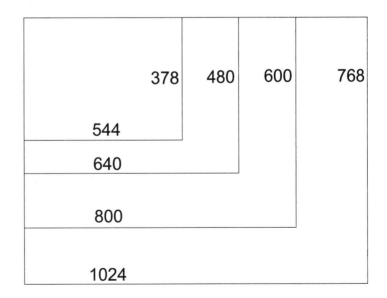

Figure 4.3   Different resolutions.

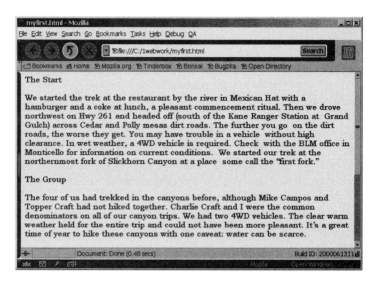

Figure 4.4   Browser with full window at 800 x 600 resolution.

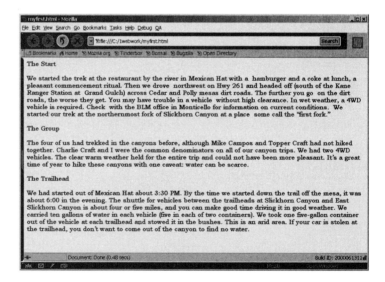

Figure 4.5   Browser with full window at 1024 x 768 resolution.

It turns out that a column of about 480-520 pixels makes the proper width for default 12-point Times New Roman (or Times) to provide maximum readability. The question is, how do you make your text column 480 pixels wide?

Cascading Style Sheets

One answer is to use Cascading Style Sheets (CSS), a Web type-setting and layout technology that experts use. Eventually, if you do a lot of text publishing, you will want to turn to CSS to make your Web pages look more like fine desktop publishing than Web pages.

There's a trick you can use to set the width of your text columns. First, you create a one-column, one-row table (one-cell table). You make the column 480 pixels wide. Then you place your text in the table. To finish, you make sure that the table border does not show in the browser.

Making a Table with Composer

Open the *myfirst.html* Web page in Composer. Scroll down and place the cursor below the text. Go Table, Insert, Table or click on the table icon.

The Insert Table dialog box will pop up. Since you need a one-row, one-column table, set the Number of rows to *1*, Number of columns to *1*, the Table width to *480*, the Border to *0*, and click *OK* (see Figure 4.6).

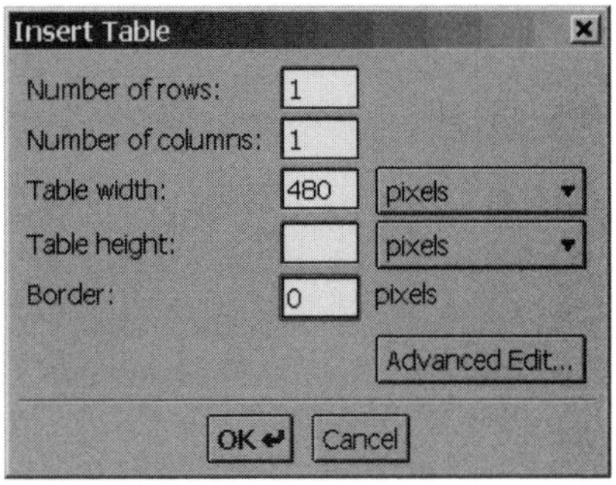

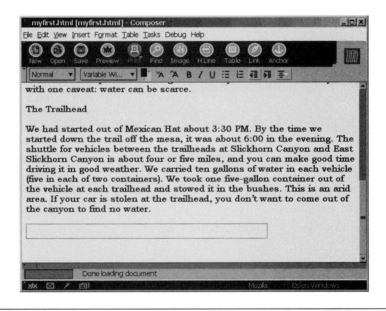

Figure 4.6   Insert Table window.

Your new table is 480 pixels wide (see Figure 4.7).

Figure 4.7   New table (outlined box).

Adjusting the Table

Next, place the cursor in the table and go Table, Table Properties. The Tables Properties window will pop up. Under Table Alignment choose *Center*. Under Borders and Spacing enter *0* (pixels) for Spacing and *10* (pixels) for Padding. Click the *OK* button. This will set up the table for adding text.

Placing the Text in the Table

First highlight all of the text and cut it (using cut and paste - see Figure 4.8).

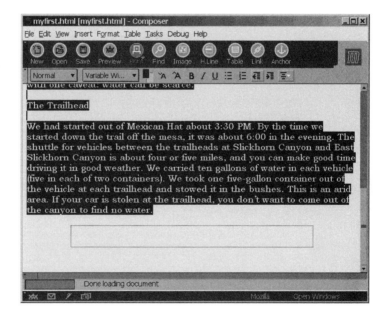

Figure 4.8   Highlight the text to cut and paste.

Paste the text into the table. Now the text is in a column 480 pixels wide (see Figure 4.9).

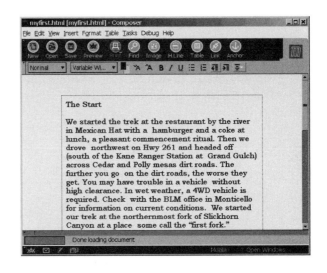

Figure 4.9   Text in a column.

Any browser can display it in any resolution. (This assumes that the browser is opened to full screen.) Test it (see Figure 4.10).

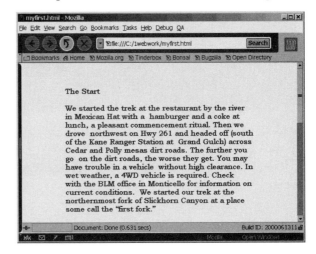

Figure 4.10   Text column displayed in browser.

Now the Web page looks like a column meant for reading. It shows in a fixed width with a margin on each side. As you will remember from your Web surfing, many websites display Web pages using a fixed-width layout. Usually the width is less than 640 pixels.

The table is in the center of the Web page by choice. You can place it on the left-hand side of the page or on the right by simply changing the alignment of the table.

Typeset the Headings

Typeset the headings. Put the cursor on the first heading (The Start). Go to the HTML formatting window just under the New icon.

It will show *Normal*. Click on the arrow, and a menu will drop down. Select *Heading 3*. The heading will now appear in a larger-than-normal size with bold type and a line space before and after. This is an HTML heading level 3. Repeat for the other two headings. Test with your browser (see Figure 4.11).

Changing the Type Size

Experiment with changing the type size. To change the font size in Composer, highlight all the text and go Format, Size, Decrease. The type size will decrease by one increment all the text that is highlighted (see Figure 4.12). Always make sure the text is easily readable after changing the font size.

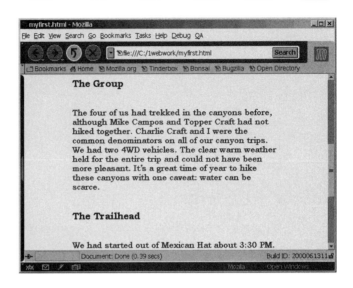

Figure 4.11   Text with headings.

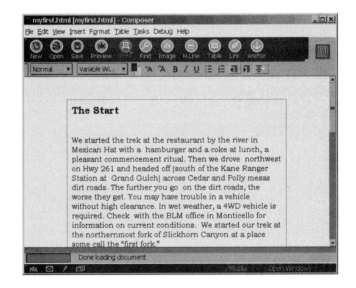

Figure 4.12   Decreased type size.

When you reduce the text (font) size one increment, the column width of 480 pixels may be too wide. Change the width so that it displays the text with 9-12 words on each line. Try 420 pixels (see Figure 4.13).

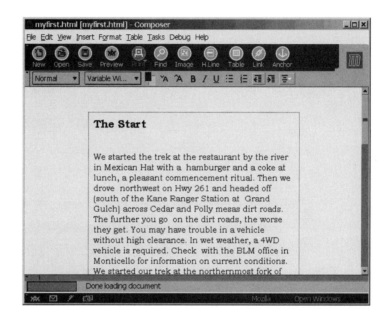

Figure 4.13   Text column 420 pixels wide with smaller font.

Likewise, if you make the font size larger, you need to expand the width of the column for maximum readability.

Making a Table with FrontPage Express

Open the *myfirst.html* Web page in FrontPage Express. Scroll down and place the cursor below the text. Go Table, Insert Table. The Insert Table window pops up. Since you need a one-row, one-column table, set the Rows to *1*, Columns to *1*, the Border Size to *0*, the Specify width to *480* (pixels), and click *OK* (see Figure 4.14).

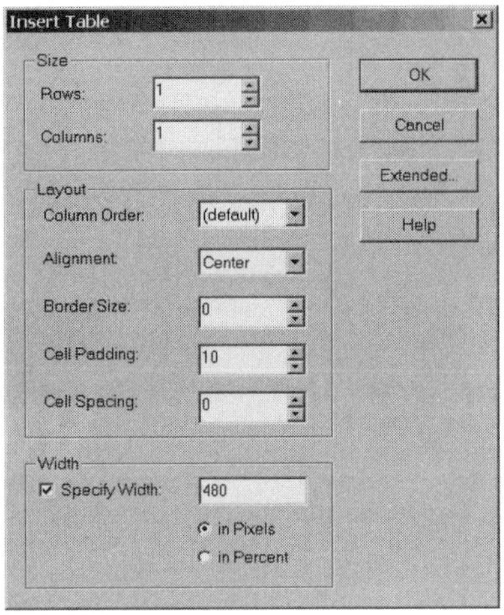

Figure 4.14   Insert Table window.

Your new table is 480 pixels wide (see Figure 4.15).

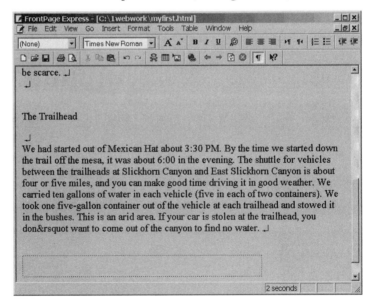

Figure 4.15   New table (outlined box).

An alternative is to click on the table icon and select the uppermost left cell.

Then go Table, Table Properties. The Tables Properties window will pop up. Set the table parameters.

Adjusting the New Table

Place the cursor in the table and go Table, Table Properties. This pops up the Tables Properties dialog box. Under Alignment choose Center. Under Layout enter *0* for Cell Spacing and *10* for Cell Padding. Click *OK*. This sets up the table for adding text.

Placing the Text in the New Table

First highlight all of the text and cut it (using cut and paste - see Figure 4.16).

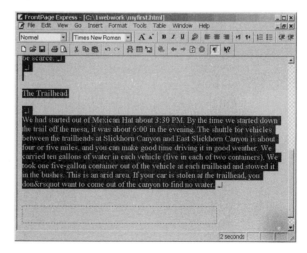

Figure 4.16   Highlighted text.

Paste the text into the table (see Figure 4.17).

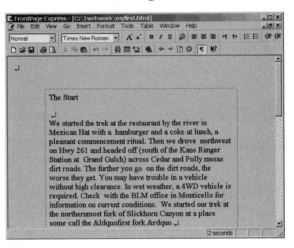

Figure 4.17   Text in the table.

Any browser can display it in any resolution. Test it (see Figure 4.18).

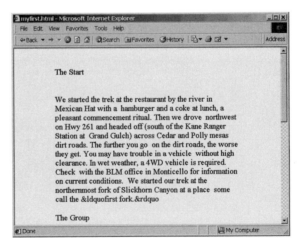

Figure 4.18   The text column in a browser.

Now the Web page looks like a column meant for reading. The column shows in a fixed width with a margin on each side. As you will remember from your Web surfing, many websites display Web pages using a fixed-width layout. Usually the width is less than 640 pixels.

The table is in the center of the Web page by choice. You can place it on the left-hand side of the page or on the right by simply changing the alignment of the table.

Typeset the Headings

Typeset the headings. Put the cursor on the first heading (The Start). Go to the HTML formatting window just under the File menu.

It will show *Normal*. Click on the arrow, and a menu will drop down. Select *Heading 3*. The heading will now appear in a larger than normal size with bold type and a line space before and after. This is an HTML heading level 3. Repeat for the other two headings. Test with your browser (see Figure 4.19).

Changing the Font Size

Experiment with changing the type size. To change the font size in FrontPage Express, highlight all the text and click on the decrease font button.

The type size will decrease by one increment (see Figure 4.20).

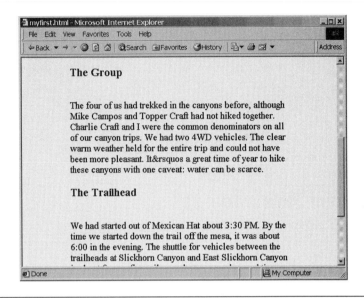

Figure 4.19   Text with headings.

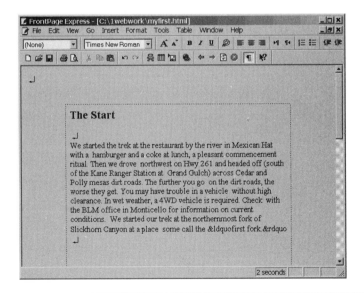

Figure 4.20   Decreased type size.

When you reduce the text (font) size by one increment, the column width of 480 pixels may be too wide. Change the width so that it displays the text with 9-12 words on each line. Try 420 pixels (see Figure 4.21).

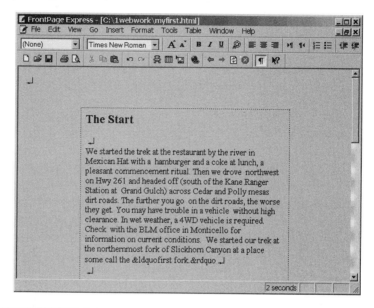

Figure 4.21 Text column 420 pixels wide with smaller font.

Likewise, if you make the font size larger, you need to expand the width of the column for maximum readability.

The HTML

For your amusement and further education, the Composer HTML version of what you have done so far follows:

```
<html><head><title>myfirst</title></
head><body>

<br>
```

```
<table cellpadding="10"
cellspacing="0" border="0"
width="480" align="center"><tbody>

<tr valign="Top"><td valign="Top">

<h3>The Start</h3>
```

We started the trek at the restaurant by the river in Mexican Hat with a hamburger and a coke at lunch, a pleasant commencement ritual. Then we drove northwest on Hwy 261 and headed off (south of the Kane Ranger Station at Grand Gulch) across Cedar and Polly mesas dirt roads. The further you go on the dirt roads, the worse they get. You may have trouble in a vehicle without high clearance. In wet weather, a 4WD vehicle is required. Check with the BLM office in Monticello for information on current conditions. We started our trek at the northernmost fork of Slickhorn Canyon at a place some call the “first fork.”

```
<h3>Group</h3>
```

The four of us had trekked in the canyons before, although Mike Campos and Topper Craft had not hiked together. Charlie Craft and I were the common denominators on all of our canyon trips. We had two 4WD vehicles. The clear warm weather held for the entire trip and could not have been more pleasant. It’s a great time

```
of year to hike these canyons with one
caveat: water can be scarce.<br>

<h3>The Trailhead</h3>

We had started out of Mexican Hat
about 3:30 PM. By the time we started
down the trail off the mesa, it was
about 6:00 in the evening. The shuttle
for vehicles between the trailheads at
Slickhorn Canyon and East Slickhorn
Canyon is about four or five miles,
and you can make good time driving it
in good weather. We carried ten
gallons of water in each vehicle (five
in each of two containers). We took
one five-gallon container out of the
vehicle at each trailhead and stowed
it in the bushes. This is an arid
area. If your car is stolen at the
trailhead, you don&rsquo;t want to
come out of the canyon to find no
water.

</td></tr></tbody></table>

</body></html>
```

This is the HTML version as authored by Composer. If you code it yourself using the HTML tutorial in Appendix II, it might look a little different.

Browser Differences

Note that the Microsoft browser doesn't display the curved apostrophe (’) or curved quotation marks (“ and ”). It shows the HTML code instead. See Figures 4.15- 4.21. This is a perpetual problem when browser makers don't use HTML standards. This particular problem resulted from a copy and paste that transferred a Composer Web page into a ForntPage Express Web page. In other words, I took a short cut to create the screen images. The outcome was that Composer 6.0, which is more shophisticated than FrontPage Express 2.0, used standard HTML code that the Microsoft browser couldn't read.

Summary

Usability and readability are essential for text. Usability in this case means that the text can be read in any browser without necessarily scrolling from side to side. This means keeping the text column width to a minimum size that any standard resolution can display without scrolling. Readability means that you need to coordinate the size of the type with the width of the text column. You can ensure both usability and readability by using a one-cell table to create a text column.

5

Adding Pictures

You can add pictures to Web pages easily. First, you must decide what pictures you want to use. The catch is that the images must be in either the GIF format or the JPEG format. For PCs the file extensions are *.gif* and *.jpg*, respectively. Here are a few of the things you might use:

Digital photographs

Text art

Clip art

Digitized art

Digital art

Digital photographs are photographs (prints) that someone digitizes, as covered in Chapter 10. You can also take digital photographs with a digital camera.

You create text art with an image editor that handles text. It's easy, and Chapter 11 covers the process. Typically, you create a heading or title and give it a drop shadow or some other artistic treatment.

You find clip art in large collections on CDs, often with accompanying catalogs (books) that enable you to make a selection more easily. Make sure that the clip art is in the GIF or JPEG file format. Clip art consists of commercial art used for specific purposes (fun or business).

When someone digitizes an existing work of art, you can use it in a Web page. Often you will find digitized art in clip art collections.

Many artists now do all their artwork on a computer, and digital art has come into its own. To obtain this type of art, you may have to hire a digital artist to create it for you on a custom basis. But some digital art also ends up in clip art collections.

These are only a few of the examples of how people use images on the Web, but they're all easy to use and can be very attractive. Composer and FrontPage Express make adding images easy.

Portable Network Graphics

Chapter 11 explains a third image format Portable Network Graphics (PNG) that you can use in your Web pages. Its use is growing, but most people still use GIFs and JPEGs.

Getting Ready

First, decide which GIF or JPEG you want to use. About 175 x 125 pixels is a convenient size. Place it in your *1webwork* folder. Name it *trailhead.jpg* (or *.gif*) if you want it to be the same as in this book (otherwise name it anything). Have your image editor on standby, ready to crop the image. You might want to read Chapter 11 about preparing images before you try this chapter.

Embedding Pictures with Composer

Open Composer and use the *myfirst.html* Web page. Next move the cursor to where you want to place (embed) the picture in the Web page. In this case it will be in the third paragraph just after the heading, The Trailhead, and just before the first sentence. Click on the image icon.

The Image Properties dialog box will pop up. Under Image Information enter the URL which is simply the image file *trailhead.jpg* (see Figure 5.1).

Click *OK* and test with your browser (see Figure 5.2).

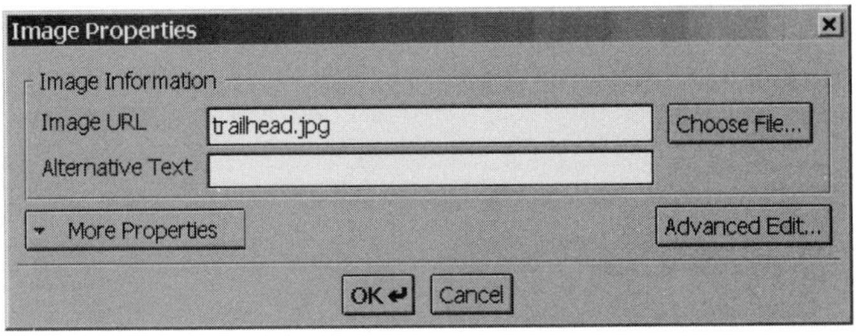

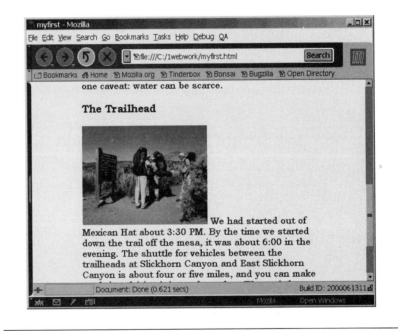

Figure 5.1   Image Properties window.

Figure 5.2   Image in Web page.

It looks good. You got off to a good start, but you will want to make this look a little better. Try having the text flow around the picture on the right. Highlight the image and click on the image icon. In the Image Properties window under Align Text to Image, select *wrap to right* and click *OK*. Test it (see Figure 5.3).

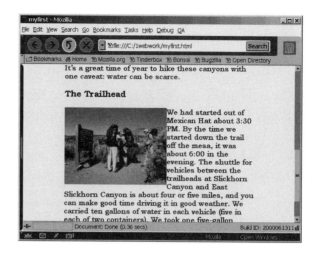

Figure 5.3   Image with text flowing around it.

You will find that it looks better as the text wraps around the image to the right. You can also chose several other ways to embed the image. Try *wrap to left* and click *OK* (see Figure 5.4).

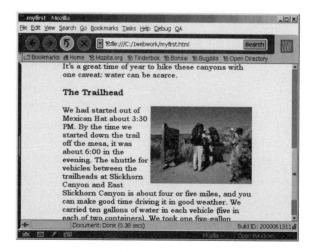

Figure 5.4   Image with text flowing around it to the left.

There are times when you want the picture to have its own space. Try placing it in the page with a line of text above and below. Place the cursor in the third paragraph before the sentence which starts: "We carried ten gallons." Press the *Enter* key twice to create a new paragraph. Place the cursor between the two paragraphs. Click on the image icon. In the Image Properties window under Image Information, enter the URL for the image file *trailhead.jpg* and click *OK*. Test it with your browser (see Figure 5.5).

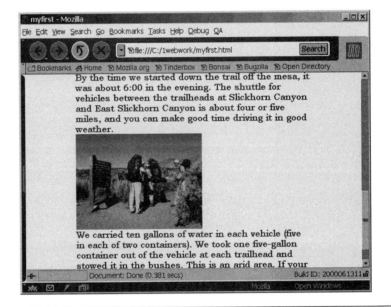

Figure 5.5   Image between two text blocks.

You can also center the image by highlighting it and clicking on the alignment icon to chose *center* (see Figure 5.6).

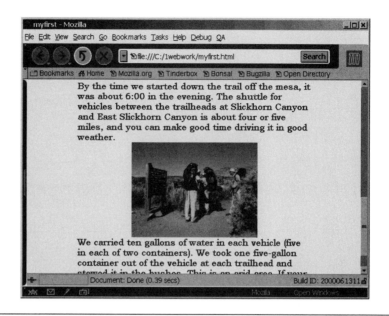

Figure 5.6   Web page with centered image.

Embedding Pictures with FrontPage Express

Open FrontPage Express and open the *myfirst.html* Web page. Next move the cursor to where you want to place (embed) the picture in the Web page. In this case it will be in the third paragraph just after the heading, The Trailhead, and just before the first sentence. Click on the image icon.

The Image dialog box will pop up. Under Browse find the image *trailhead.jpg* and open it (see Figure 5.7).

Figure 5.7   Image window.

Test with your browser (see Figure 5.8).

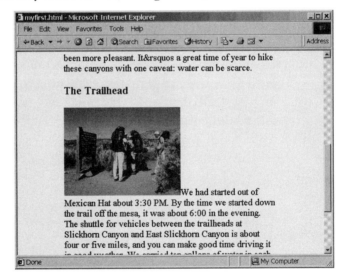

Figure 5.8   Image in Web page.

It looks good. You got off to a good start, but you will want to make this look a little better. Try having the text flow around the picture on the right. Highlight the image, right click, and select Image Properties, Appearance, Layout, Alignment, *Left,* and click *OK.* Now test it with your browser (see Figure 5.9).

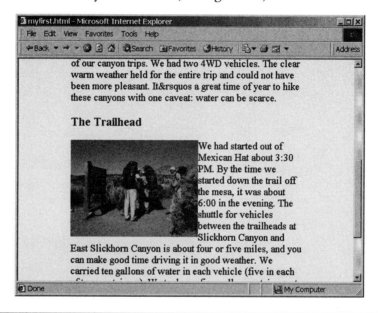

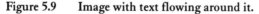

Figure 5.9   Image with text flowing around it.

You will find that it looks better as the text wraps around the image to the right. You can also chose several other ways to embed the image. Try *right* and click *OK* (see Figure 5.10).

There are times when you want the picture to have its own space. Try placing it in the page with a line of text above and below. Place the cursor in the third paragraph before the sentence which starts: "We carried ten gallons." Press the *Enter* key twice to create a new paragraph. Place the cursor between the two paragraphs. Click on the image icon. In the Image dialog box, open the image file *trailhead.jpg*. Test it with your browser (see Figure 5.11).

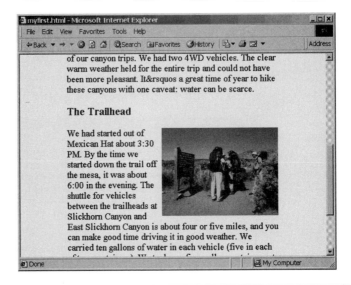

Figure 5.10   Image with text flowing around it to the left.

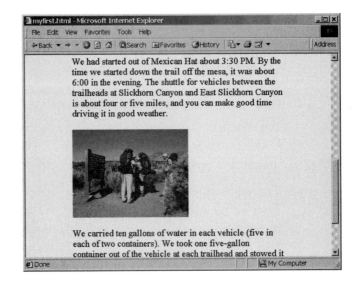

Figure 5.11   Image between two text blocks.

You can also center the image by highlighting it and clicking on the center icon (see Figure 5.12).

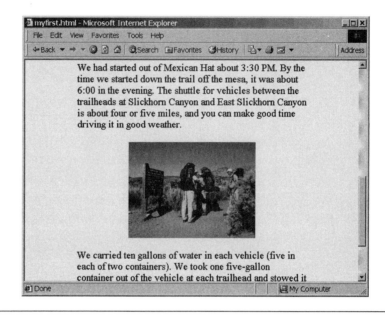

Figure 5.12   Web page with centered image.

Refinements for Embedding Pictures

You can change the way an image displays by changing its properties. This comes in handy for creating attractive Web pages.

Composer

You noticed that the margin of space surrounding the wrapped image (see Figure 5.3 earlier) was so thin as to be distracting. You can add space to the margin. Highlight the image. Click on the image icon. Go Spacing, Left and Right, enter *15*, and click *OK*.

This creates a 15-pixel space between the image and the text (see Figure 5.13).

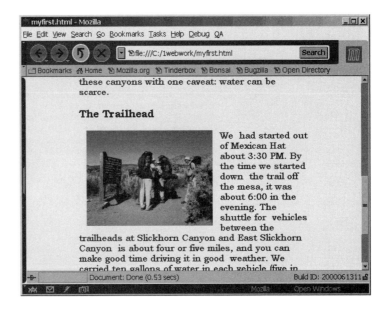

Figure 5.13   Wrapped image with space.

FrontPage Express

You noticed that the margin of space surrounding the wrapped image (see Figure 5.9 earlier) was so thin as to be distracting. You can add space to the margin. Highlight the image and right click. Go Appearance, Layout, Horizontal Spacing, enter *15*, and click *OK*. This creates a 15-pixel space between the image and the text (see Figure 5.14).

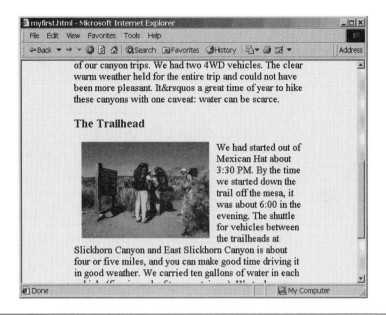

Figure 5.14   Wrapped image with space.

Correct Pixel Dimensions

Be aware that when Composer or FrontPage Express bring in an image, they automatically set the correct pixel dimensions. For instance, the *trailhead.jpg* photograph is 253 x 186 pixels. Suppose you do some work on the photograph in your image editor and crop it (see Figure 5.15).

Figure 5.15   Cropped photograph.

The pixel dimensions are now 172 x 153 pixels. You save the photograph and keep the same file name for the cropped photograph. The browser may not automatically change the size of the photograph to the pixel dimensions of the cropped version. This is not good for several reasons:

- A small photograph enlarged will lose quality (e.g., the cropped photograph enlarged to the size of the original).

- A large photograph reduced may lose quality.

- If the aspect ratio is different (pixel width to pixel height), the photograph will be distorted.

- A combination of the above factors may result in a bizarre display of the photograph.

Therefore, make sure that the pixel dimensions change for the cropped version. If not, go to the photograph in Composer or FrontPage Express and highlight it. Delete it (i.e. unembed it), but don't move the cursor. Go through the process of embedding it again. When you go through this process, Composer or FrontPage Express will definitely set the proper pixel dimensions for it. The photograph will display properly (see Figure 5.16).

Figure 5.16   Web page with cropped photograph.

In the alternative, you can simply change the properties of the image by manually changing the pixel dimensions. You can get the pixel dimensions of the image (after cropping) from your image editor.

Summary

Putting a picture in a Web page is almost as simple as just specifying the image file. You can make some adjustments such as wrapping left or right, but it's not a difficult process. The most difficult part is finding an image you want to use and getting it ready. But even that's easy, as Chapter 11 explains.

6

Adding Links

Adding links is easy and straightforward. Using proper URLs (Universal Resource Locators) is a bit more complicated, but this chapter covers URLs comprehensively.

A link goes to:

Another Web page (HTML file)

An anchor in another Web page

An anchor in the same Web page

Another file (e.g., a GIF file)

For simplicity, the book uses the example of another Web page. So, create another Web page with the file name of *roads.html*. To create it:

Open Composer or FrontPage Express.

Press the *Enter* key twice.

Type the following text:

Target page: roads.html (maps of dirt roads)

Save it as *roads.html* to the folder *1webwork*.

When you test it in your browser, it appears as Figure 6.1 shows.

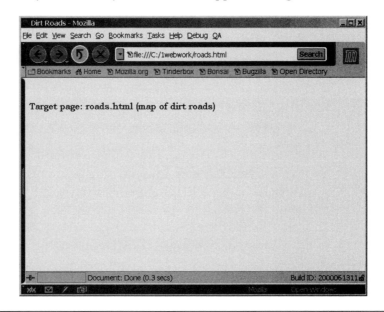

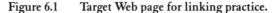

Figure 6.1   Target Web page for linking practice.

Now you have a Web page to which you can link from *myfirst.html*.

Creating a Link with Composer

Open *myfirst.html* in Composer. Look at the first paragraph. Highlight the words "dirt roads." Click on the link icon.

The Link Properties window will pop up. Go Link to, enter *roads.html,* and press *Enter.* Since the *roads.html* file is in the same folder as *myfirst.html*, the URL is simply the file name (see Figure 6.2).

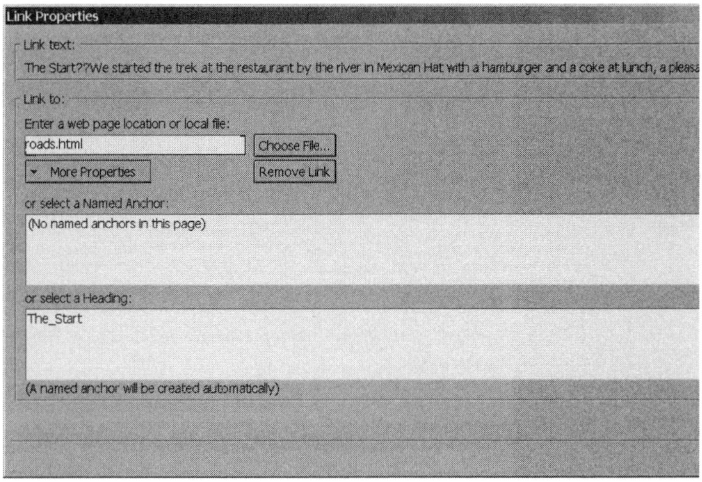

Figure 6.2   Link Properties window.

Now the words "dirt roads" form the trigger for a hyperlink (technical name for link). Look at this Web page in your browser. Notice that the words are a different color than the other words (see Figure 6.3).

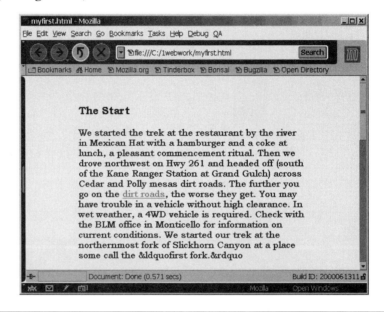

Figure 6.3   Text with link.

Text is normally black, and links are blue (default) differentiating them from the rest of the text. (The words will be underlined, too, if you have not turned off the link underlining in your browser.) Click on the words "dirt roads" and the link will immediately take you to the Web page *roads.html*. Once you have used the link, the link words change to another color (default: purple).

Creating a Link with FrontPage Express

Open *myfirst.html* in FrontPage Express. Look at the first paragraph. Highlight the words "dirt roads." Click on the hyperlink icon.

The Create Hyperlink window will pop up. Go World Wide Web, URL, enter *roads.html,* and click *OK.* Since the *roads.html* file is in the same folder as *myfirst.html*, the URL is simply the file name (see Figure 6.4).

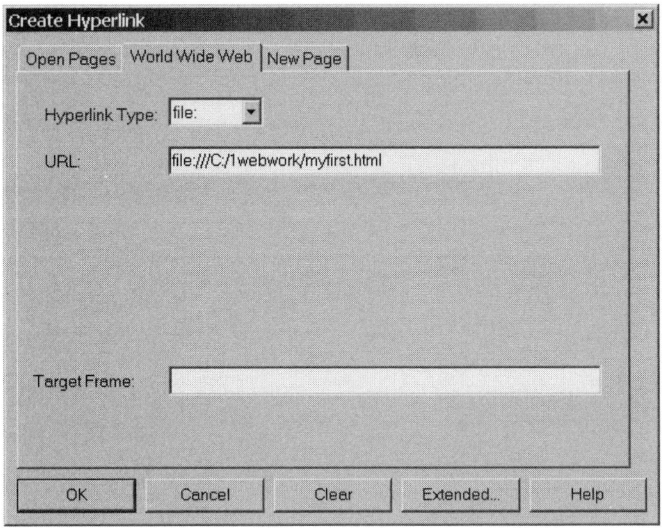

```
Create Hyperlink                                               [x]

 Open Pages   World Wide Web | New Page |

   Hyperlink Type:  |file:         |▼|

   URL:              |file:///C:/1webwork/myfirst.html          |



   Target Frame:     |                                          |


     OK          Cancel        Clear      Extended...     Help
```

Figure 6.4   Create Hyperlink window.

Now the words "dirt roads" form the trigger for a hyperlink (technical name for link). Look at this Web page in your browser.

Notice that the words are a different color than the other words (see Figure 6.5).

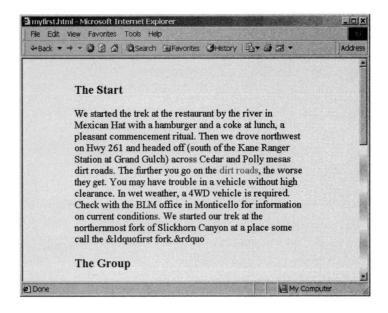

The Start

We started the trek at the restaurant by the river in Mexican Hat with a hamburger and a coke at lunch, a pleasant commencement ritual. Then we drove northwest on Hwy 261 and headed off (south of the Kane Ranger Station at Grand Gulch) across Cedar and Polly mesas dirt roads. The further you go on the dirt roads, the worse they get. You may have trouble in a vehicle without high clearance. In wet weather, a 4WD vehicle is required. Check with the BLM office in Monticello for information on current conditions. We started our trek at the northernmost fork of Slickhorn Canyon at a place some call the &ldquofirst fork.&rdquo

The Group

Figure 6.5   Text with link.

Text is normally black, and links are blue (default) differentiating them from the rest of the text. (The words will be underlined, too, if you have not turned off the link underlining in your browser.) Click on the words "dirt roads" and the link will immediately take you to the Web page *roads.html*. Once you have used the link, the link words change to another color (default: purple).

Image Tricks

Keep in mind the two following image tricks that you may find useful from time to time.

Image Link

Who says that a link has to consist of a word or a group of words? It can be an image too. Rather than highlight a word or a group of words, highlight an image. Then proceed to create a link. Once you have turned an image into a link, a click on the image will take a website visitor to the target of the link (e.g., another Web page).

Linked Image

You can link to an image file just as you can link to a Web page. The image file name takes the place of a Web page file name in the URL. The browser will display the image by itself on a Web page (see Figure 6.6) in the upper left-hand corner.

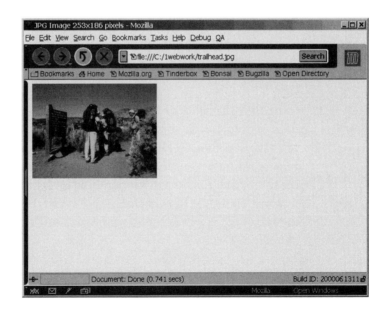

Figure 6.6   Browser display resulting from a link to an image.

Learning about URLs

A URL is simply an address for a file available on the Internet. It's more than you need to know to review the domain name system exhaustively. Nonetheless, this chapter covers the basics in a simple way.

Absolute Reference

Use the following domain address as an example:

http://www.ebaythesmartway.com/temp/index.html

The *http://* indicates that the file is on the Web and is to be linked via Hypertext Transfer Protocol (HTTP), the Web network transmission protocol. The *www.ebaythesmartway.com* is the unique domain name address. Note that this part of the URL is not case-sensitive (it can be in upper- or lowercase characters). The appropriate folders (and target HTML file) at the eBay the Smart Way website show after the domain name and the forward slant.

/temp/index.html

Note that this part of the URL is case sensitive. Capitalization does matter. Get the uppercase and lowercase right and save yourself a lot of trouble. The URL names the file, and it names the subfolders from the root folder (the domain folder) as a path to get to the target file. Each subfolder and the target file are separated by a forward slant (/). In this case, the domain is the root folder, and the target file is in a subfolder named *temp* (short for eBay auction ad template).

The Name's Not the Same

The folder (the Web root folder) for the domain is not necessarily named ebaythesmartway *on the ISP's hard drive. It may have a name such as* public_html *or* virtual_html. *On your hard drive, however, name the root folder the same as the domain name (e.g., ebaythesamrtway) to keep things simple.*

When you express a Web address including the transmission protocol (HTTP) and the target file (*index.html*), it's an *absolute* reference. Since each domain name is unique, each subfolder of a parent folder is unique, and each file in a folder is unique, you have absolutely defined where the target file is located. But there is another way to reference Web addresses.

Relative References

Within a domain, you can make your references relative to the folder structure of the domain. Study the folder structure for Huge Lender (*hugelender.com*).

```
⊟ 🗀 loans
   ┈ 🗀 administration
   ⊟ 🗀 applications
      ┈ 🗀 brokers
      ┈ 🗀 online
      ┈ 🗀 printed
   ⊟ 🗀 closings
      ┈ 🗀 escrow
      ┈ 🗀 office
      ┈ 🗀 onsite
   ⊟ 🗀 rates
      ┈ 🗀 auto
      ┈ 🗀 homes
```

Advance

If you want the navigation path to go from *index.html* (a Web page) in the folder (*loans*) to *fha.html* (another Web page) in the subfolder *homes*, you express the link as follows:

rates/homes/fha.html

In contrast, the absolute URL is:

http://www.hugelender.com/loans/rates/homes/fha.html

Keep in mind that the absolute URL doesn't work on your own computer (where you keep a parallel website), but the relative link works on both your computer and the Web host computer.

Retreat

Suppose you place a link in *fha.html* that goes back to *index.html* in the root folder (*loans*). How do you express that? You use the expression ../ to go back up the folder tree. The link from *fha.html* to *index.html* is:

../../index.html

The first ../ goes from the *homes* subfolder to the *rates* subfolder. The second ../ goes from the *rates* subfolder to the *loans* folder.

Retreat and Advance

Now for the finale! Suppose you want to put a link to *fha.html* (in the *homes* subfolder) from the Web page *fha-app.html* in the *online* subfolder. The relative link follows:

../../rates/homes/fha.html

The first two ../ take you up the tree (to the *loans* folder from the subfolder *online*); and the *rates/homes* take you down the tree (from the *loans* folder to the subfolder *homes*).

Test Immediately

This is a simple straightforward system of linking Web pages inside a website. When you put it into practice, however, it sometimes gets a little tricky. Always check your links immediately after you create them to see if they work properly (remember testing in Chapter 3).

Relative links work effectively in Web pages on your own computer or in the Web pages on your Web host computer. This enables you to keep the parallel websites essential to efficient and sensible Web work (see Chapters 18 and 19).

Good Practice

When linking to your own Web pages within your website, use relative references. It's generally easier. When referring to Web pages outside your website elsewhere on the Web, use absolute references. It's the only way to get there.

File Names

Windows 95, 98, NT 4.0, 2000, and Mac OS allow flexible file names with almost unlimited characters. Nonetheless, there are still people and software that use the 8.3 (DOS) configuration for naming files. That means up to eight characters with a three-character extension (not case sensitive):

fastcars.htm

In this case, even the Web extension *.html* is shortened to *.htm*. If you desire to accommodate these people, you need to name your files appropriately. They are probably such a small remnant population on the Web, however, that you can safely ignore them.

Reminder

Remember that on the Web, files names are case sensitive. I always make all my file names lowercase just for more efficient typing and to avoid confusion. Also, no spaces are allowed in Web file names, but some people use the underline character in place of a space.

Anchors

What is an anchor? It's a target within a Web page. It's a place to go. And it has a unique name within the Web page. A link can take you to an anchor.

An anchor has a prefix of the character #. Thus, if there is an anchor named *april* in the Web page *fha.html*, you can link to the anchor with the following absolute URL:

http://www.hugelender.com/loans/rates/homes/fha.html#april

A relative link from the *loans* folder to the anchor is as follows:

rates/homes/fha.html#april

The following sections show how to create an anchor in a Web page for Composer and FrontPage Express.

Composer

Open *myfirst.html* in Composer. Place the cursor before the second heading (The Group). Click on the anchor icon.

The Named Anchor Properties window will pop up. For the Anchor Name, enter *group* and click *OK*. An anchor marking will appear in the page.

Now go to the first word in the first paragraph (We). Make it into a link that goes to the anchor. The URL for the relative link is simply:

#group

If you were linking to the anchor *group* from outside the Web page, the URL would include:

myfirst.html#group

In your browser, test the link to the anchor you have made. Click on the word We, and the browser will bring the heading The Group to the top of the browser window (see Figure 6.7).

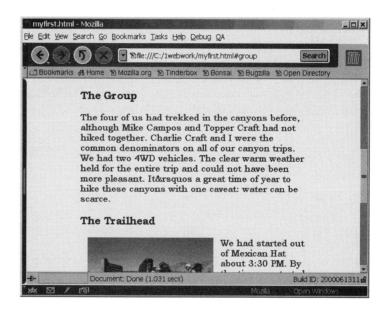

Figure 6.7   Browser display after clicking on the link to the anchor.

FrontPage Express

FrontPage Express does not provide a well-specified way to create an anchor other than using HTML. Consequently, you will have to add the HTML markups to your Web pages and understand how they work. To insert an HTML markup in FrontPage Express go Insert, HTML Markup, and enter the markup you desire to use. See Appendix II for an HTML tutorial.

Another Way

You can also use the Extended Attributes window activated by the Extended button on the Create Hyperlink window. But you need to know for HTML purposes that the attribute name for naming an anchor is name.

Creating an Email Link

You have seen forms in Web pages that enable you to send an email message. Website visitors find such forms awkward to use. The forms themselves add a process to Web page making that few beginners ever use; that is, the forms require a CGI script (see Chapter 21). But you have a better way to accomplish the same purpose easily. Use an email link.

```
<a href="mailto:
staff@camcordersforall.com">Contact
Us</a>
```

As you can see, the *href* is not a URL. It's an email address. When a website visitor clicks on this link, his or her email program pops up with the addressee (*staff@camcordersforall.com*) already on the *To:* line. Most website visitors feel more comfortable using their email programs to send information or messages than using an email form in a Web page.

Don't Use Info@

When you use the email link, don't use the email address info@. This is traditionally reserved for auto responders (bots), a technique for automatically delivering information by email in response to email inquires. If you do use info@, it will be confusing to many people.

Summary

In Composer and FrontPage Express, creating a link is easy. The toughest part is getting the Web address right, and that's easy, too, although sometimes it takes a little thought.

Most people don't use anchors often, but they serve a useful purpose when you need them. Keep them in mind for navigational use inside Web pages.

7

Fill-in-the-Blank Web Pages

If making Web pages seems overly complicated or time-consuming when using Composer or FrontPage Express, you can find places on the Web where you can create a Web page by answering a questionnaire. These Web pages or miniwebsites are often hosted free. If you're looking for something simple, one of these may suit you just fine.

To otherwise save time and effort in making Web pages, you can use ready-made Web pages (templates) that have blanks for you to fill in. This is quite easy, and can save much time when you make many similar Web pages, particularly for the same website.

Fill-in-the-Blank Web Host

In a book, it's risky to illustrate an online scheme for doing anything, because online schemes, and instructions for using them, change regularly without notice. Consequently, you can read through this chapter to get the flavor of using a fill-in-the-blank Web host rather than to get a step-by-step tutorial. Plenty of Web portals (major websites) and some ISPs offer free Web hosting services via a fill-in-the-blank authoring scheme. This chapter will illustrate one Web hosting opportunity, GeoCities (now part of Yahoo!), as a prototype of this type of Web hosting service.

The first thing to do is sign up and get a login and password (see Figure 7.1).

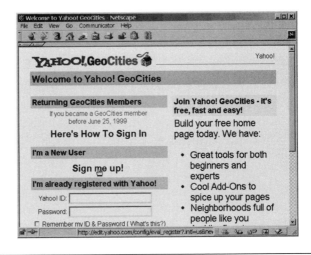

Figure 7.1   Signup page.

Next you move on to building your website. You have a choice between the PageWizards and the PageBuilder (see Figure 7.2).

Figure 7.2   Choice of ways to build Web pages.

PageWizard

The PageWizard is the easiest. You have your choice of page layouts (see Figure 7.3). I picked the *Techie*.

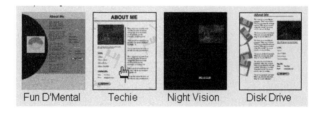

Figure 7.3   Choice of Web page layouts.

It's just a matter of filling in blanks in forms (see Figure 7.4).

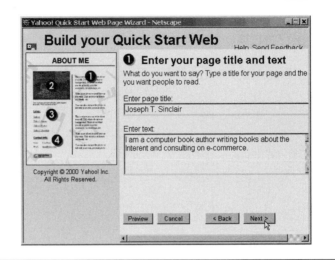

Figure 7.4   Fill in the blanks.

When you finish, GeoCities gives you your Web address.

http://www.geocities.com/sinclair_39/index.html

Because the information you provide fills in a template, the finished Web page can look very attractive (see Figure 7.5).

Page Builder

GeoCities also provides PageBuilder to make creative Web pages. Although it uses templates, you do the work and can change the templates. PageBuilder is a Web authoring program (a Java applet) which is not difficult to learn but nonetheless is certainly no easier to learn than Composer or FrontPage Express. This program starts with an open template that includes sample text (see Figure 7.6).

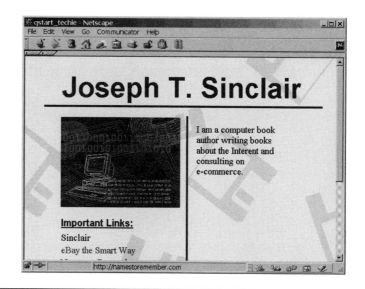

Figure 7.5   The finished product.

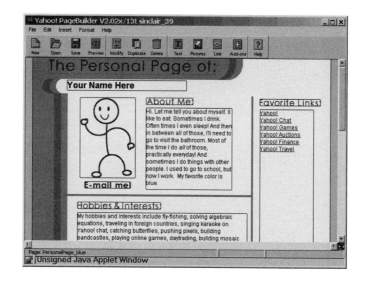

Figure 7.6   PageBuilder template.

You remove the existing text (highlight and *Delete*) and add your own (see Figure 7.7).

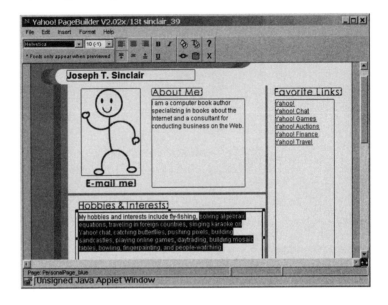

Figure 7.7   Using the template.

You can add a text box and text, add a photograph, delete a text box, or do almost anything you want to do (see Figure 7.8).

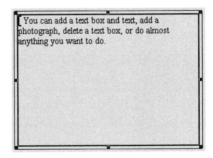

Figure 7.8   Using PageBuilder.

You can also start from scratch with a blank Web page and build the entire page yourself.

The Rest of the Story

When I used PageBuilder the first time, it crashed my operating system (Windows 2000) as some Java programs are wont to do occasionally. Thereafter, PageBuilder worked OK, at least for short periods of time. This illustrates the current inconveniences of working online to do projects such as building websites. If it's a small website, that's fine. If it's a large project, you may want to opt for offline software.

Multiple Web Pages

You aren't limited to one Web page at GeoCities. You can do multiple Web pages and link them. Thus, you can build a real website at GeoCities. For no cost, this is a good deal if it fits your purposes. To get started go to *http://geocities.yahoo.com/home*.

Templates

A template Web page is simply a predesigned Web page waiting for the content to be filled in. Once you put in the content, the Web page comes to life. You can create a template just by taking the content out of one of your existing Web pages or from any Web page on the Web. You can also find templates on the Web. Templates come with a wide variety of software. Consequently, you shouldn't have any trouble finding or making a template to suit your purposes.

Composer and FrontPage Express

Try making a template with *myfirst.html*. Highlight all the headings and text, and press the delete key. The text disappears, and a one-cell table with no content remains. You now have an effective template for a series of Web pages on a website. Just copy some other content and paste it into the blank table in the template.

Voila!, You now have a new Web page. It not only looks good, but it matches the layout of the original Web page and gives your website a unified and well-managed look. Naturally, templates can get much more elaborate than this very simple example. Nevertheless, you can see how this takes the Web page formatting work you've done already and turns it into something you can reuse. (Note that you do have to do some typesetting, such as create headings, after you fill in the template.)

Composer

You can access Netscape's template website to choose a template for use in Composer. Because it was not yet activated in my beta version of Composer, I cannot provide a complete explanation of this feature. However, go New, and look for *Page Using Template* or something similar; you'll be on the right track.

FrontPage Express

Can FrontPage Express be any easier? Perhaps. Try the Personal Home Page Wizard. Go File, New, and select *Personal Home Page Wizard* in the New Page dialog box that pops up and click *OK*. The Personal Home Page Wizard will pop up.

Make your selections in the Wizard and click *Next>*. Make your selections and inputs in succeeding windows. After less than a dozen windows, you have a new Web page. Slick! Alas, it's probably not a Web page that you will want to own.

HTML

An HTML template starts with a normal Web page from which the content has been removed such as in the earlier example for *myfirst.html*. The HTML for the simple template follows:

```
<html><head>

<title>My First</title>

</head>

<body bgcolor="#FFFFFF">

<p> </p>

<table border="0" cellpadding="10"
cellspacing="0" width="480">

<tr><td> </td>

</tr></table>

</body></html>
```

Now add some instructions using the <--! comment --> markup. Someone using the template can read the comments, but the browser doesn't display the comments. The following is the *myfirst.html* template with instructions added using the comment markup:

```
<html><head>

<title>My First</title>

</head>

<body bgcolor="#FFFFFF">

<p> </p>

<table border="0" cellpadding="10"
cellspacing="0" width="480">

<tr><td>
```

```
<!-- Enter text below to take the
place of the x. The text will appear
in a text column 480 pixels wide. -->

x

<!-- Enter text above -->

</td>

</tr></table>

</body></html>
```

If you use this Web page in its HTML format, all you need to do to add content is copy and paste it into the proper place. You will also have to add the normal text typesetting markups such as for headings and paragraphs.

Summary

If you need something simple for no expense, a free fill-in-the-blank Web page host offering may work well for you. But beware. More elaborate online authoring programming at fill-in-the-blank Web hosts may be more difficult to use than Composer or FrontPage Express.

In any event, use templates to create Web pages and save time and energy. You can easily make templates from existing Web pages.

II

Web Page Skills

8

Making Text Look Good

Just because you're on the Web doesn't mean you can forget the rules of typesetting and layout. Many readers learned these rules when they mastered desktop publishing. Other readers never learned desktop publishing. The rules this chapter sets forth will acquaint the uninitiated with some proper techniques for making your text on the Web readable and attractive. Reading this chapter will also provide a useful review for those who have already learned desktop publishing.

Communicating with Text

You hear a lot of conversation along the lines of, "Text is dead. People don't read any longer. Multimedia is the new publishing medium." It sounds good and certainly defines the times. But it's not true. Text remains the most important medium for the Web. For instance, you can read the script of a video in much less time than it takes to listen to it being read or watch the video. Text is relatively fast and efficient. It takes teams of people to produce sound and video presentations; often one writer creates an entire textual work by himself or herself. Consequently, text can be, and often is, less expensive and more efficient. Text remains very useful no matter how much sound or video you use at your website.

Therefore, pay attention to your use of text. Typeset carefully. The goal has to be to make your text as readable as possible. Otherwise, what's the point of using text? And keep in mind that good typesetting enhances the appearance and appeal of a wide variety of multimedia presentations.

What Visitors Have

To start your typesetting strategy, realize your limitations. You can only count on all your website visitors having the following fonts:

PC: Times New Roman, Arial, Courier New

Mac: Times, Helvetica, Courier

As you might suspect, these fonts are comparable (Times New Roman to Times, Arial to Helvetica, and Courier New to Courier). Netscape and Microsoft have set Times New Roman and Times (almost identical) serif fonts as the defaults for their browsers. They feature Arial (a version of Helvetica) and Helvetica for a standard sans serif font. They also feature Courier New and Courier for standard monospaced fonts. This is what you have to work with. You cannot count on your website visitors having any other fonts. Consequently, if you typeset with other fonts, your Web pages may not display for many website visitors the way you intended.

As the chapter later explains, you can use advanced typesetting techniques to embed fonts in Web pages so that your website visitors can use them to read your specialized typesetting, but such Web typography is the realm of advanced Web developers. Until you're ready to tackle learning the use of advanced Web typography, limit your Web pages to the serif, sans serif, and monospaced fonts mentioned in this section.

Layout

The first rule of layout is to make a readable column. You already mastered that technique in Chapter 4. Make your columns a certain width (expressed in pixels) appropriate to the text font size. Remember, the column should be 9-12 words on each line for readability. Larger font sizes will require wider text columns.

Another rule of layout is to make your Web pages attractive. Text that goes from left to right (without margins) fills the whole page. That tends to overwhelm readers and make text difficult to read. When you place text in a column more narrow than the browser display, you create white space on either side of the column (margins). White space brings visual relief to readers.

Naturally, you need to break up text by creating paragraphs. On the Web, make your paragraphs short wherever practical. Unbroken text scrolls forever on the Web, unlike in books or magazines where long paragraphs must eventually break at the end of the page. Although technically a Web page is the entire Web document, which can be any length, psychologically a Web page is what a reader sees in the browser display before he or she begins to scroll. Paragraphs that fill an entire browser display seem to go on exhaustingly. Make most of your paragraphs shorter than one browser display if practical.

Use headings generously. Headings break up text and provide additional navigation support for the content. Without physical pages to break up the text rhythmically, a generous number of headings provide visual relief.

Plain ungarnished Web pages tend to have a boring look on the Web, even though they might not in a book. In a book, you expect only black and white, normally few illustrations, and plenty of text. On the Web where one can easily provide color graphics and even sound or video, you expect a little more.

On the other hand, too much visual garnishment can look gaudy and unattractive. "Keep it simple" is a good rule for most situations.

With a Grain of Salt

You will hear some Web gurus say that long pages of text don't work on the Web, that you need to keep it short. Take such advice with a grain of salt. It's true that in some Web presentations short blocks of text work well and are appropriate. But there's nothing wrong with long, well-written text passages nicely typeset for readability. It depends on your purpose and the level of interest your target audience has in your presentation. With good writing and high interest from your audience, you can publish long Web pages effectively.

Steal That Web Page

Even though you can copyright your content, you can't copyright your layout. Anyone can copy your finely tuned layout just by saving your Web page to their hard drive. That works in reverse too. You can copy the layout from any Web page just by saving it to your hard drive. Then you can substitute your content for the existing content. In other words, you use the saved Web page as a template.

Is this a common practice? You bet! The way it usually works, however, is that you find a Web page you like, save it, and use it to create a template that suits your purposes more closely than the original (i.e., you modify the layout). Sometimes you can modify the layout of someone else's Web page more easily than starting from scratch.

Be Careful

Many websites show a quasi-attractive layout and a dull appearance. Be careful that you don't make a template out of an ordinary Web page from such a website. Seek a website that has attractive and readable Web pages.

Search for Templates

Computer book CDs, HTML software documentation, and other Web instructional resources provide templates for layout. You can start with one of these to make your own templates. Other sources of ideas for templates are printed magazines and books. Unfortunately, you will need to create from scratch any templates based on printed material, but at least that way you'll have an idea with which to work.

Typesetting

Typesetting is an old art. Today's most popular typeface for text Garamond is about 500 years old. When typesetting works well, you don't notice it. Your reading experience is smooth. When typesetting is deficient, you not only notice it but you usually find reading uncomfortable. With that in mind, you will want to make your typesetting practices sound. A few typesetting basics follow, but you need to learn as much about typesetting as practical to do a credible job on the Web.

Not Typewriting

Neither desktop publishing nor Web typesetting is exactly like typewriting (using a typewriter). A typewriter has many limitations in regard to typesetting that desktop publishing and Web publishing do not. Therefore, typeset your Web pages like a book, not like a typewriter document. Use italics, not underlines, for emphasis and citations. Use bold, not uppercase characters, for headings.

Follow the Traditional Guidelines

Typesetting can be a complex art, particularly for typesetting special books. But by following a few simple guidelines, you can make your text look professional.

Italic

Use italics for emphasis and for the common uses set forth in style manuals, such as for book titles.

Bold

Use bold for headings, headlines, and for warnings. Do not use it for emphasis. Bold is disruptive for reading. If you use bold for emphasis inside a text block, it will make reading more difficult, not easier, to understand.

Bold Italic

Use bold italics only as substitute for bold.

All Caps

Don't use "all caps;" that is, text made up entirely of capital letters. People find it difficult to read. All caps is strictly a typewriting technique. Specifically, don't use all caps for headings or headlines.

Superscripts and Subscripts

The Web supports superscripts and subscripts. Use them where appropriate.

Bullets

The Web supports bulleted lists. These can dress up your text and make it look professional.

Numbers

The Web supports numbered lists. Numbered lists are useful to readers.

Border

Use borders to create boxed text. Use boxed text for sidebars, special instructions, and other appropriate uses. You can create boxed text by putting text inside a one-cell table and showing the border for the table.

Type Size

You can change the type size for your Web page text. For easy reading, set the type size to normal, which is 12 points. A *+1*, *+2*, or *+3* increment will make the type size larger for special uses such as headings or headlines. A *-1*, *-2*, or *-3* increment will make the type size smaller for uses such as block quotes. Be careful when you use smaller type sizes. People find them difficult to read. In fact, you can make type small enough on the Web so that most people will find it uncomfortably difficult to read. Why would anyone want to do that? Who knows? It's one of the great mysteries of the Web. Yet, you don't have to look far on the Web to find text that's too small to read.

Rules

At one time early in Web history, people used rules (straight horizontal lines) quite a bit. It became trite to do so, and you don't see rules used often any longer. But don't be afraid to use them occasionally when appropriate to separate different sections of text.

Underlines

Don't use underlines in Web pages. An underline designates a link. If you put underlines to other uses, you will confuse your website visitors.

Add an Image

How do you add an image to make text look better? It's simple. Add a small logo or trademark in the upper portion of the Web page. It makes the text page look better and gives it a stamp of authenticity that it otherwise lacks. This works well for recognizable logos and trademarks, but it works for unknown images too. If you don't have a logo or trademark, create one for your website and use it for text pages that would otherwise be without an image.

You can also add abstract or design images as Web page dressing, which can make text pages more attractive. However, this takes considerably more design skill than just adding a logo or trademark. You might want to ask your favorite digital artist to create something for you.

Advanced Web Typesetting

The typesetting supported by HTML and Web authoring is basic and sometimes limited. Web standards, however, support advanced typesetting and layout. The standard is Cascading Style Sheets (CSS) which supports fine-grained typesetting and layout and is not difficult to use.

In addition, Bitstream's TruDoc and Microsoft's font embedding enable you to use the fonts of your choice and embed them in a Web page so that readers will be able to see your Web page typeset as you intended with your choice of fonts. You can get plenty of information on the use of this full-fledged Web typesetting technology in my *Typography on the Web* (AP Professional, 1999).

Text for Tutorials

Type in the following text for use in the Composer or FrontPage tutorials that follow later:

Logistics

Most of our food was dry food from the supermarket packed in Ziploc bags. In a pinch, you can also use the Ziplocs to carry extra water. Although we had tents, we slept in the open almost every night (due to good weather). Our packs ranged from about 40 to 55 pounds (including food and 11 pounds of water). The following list supplements normal backpacking equipment with items specifically for desert canyon trekking:

Extra water bottles and water. Usually six one-quart bottles of water are enough, but some treks require more.

Bandanas. Bandanas come in handy for a variety of purposes. One is air conditioning; wet a bandana and tie it around your forehead.

Large shade hat. You need to keep your head out of the sun on any trek, but it's especially important to do so in desert canyons.

This is not much extra equipment. In fact, the equipment for desert trekking is much the same as for general backpacking. You may want to wear lightly-colored clothes in the desert to reflect the sun.

Forty Nights

In my last forty nights in the canyons, it has rained only two nights. One night was an on and off drizzle, the other a light rain. For both nights a tarp worked just fine.

For group cooking, you will need the following basic equipment for heating water for soup and drinks and for cooking pot dinners:

Backpacking stove and fuel.

Cigarette lighter for lighting stove.

Three pots, one four-quart and two two-quart, with covers and a potholder.

One cup and three spoons.

Each individual eats everything with his or her own cup and spoon and washes them separately from the group cookware.

The topo maps you need are:

Slickhorn Canyon East

Pollys Pasture

Slickhorn Canyon West

Sorry it's so much typing, but there are many lessons to be learned with this reasonably small amount of text.

Using Composer

Open *myfirst.html* in Composer. Highlight and delete all the content (text) in the one-cell table. In other words, make a template as described in Chapter 7. Type in the text provided earlier in this chapter. Now you're ready to get to work.

Bold and Italic

In the first paragraph, highlight the word "supermarket." Click on the italic icon.

The word will change to italic type. Highlight the word "Ziploc." Click on the bold icon.

B

The word will change to bold type. (Note that this is not a correct usage of bold but will suffice for an illustration.)

Change Type Size

Highlight the word "pinch." Click on the type size decrease icon (on the left).

ᴬ ᴬ

The type size will decrease by one increment. (Click on the type size increase icon on the right, and the type size will increase by one increment.)

Change Typeface (Font)

Highlight the word "Ziplocs." Go to the typeface window under the Preview icon, and click on the arrow.

Variabe Wi... ▼

Select the typeface Arial. The word now appears in the Arial typeface.

Headings

You already learned how to make HTML headings in Chapter 4 (headings set at level 3). Using the HTML headings is a good practice (levels 1-6). But there is another way to create headings.

Increase the type size of the heading and make it bold. Put a line space before and after by pressing the *Enter* key. Use this technique to make "Logistics" a heading and also "Forty Nights."

Centering

Place the cursor on the heading Logistics, click on the alignment icon, and select *Center*. This centers the heading. Normally you don't center headings, but you do often center titles.

Bulleted Lists

Place the cursor in front of the sentence that starts "Extra water bottles and water." Press the *Enter* key. Do the same for the three sentences that start with "Bandanas" and "Large shade hat" and "This is not much." Put the cursor on the first sentence and click on the bulleted list icon.

Do the same for the next *two* sentences. Test the result in your browser (see Figure 8.1).

Rules (Horizontal Lines)

Place the cursor before the sentence that starts "The topo maps you need." Go Insert, Horizontal Line. This inserts a rule separating this last paragraph from the remainder of the text. Figure 8.2 shows the rule. Note that Composer gives you control over how a rule will be displayed (e.g., color, width). The default setting is a full-width, shadowed rule.

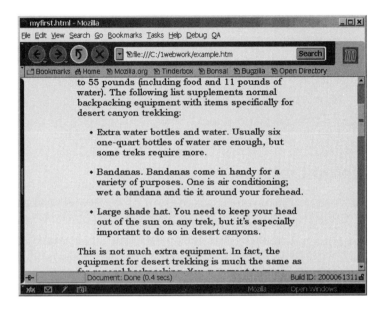

to 55 pounds (including food and 11 pounds of water). The following list supplements normal backpacking equipment with items specifically for desert canyon trekking:

- Extra water bottles and water. Usually six one-quart bottles of water are enough, but some treks require more.

- Bandanas. Bandanas come in handy for a variety of purposes. One is air conditioning; wet a bandana and tie it around your forehead.

- Large shade hat. You need to keep your head out of the sun on any trek, but it's especially important to do so in desert canyons.

This is not much extra equipment. In fact, the equipment for desert trekking is much the same as

Figure 8.1   Bulleted list.

Numbered Lists

Place the cursor in front of the list item "Slickhorn Canyon East." Press the *Enter* key. Do the same for the two items that start with "Pollys Pasture" and "Slickhorn Canyon West." Put the cursor on the first item and click on the numbered list icon.

Do the same for the next two items. Test the result in your browser (see Figure 8.2). You will have a traditional numbered list, which gives your text a nice change of scenery.

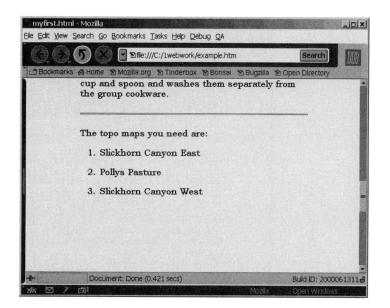

Figure 8.2   Numbered list in the paragraph below the rule.

Unnumbered Text

You can use the move-to-the-right icon to create unnumbered lists
and sidebars.

Lists

Place the cursor in front of the list item "Backpacking stove." Press
the *Enter* key. Do the same for the sentence that starts with "Each
individual." Put the cursor on the first item and click on the move-
to-the-right icon.

Test the result in your browser (see Figure 8.3).

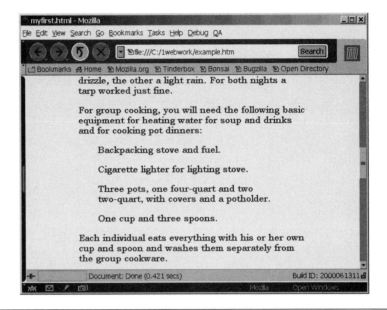

Figure 8.3   Unnumbered list.

Sidebars

To create a sidebar, treat the sidebar heading as an unnumbered list item and the sidebar body of text the same way. Make the heading bold. See an example in Figure 8.4.

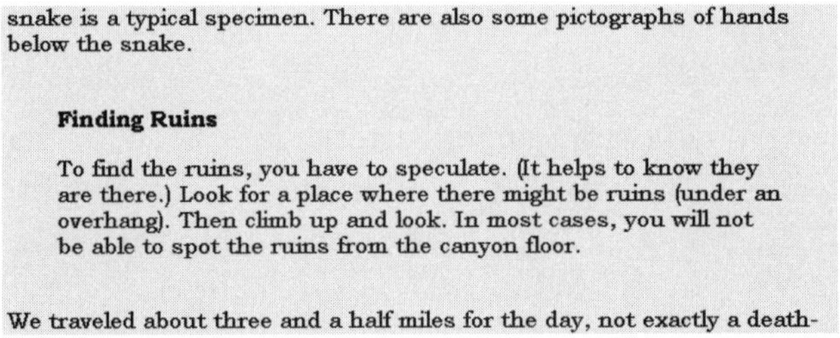

snake is a typical specimen. There are also some pictographs of hands below the snake.

Finding Ruins

To find the ruins, you have to speculate. (It helps to know they are there.) Look for a place where there might be ruins (under an overhang). Then climb up and look. In most cases, you will not be able to spot the ruins from the canyon floor.

We traveled about three and a half miles for the day, not exactly a death-

Figure 8.4   Sidebar created similarly to an unnumbered list.

Using FrontPage Express

Open *myfirst.html* in FrontPage Express. Highlight and delete all the content (text) in the one-cell table. In other words, make a template as mentioned in Chapter 7. Type in the text provided earlier in this chapter. Now you're ready to get to work.

Bold and Italic

In the first paragraph, highlight the word "supermarket." Click on the italic icon.

The word will change to italic type. Highlight the word "Ziploc." Click on the bold icon.

The word will change to bold type. (Note that this is not a correct usage of bold but will suffice for an illustration.)

Change Type Size

Highlight the word "pinch." Click on the type size decrease icon (on the right).

The type size will decrease by one increment. (Click on the type size increase icon on the left, and the type size will increase by one increment.)

Change Typeface (Font)

Highlight the word "Ziplocs." Go to the typeface window under the Go menu, and click on the arrow.

Times New Roman ▼

Select the typeface Arial. The word now appears in the Arial typeface.

Headings

You already learned how to make HTML headings in Chapter 4 (headings set at level 3). Using the HTML headings is a good practice (levels 1-6). But there is another way to create headings. Increase the type size of the heading and make it bold. Put a line space before and after by pressing the *Enter* key. Use this technique to make Logistics a heading and also Forty Nights.

Centering

Place the cursor on the heading (Logistics), and click on the center icon. This centers the heading. Normally you don't center headings, but you do often center titles.

Bulleted Lists

Place the cursor in front of the sentence that starts "Extra water bottles and water." Press the *Enter* key. Do the same for the three sentences that start with "Bandanas" and "Large shade hat" and "This is not much." Put the cursor on the first sentence and click on the bulleted list icon.

Do the same for the next *two* sentences. Test the result in your browser (see Figure 8.5).

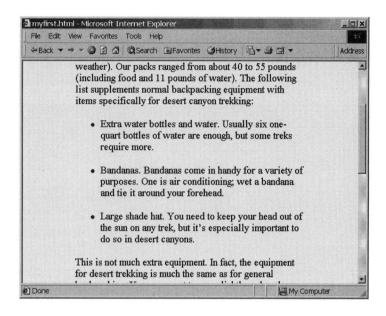

Figure 8.5   Bulleted list.

Rules (Horizontal Lines)

Place the cursor before the sentence that starts "The topo maps you need." Go Insert, Horizontal Line. This inserts a rule separating this last paragraph from the remainder of the text.

Numbered Lists

Place the cursor in front of the list item "Slickhorn Canyon East." Press the *Enter* key. Do the same for the two items that start with "Pollys Pasture" and "Slickhorn Canyon West." Put the cursor on the first item and click on the numbered list icon. A browser automatically numbers the items for you.

Do the same for the next two items. Test the result in your browser (see Figure 8.6).

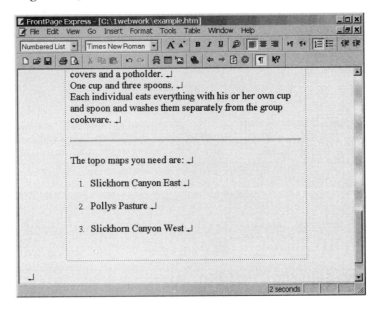

Figure 8.6   Numbered list in the last paragraph below the rule.

Unnumbered Text

You can use the move-to-the-right icon to create unnumbered lists and sidebars.

Lists

Place the cursor in front of the list item "Backpacking stove." Press the *Enter* key. Do the same for the sentence that starts with "Each individual" and each list item in between. Highlight all the items and click on the move-to-the-right icon.

Test the result in your browser (see Figure 8.7).

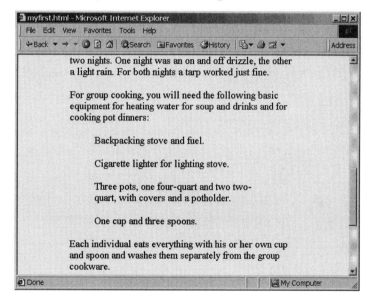

Figure 8.7   Unnumbered list.

Sidebars

To create a side bar, treat the sidebar heading as an unnumbered list item and the sidebar body of text the same. Make the heading bold. See an example in Figure 8.8.

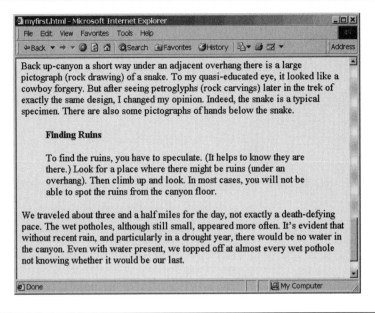

Figure 8.8   Sidebar created similarly to an unnumbered list.

The Future of Text

The future of text on the Web looks promising. As more and more webmasters used advanced Web typesetting, readable text will become the norm rather than the exception on the Web. Software technology such as Bitstream's TrueDoc and Microsoft's ClearType make Web type more readable without special hardware. Normal monitors still have a little room to improve resolution, and presumably manufacturers will eventually sell normal monitors that display text a little sharper. Active matrix LCD monitors have even more room for improvement. In addition Microsoft's ClearType works much better with flat panel monitors than with normal monitors. Consequently, we can expect flat panel monitors to display text a lot sharper in the future. All of which is to say that reading will improve on the Web, not disappear leaving behind a multimedia whirl. So, take text on the Web seriously. Make it readable. And enjoy the reality that text is a cost-efficient Web medium that every literate person can use.

Summary

Observing a few basic typesetting rules will go a long way toward making your text readable on the Web. Learn the rules and use them. If you want people to read your Web pages, give them a break. Make your text readable.

9

Adding Color

Color adds a wonderful dimension to publishing, and you can use color on the Web. Digital color is a complex topic. This chapter takes a look at digital color but covers only the practical basics. The most important effect to achieve with color is to brighten up the page without impairing readability and to keep color designs consistent from one Web page to another and from one browser to another.

Color Basics

The main ingredient of proper color use is cultural; that is, good taste remains important. Choose your color combinations with care. The two most important combinations are the text (foreground) color and the background color. But also keep in mind that the colors for additional Web page design elements must fit into your color scheme.

Color Combinations

Text colors and background colors are essential design elements of an attractive website or group of Web pages. Where text is present, keep readability in mind. To be readable, the text color and the background color must contrast. For instance, in Figure 9.1 the turquoise text on a sky blue background does not contrast enough with the background to be readable.

Figure 9.1   Turquoise on sky blue.

Change the text color to dark red, however, and it's readable (see Figure 9.2) because the combination has greater contrast.

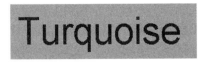

Figure 9.2   Dark red on sky blue.

What's wrong with this dark-red-on-sky-blue combination? Even though it's readable, it's not attractive. It might be attractive with the right artistic treatment, but generally it's not a pleasing combination in American culture.

That leads to the conclusion that choosing attractive color combinations that contrast sufficiently to support readability is based on judgment, not on technical formulas. Table 9.1 includes some proven combinations that support readability and apparently are not offensive.

Table 9.1   Color combinations for readability.

	Text Color	Background Color
Monochrome monitor	green	black
Monochrome monitor	yellow	black
Word for Windows	white	dark blue
WebTV	light colors	black
Author's choice	black	medium green
Variation	dark blue	medium green
Used by many	black	light gray
Also used by many	black	medium gray

You will note that white is conspicuously missing in Table 9.1 with one exception (white on dark blue). Normal monitors (cathode ray tubes - CRTs) blast light at your eyes. The white light is particularly irritating. If you tone it down a little, however, it helps readability.

If you're set on using a white background, use a light gray, cream, pastel green, rose, or pastel blue background instead. Avoid white text on a dark background (even though Microsoft offers white on dark blue as an elective in Word for Windows).

Author's Experience

My eyes quickly get strained when I have to read on white backgrounds (more often than I would like). Nonetheless, I can read

*and write for 14 hours in a day without eyestrain using black
text on a medium green background.*

The Great White Problem

Most people creating Web pages use black type on a white background by default. They don't set a color background, and the default color is white. Likewise, most people using the Web read on a white background simply because that's the default. They don't know how to change the background color. Consequently, most people on the Web read black type on a white background. It's no wonder that people get eyestrain or headaches and don't like to read on the Web. You can help change this by providing a background that gives some relief to your poor readers.

Web Color

Digital color comes with numerous systems of designations. Of those, this chapter covers the only two you will need to know. Although Composer and FrontPage Express provide you with color charts, you will need to know how to use the numerical designations in order to use an assortment of *browser-safe* colors.

RGB

Most of the image editing software designates color with the RGB (Red Green Blue) system. You assign a number from 0 to 255 for each of the three colors, and together they comprise a specific color. Table 9.2 contains some normal colors.

Table 9.2   RGB color chart.

RGB	Red	Green	Blue	Yellow	Gray	Black	White
R	255	000	000	255	204	000	255
G	000	255	000	255	204	000	255
B	000	000	255	000	204	000	255

Examples of other conventional colors are turquoise (000,255,255), fuchsia (255,000,255), powder blue (153,204,255), pastel green (204,255,204), rose (255,255,204), and cream (255,255,204).

The problem with colors is that different browsers may display colors differently. What you see in your browser (while testing) may not be what someone else sees in their's. However, there are browser-safe colors that look the same in every browser. They are any colors designated with the following RGB numbers:

000, 051, 102, 153, 204, 255

Thus, medium green (000,204,102) is a browser-safe color. It displays as a dependable Kelly green in every browser. But this royal blue (049,028,231) is not a browser-safe color. It might look just right in your browser but different in someone else's browser.

Consequently, use browser-safe colors as much as possible, or take your chances.

Hex

Unfortunately, the Web uses the Hex number system. If you use non-browser-safe colors, you need to get an RGB-Hex converter program such as RGB2Hex, a freeware program downloadable at *http://download32.com/proghtml/99/9905.htm* and other locations.

Alternatively, you can use a simple way to designate colors with Hex numbers, but only if you use exclusively browser-safe colors. The RGB and Hex equivalents for browser-safe colors are as follows:

RGB   Hex

000 = 00

051 = 33

102 = 66

153 = 99

204 = cc

255 = ff

Thus, using only browser-safe colors, you can memorize the RGB-Hex equivalents to use them in your Web pages. For example, Table 9.3 shows the same colors as Table 9.2 in Hex numbers instead of RGB numbers.

Table 9.3   Hex color chart.

Hex	Red	Green	Blue	Yellow	Gray	Balck	White
R	ff	00	00	ff	cc	00	ff
G	00	ff	00	ff	cc	00	ff
B	00	00	ff	00	cc	00	ff

Examples of other normal colors are turquoise (00,ff,ff), fuchsia (ff,00,ff), powder blue (99ccff), pastel green (ccffcc), rose (ffcccc), and cream (ffffcc).

Why Color Designations?

Why include color designations in this chapter? If you learn HTML (see HTML tutorial in Appendix II), you will be able to read the HTML in any Web page (see Appendix III). By learning the color designations, you will be able to read the Hex color designations in any Web page. You can learn a lot by analyzing other people's Web pages, and you analyze them by looking at the HTML.

Composer Colors

The built-in color chart in Composer consists of 70 colors. This makes things convenient unless you want to use browser-safe colors. You pop up the color chart by clicking on the color icon.

The top square is for text color, the bottom square for background color. Just chose your colors from the Composer color chart (see Figure 9.1).

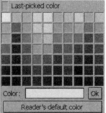

Figure 9.1   Composer color chart.

If you use browser-safe colors, you will need to use the numerical designations for color. Go Format, Page Colors and Background, Advanced Edit, HTML Attributes, enter hex numbers for colors, and click *OK*.

FrontPage Express Color

For text colors, highlight the text for which you desire to change the color. FrontPage Express provides a color chart when you click the color icon.

Don't assume the colors are browser-safe. Many are not. Instead click on the Define Custom Colors button. Click on a blank (white) box under Custom colors. Then define a color using RGB numbers on the right-hand side of the color generator. Finally, click on the Add to Custom Colors button. Your color will appear in the blank box and will be selected. Click *OK*.

For background colors, go Format, Background, Background, Background, click on arrow and select Custom. You will get the color chart. Select the color as you do for text. You can do the same for the general text color.

Background Pictures

Putting in a background image and tiling (repeating a small image horizontally and vertically) it is a very popular technique on the Web. See the tile GIF below and the tiled background in Figure 9.2.

Gray Weave.gif

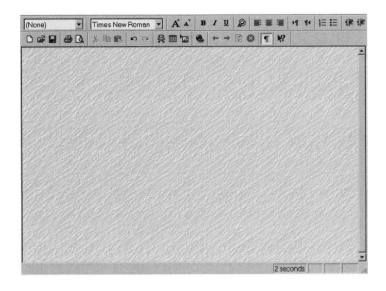

Figure 9.2   A tiled background.

Unfortunately, it invariably impairs reading and doesn't make sense. Why use this artistic technique, no matter how attractive it might look, if it defeats the purpose you set out to accomplish? Sometimes a faint watermark background works OK, but even most watermark backgrounds are too strong and interfere with easy reading. Thus, the best backgrounds for text are plain browser-safe colors.

Design Elements

This chapter does not cover color design elements. That's art, and you can find information on color design in a multitude of Web design books. You can even find packages on the Web that include color design elements for Web pages. There are a few things to keep in mind:

- To give your Web pages a professional look, hire a digital artist to create some Web page design elements.

- If you can't afford a digital artist, keep your design simple. Or, find a package of color design elements you can use.

- Make sure the design elements you use fit into your text-background color scheme.

- Avoid Web page clutter.

Chapter 8 suggests using a small image (e.g., logo) to give Web text pages a professional look, and Chapter 11 covers making text graphics, which can add elegance to Web pages. Naturally, these additions must fit your text-background color scheme.

Summary

The use of a white background, particularly for reading, is not advisable. Use browser-safe colors not only to make your Web pages more readable but to brighten them up. Memorize the browser-safe RGB and Hex numbers to avoid using colors that are inconsistent from one browser to another.

10

Getting Digital Photographs

You have many choices when you digitize your photographs or take digital photographs. This chapter will cover many of these choices and also tell how you can acquire the photographs of others in digital form. Color photographs provide you with one of the easiest and least expensive means of dressing up your website. They look great. Take advantage of this great Web capability and give your website the look of an attractive magazine.

Digitizing Photographs

Once you have taken a roll of film, you have at least five different methods of digitizing the photographs.

Ordinary Scanner

Home-office scanners cost between $50 and $300 and make an effective method of digitizing ordinary prints. The quality is not high, but with a little care, the quality may be acceptable. Be careful, experiment, and see what works. The purchase of such a scanner is a modest and worthwhile investment if the quality suits your purposes. Using this method, you must have your photographs developed and printed before you can scan them.

Film Scanner

You can have your film negatives scanned on a film scanner at a professional photo processor. This is a reasonably priced method for good quality. Such a scanner will cost between $1,000 and $4,000 should you desire to purchase one for your home or office.

Professional Scanner

A professional scanner achieves the highest quality. Such scanners usually exceed $25,000 in price and are owned by service bureaus. This is a high-price method of digitizing high-quality prints that far exceeds the quality requirements of the Web.

Kodak Picture CD

Perhaps the easiest way to digitize photographs is to have a photo processor digitize them for you and deliver the results on a CD. Kodak Picture CD, available at most photofinishers, does just that. For a low price (about $9) you get thumbnail prints and 1536 x 1024-pixel digitized photographs (JPEGs). This size is more than adequate for most Web work. This is a high-quality process at a low price. You can't beat it for cost-effectiveness. But Kodak Photo CD is higher quality.

Kodak Photo CD

If you need sizes other than 1536 x 1024 pixels, Kodak continues to offer its original digitizing service, which includes the following pixel resolutions:

Wallet 192 x 128

Snapshot 384 x 256

Standard 768 x 512

Large 1536 x 1024

Poster 3072 x 2048

These are Photo CD files (PCD - *.pcd*) which you can convert to the type of image files you need for image editing and for Web pages. This is enough quality for the most demanding photographic work, and the higher resolutions exceed the quality you need for the Web. Although more expensive than Kodak Picture CD, this is a high-quality service at a good price available at most photofinishers.

Digital Cameras

For the Web, using a digital camera provides convenience that scanning cannot. You shoot your photographs and transfer them directly to your computer.

Consumer Digital Cameras

Consumer digital cameras, generally under $1,000, provide adequate quality for many Web purposes. The quality in this market gets higher every year. Most consumer digital cameras are point-and-shoot and easy to use.

If you buy one of these cameras, make sure that you know how you can transfer the pictures from the camera to your computer. You don't want to get stuck with a transfer method that's difficult, slow, or impossible. Also, pay attention to memory (storage). You want a storage *capacity* that's adequate and expansion storage capability that's *inexpensive*.

Floppy Disks

There's a lot to be said for digital cameras that use floppy disks. The memory is cheap and the transfer is simple.

Consumer digital cameras usually deliver the image files in a format you can put on the Web without conversion. This is a handy convenience for those who do not want to do a lot of digital image processing.

At the low end of the consumer price range, the resolution is usually 640 x 480 pixels. More expensive cameras provide resolutions as high as 1600 x 1200 pixels.

Professional Digital Cameras

These cameras range in price from $3,000 to $45,000. To begin to match the quality achieved with a high-quality 35mm camera, you will need to spend over $10,000 for a digital camera. Consequently, a purchase at the bottom of the professional price range (around $3,000) is no assurance that you will be happy with the camera's quality for conventional photographic use. On the other hand, the quality achieved by a $3,000 digital camera is adequate for most Web work.

Camcorders

Many camcorders, even analog camcorders, use a digital system for capturing images that can be used to capture one image at a time. In other words, you can use the camcorder to take digital snapshots. The resolution is low. If you have an analog camcorder, see if it will take digital snapshots and how you can transfer the snapshots to your computer. If you have a digital camcorder, chances are high it will take snapshots. You may find a camcorder adequate for some of your Web photographic requirements.

Image Files

Different cameras and camcorders use different image file formats to take photographs. If a camera takes GIF or JPEG files, you can use the pictures on the Web without further processing. This is convenient. If the camera saves the pictures in another image file format, however, you will have to use an image editor to go from one file format to another. You simply open the photograph file in its normal format and then save it to the format you need to use (GIF, JPEG, or PNG) for your website.

Stock Photos

"Stock photos" is a generic name for photographs taken by someone else that you can purchase the right to use. You can purchase these photographs by four different means:

Stock Photo Bureau Usually you purchase one photograph at a time from a huge collection of photographs taken by professionals. The quality is high, and so is the cost. The photographs are intended for commercial use.

Stock Photo Collection These are small collections of high-quality photographs on CDs put together by stock photo bureaus. The cost is high. The photographs are intended for commercial use.

Photograph CDs These are large collections of photographs that vary greatly in quality. The cost is low. Some are intended for non-commercial use and require a royalty to be paid only when used for commercial purposes. If you want to use them on a business website, make sure you buy collections labeled "royalty free."

Clip Art CDs These are collections of clip art. They often include a large collection of photographs. The quality varies greatly. The cost is low. Make sure the photographs are royalty free.

These are great resources for putting photographs on your website, a source to fit every budget. You can often improve the low-quality photographs with a little image editing (see Chapter 11).

Quality

What is high quality for digital photographs? You can say that higher resolution provides greater quality. In a sense, that's true. But that's not the whole story.

Resolution

A Photo CD Snapshot (384 x 256 pixels) uses 98,304 pixels to define a photograph. A Photo CD Standard (768 x 512 pixels) uses 393,216 pixels to define the same photograph. Assuming both versions of the photograph are the same physical size (same size print), the Standard will create a higher resolution image. On the screen of a computer monitor, however, the Standard is just a larger photograph. Consequently, resolution isn't necessarily a determinant of display quality for computer users.

Devices

The primary determinant of quality is the camera or scanner. How well does the camera or scanner use the pixels available to define the photograph? Just like some camera lenses are better than others for 35mm cameras, some digital cameras and scanners are better than others for creating sharpness and high quality.

The Aesthetic Factor

Assuming a reasonable level of quality in cameras and scanners, however, the real determinant of quality is the photographer. Knowledgeable photographers take better photographs. Thus, if you can't afford to use a $75,000 scanner, you can at least read a $35 book on how to improve your photography. A good amateur photographer, a 35mm camera, and Kodak Picture CD can produce some remarkably high-quality photographs for the Web.

Summary

Images are the spice of the Web, and digital photographs provide the most cost-effective means of adding images to your Web pages. If you have a scanner, use it to digitize some photographic prints. If not, have a roll of film processed to include a Kodak Picture CD. Try it! You'll like it.

11

Preparing Pictures

This is a large, complex topic that only an insane author would dare to cover in a basic book on Web page authoring. Indeed, the spectrum of learning for color and digital color is wide and deep. The amount to learn is never ending. But it's so amazing what you can do with a few simple techniques that it can't be left out of this book. This chapter presents a few basic image editing techniques that anyone can use with low-cost or free software to manipulate and improve digital photographs and other digital color graphics.

Web Image Files

Web image files come in three varieties, and you need to make sure that the one you use provides the characteristics you want.

GIF

A Graphics Interchange Format (GIF) image file contains only 256 colors (8-bit color), a minimum for making photographs look real. In addition, a GIF automatically compresses to about 50 percent (without a loss of quality) making it quicker to download.

Many people use GIFs, but today GIFs may not get the job done for you. For instance, many people today have computer color systems that display 64 thousand colors (16-bit color) or even 16 million colors (24-bit color). Why use GIFs when they can't take advantage of advanced color systems? For instance, photographs with thousands of colors look better than photographs with 256 colors.

GIFs still make sense to use for simple Web page design elements that don't need a wide range of colors. They also make sense to use when you need to keep download times short.

JPEG

Joint Photographic Experts Group (JPEG) image files contain as many colors as it takes to define an image. But JPEGs do not have automatic built-in compression, and they generally take longer than GIFs to download. Nonetheless, you can manually compress JPEGs so that they are smaller files than they were, but the compression is *lossy*; that is, image quality deteriorates in the compression process. Even though you can achieve a certain level of compression without a noticeable loss in quality, if you compress an image too much, it will affect its appearance.

In most cases, use JPEGs (without compression) for photographs and artwork that uses a wide spectrum of color. They will display better. Be sensitive, however, to download times. In most circumstances, website visitors don't like to wait a long time for images to download.

PNG

A Portable Network Graphic (PNG) image file is a Web standard intended to replace GIFs. There are legal problems with GIFs that motivated the establishment of an advanced image file format as a new Web standard. Expect PNGs to grow in popularity. The standard was designed specifically to be a network image format and will provide a great deal of flexibility in the future as creating and editing images for the Web become simpler yet more sophisticated.

PNGs can handle 24-bit color (16 million colors) and do much more. Before long, some of the advanced processes in image editing programs will work only with PNGs.

Choosing an Image Editor

You need an image editor. Even some low-cost image editors provide tremendous capabilities. High-end image editors such as Adobe Photoshop are marvelous digital darkrooms that far surpass the capabilities of physical darkrooms at a small fraction of the cost. Learning all the capabilities and techniques for using a program like Photoshop and the many Photoshop plug-in programs from third-party software vendors takes a very long time.

If you're a professional photographer, go for the high end. You have your work cut out for you. For the rest of us, almost any image editor is not only useful but probably more than we'll ever master. It's really a matter of preference. Try a few image editors, and find one that's fun to use. The image editor should be able to do the following basic tasks

1. Change the contrast

2. Change the brightness

3. Crop

4. Resize

5. Add text

6. Convert graphic file formats

I prefer image editors that change the contract and brightness as you move a slider. They are so cool! You don't have to wait to see the change. Cropping small portions out of existing images is a standard capability of image editors, as is the ability to convert images into various digital file formats.

This is definitely fun stuff, and it's important to find an image editor that's fun for you. You can find them in shareware collections on the Web, usually for under $50. Macromedia (*http://www.macromedia.com*) sells Fireworks and Jasc (*http://www.jasc.com*) sells Paint Shop Pro, two capable and reasonably priced image editors with features designed especially for the Web.

This chapter uses IrfanView 3.17, a popular freeware image editor. See Chapter 2 for downloading instructions. Although I don't necessarily recommend IrfanView for the long haul, it's adequate for the short coverage provided by this book, and it's free.

MGI PhotoSuite SE

This chapter also uses this MGI photo editor for text images since IrfanView doesn't create text. This MGI program is often bundled with other products.

Using an Image Editor

Like most other programs, to use an image editor, you open the program and then you open the image file you want to edit. For this chapter, you need to use an image. The best image for learning is a digital color photograph. If you don't have one, find one on the Web.

Go to any website that has a photograph. Put your cursor over the photograph and left click on it. Go Save Image, and the image will be accessible wherever you save it. (Save it to your *download* folder.)

Where?

One of the more practical questions is where to store the image files? Chapter 18 gives some suggestions. For now, however, we're not concerned with storing Web images in a website system of folders. Rather, we're faced with putting an image workshop somewhere that we can easily remember to store files. I like to store my work in progress in a folder named *artwork*.

I have a subfolder named *art* for my website where I store the Web page images (e.g., JPEGs and GIFs).

I also have a subfolder named *artwork* (below the *art* subfolder) where I store all my image files that I use to create the JPEGs and GIFs with my image editor. This works well. When I use my image editor, I always know where to save image files (to *artwork*). When I have an image in its final form ready for display in a Web page, I move it to its appropriate website folder (e.g., *art*). So, for this chapter, make the image workshop folder *artwork*, a subfolder of the *art* folder.

When you save the photograph from the Web, make sure you save it to the *artwork* subfolder of the *art* folder.

Saving Images

You can alter an image permanently in an image editor, whether intentionally or unintentionally. Always keep images in a permanent archive folder (unless they're on a CD). Never remove one to work on it. Always copy it to another folder instead leaving the original in the archive unaltered. (We will ignore this practice for this chapter.)

Rather than Save your work on an image, do a Save As to assign the revised image a new name. Thus, you may have a series of image files as you work on one image, each representing the progression of your work (e.g., *horse.gif*, *horse2.gif*, *horse3.gif*, *horse4.gif*). If you don't like what you've done, you can go back. This turns out to be a very efficient way to work on image files that saves a lot of time and headaches.

Undo

Undo is very handy for image editing too. When you make a mistake, try the Undo. It gets you back to a prior version of your image work, which can often be a lifesaver. Image editing programs with multiple levels of Undo make editing easier.

Contrast

After you open the image file you want to edit, find the contrast control in your image editor. With the contrast control, you can make the image sharper. By using a slider that shows the change instantly, you can easily adjust the contrast to your liking. I find that boosting the contrast a fair amount often gives photographs a much sharper appearance.

For IrfanView, open an image and go Image, Enhance colors and a window will pop up with some nice sliding controls. Play with the contrast by putting the cursor in the Contrast slider, pressing the mouse button, and sliding. You will see it change before your very eyes (see Figure 11.1).

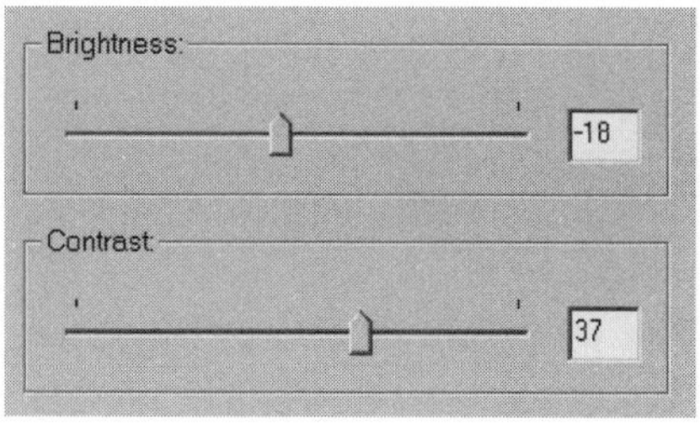

Figure 11.1   Enhance colors sliders.

When you adjust the brightness (covered next), it affects the contrast. As a consequence, you will have to go back and forth between contrast and brightness adjustments until you have adjusted the photograph to an appearance that suits your purposes (e.g., making the photograph as attractive as possible).

Brightness

The next control of interest is the brightness control. Often you will find it together with the contrast control. I find that decreasing the brightness just a little often gives a photograph a richer look. Unfortunately, every photograph is different and every taste is different. You need to make your own judgements as to the adjustments you make.

For IrfanView, play with the brightness by putting the cursor in the Brightness slider, pressing the mouse button, and sliding. You will see it change immediately.

Again, you will need to coordinate your brightness adjustments with your contrast adjustments to achieve the look you want for a particular photograph.

Gamma

You can also use another similar adjustment, gamma, also on the Enhance colors window of IrfanView. This is more for experts and makes the adjustment a three-way effort instead of a two-way effort. But if you learn how to use gamma, adjusting it will make a difference in some photographs.

Cropping

Cropping is simply cutting a small piece out of a larger image. Almost all image editors provide cropping, and it's handy.

For IrfanView, simply place the cursor on the image and pressing the mouse button, drag the cursor down and to the right. You will open a crop window. Release the mouse button to set the cropping frame. If you don't like the way the cropping frame is set, move the cursor outside the image, click, and start over (see Figure 11.2).

Figure 11.2   Setting the cropping frame.

Once the cropping frame is set where you want it, go Edit, Crop. Everything outside the cropping frame disappears (see Figure 11.3).

Figure 11.3   Cropped image.

Just Right

One useful function of cropping is correcting your photographs. We all try hard to get photographs framed just right when we take them. However, we don't always succeed. Cropping provides a second chance to get a photograph framed just right.

Resizing

Resizing *large to small* works reasonably well. The quality doesn't stay the same, but often the quality remains high. Resizing from *small to large* doesn't work well. If you're expecting high quality, don't waste your time.

For IrfanView, go Image, Resize/Resample for the Resize/Resample image window. It provides a number of options for enlarging an image. If you don't want the shape of your image to be distorted, make sure the Preserve aspect ratio box is checked. Simply enter a new number into either Width or Height, and click *OK*. The enlarged or reduced image will pop up immediately for your inspection (see Figure 11.4).

Figure 11.4   Enlarged image (fuzzy).

Sharpen

IrfanView has a special function it calls *sharpen*. Other software also includes this function, but you can not expect it to be uniformly defined or work the same from one program to another. Its purpose is to make an image sharper.

For IrfanView, go Image, Sharpen. IrfanView will sharpen the image immediately. If you don't like what it did, go Edit, Undo. The image will go back to its original state.

This turns out to be a handy function to use for digital photographs for those who are less familiar with photo processing. You don't have to fool around with contrast and brightness (or gamma). One easy function creates a sharp photograph. If it doesn't work well, you can always do some custom work with contrast and brightness.

Blur

The opposite of sharpen is blur. Many image editors provide a blur function as well as many other visual treatments. Experi-

*ment with your image editor to see what it can do. It's great
fun!*

Making Text Images

As discussed earlier in the book, you don't have much choice in
typefaces for the Web by means of HTML. You can count only on
website visitors having Times New Roman (Times), Arial (Helvetica), and Courier New (Courier). If you want to use other typefaces for titles or headings, you will have to make text images.

Most image editors enable you to render text as text images. Text
images are pictures of text and do not require website visitors to
have the proper fonts. When you make text images, nothing limits
you to the ordinary. In effect, you are creating art and can use all
the techniques that artists use. As a practical matter, you will probably keep your text images simple, and this chapter covers only
elementary techniques.

Since IrfanView doesn't create text, this chapter features MGI
PhotoSuite SE (photo editor) to illustrate the creation of text
images. Most image editors work about the same for the basics.
Open MGI PhotoSuite SE and go File, New Photo, and the New
Photo window will pop up. Set the size of your image, and click
OK. A blank (white) rectangle appears (see Figure 11.5).

Move the cursor to the color chart on the right side and click on
the color chart. An "F" (for foreground color) will appear in the
color pixel that you select.

The alternative for setting color is to set it to your own specifications. Two rectangles in the lower left-hand corner represent the
foreground color (text) and the background color. Click on the
foreground rectangle, and a color generator will pop up, enabling

you to set your the color. (See Chapter 9 for information on how to
set colors particularly browser-safe colors.)

Figure 11.5   Blank image.

If you want to have a transparent background, don't set a background color (more on transparent backgrounds later). Otherwise,
use the foreground color function to create a background layer of
color. (Remember, you want your background color to match that
of the Web page into which you plan to place the text images.)
Click on the paint can icon.

Move the cursor to the blank image and click. The image frame
will fill with the color that shows in the foreground rectangle.

For the text, set the foreground color again and click on the text
icon.

The Text window will pop up enabling you to create text of any
size with any font in your computer. Type in the text and click *OK*.

The text will appear in the upper left-hand corner of the blank image. Move the cursor to the text, press the mouse button, and drag. Let up on the mouse button to put the text in place. Click outside the text area to permanently affix the text inside the image frame (see Figure 11.6).

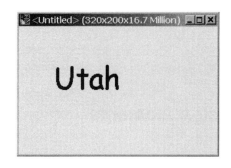

Figure 11.6   Text image.

You have created a text image with any font on your computer, and the image requires no font on a website visitor's computer to display. These are appropriate for titles, navigation images, and other website art. All that's left to do is crop. Click on the cropping icon.

Move the cursor to the image, press the mouse button, and move down and to the right to define a rectangle that you want to crop out of the image. Let up on the mouse button and go Edit, Trim. The image changes immediately. If the crop wasn't correct, go Edit, Undo, and try again.

Fancy

You can do some fancy things with type. For instance, do your text in black. Then do it again (identical) in another color, say green. Move the green text over the black text so that the black text shows just a little around the edges on two sides. This creates a drop shadow effect.

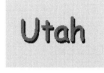

It makes the text seem to float on the page.

Making Design Elements

Making design elements for Web pages is artists' work. Certainly, design elements can make Web pages look much better. If you cannot afford to hire a digital artist, however, you will do best to keep your design elements simple. It doesn't take much to create attractive Web pages, and if you go overboard on the design elements, you may end up with a cluttered look.

To create simple design elements, use an image editor, create geometric shapes, fill them with color, and incorporate them into a Web page.

Changing Colors

Using an image editor, you can change colors inside an image. You change colors by changing one pixel. All adjacent pixels of the same color will change too. In some image editors, you set the change to affect all adjacent pixels within a certain color range.

Be careful when changing colors. One mistake can ruin your image. If you can *Undo* the mistake or if you haven't saved the image after the change, you can recover. Otherwise, you may be stuck with a strange-looking image.

Making Transparent GIFs

GIF images have 256 colors. You can make one of those colors effectively transparent; that is, the background of the Web page will show through the "transparent" color. Use this clever technique to make text images.

For instance, suppose you create a dark blue text title over a light green background. Make the green of the background the transparent color. When the text image displays, the Web page will show through where the green would otherwise be. The text appears to be part of the Web page no matter what color the Web page is.

The advantage of a text image with a transparent background is that you can use it on a Web page of any color. (Another way to create the same effect is to make the background color of the text image the exact same color as the background color of the Web page. Such a text image will work only on a Web page that has the same exact color as the background color of the text image.)

IrfanView doesn't create text or transparent GIFs. So, this chapter will illustrate transparent GIFs with MGI PhotoSuite SE. Start with a default (blank) image. Don't add a background. Add text as normal. When you save, select GIF as the file format and check the *Transparent Background* box (see Figure 11.7).

This will produce a transparent GIF, which you can use in a Web page with any color background. Keep in mind that this works only with GIFs. Many people use transparent GIFs on their website. They make handy text images and logos which have become staples for creating attractive Web pages.

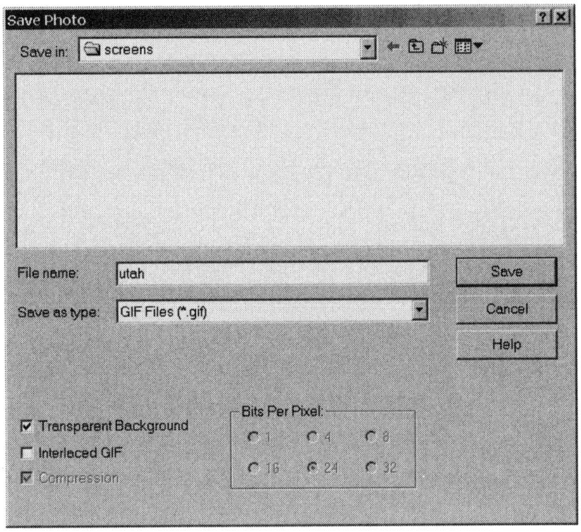

Figure 11.7   Save with transparent background.

Planning

Keep your website visitors in mind when you plan your images. They don't like long downloads. Table 11.1 gives you an idea of how long it takes to download 100K of Web page and image files at various bandwidths.

Table 11.1   Download times for 100K.

Bandwidth	Seconds	Description
28.8	35	old modem
56	18	new modem
ISDN	8	old digital line
DSL (minimum)	3	new digital line
Ethernet	1	network

Web pages don't weigh in too heavy, but image files can get pretty large. A 100K-Web page (text and images) is hefty and will take 35 seconds to load with a 28.8 modem. Lighten up.

One way to keep your Web pages rich with images yet light in weight is to use small icons, small logos, and thumbnail photographs. For instance, a thumbnail photograph can be a link to the full-size photograph. You can also use redundant images. For instance, if you use the same red bullet image to set off items in a list, it loads only once, even though it can appear as many times as you need it. A Web page without images looks pretty bleak, but a Web page with just a few small images can be attractive.

Summary

With a few simple editing techniques and almost any image editor, you can improve your digital photographs and other images dramatically. This is a fun process, and there's not much to learn for the basics. (If you want to become an expert, you have many years of learning and experience ahead of you.) Try your hand at image editing. Don't think it's only for experts.

12

Adding Navigation Menus

Usable websites require easy navigation. Except for simple websites with just a few Web pages, you normally need to provide an easy navigation system. You can do it with links in the text. You can do it with a line of links. You can do it with individual images used as links. Or, you can do it with a imagemap, a system of using one image for multiple links. You have another choice, however, which you will find easy to create and your website visitors will find easy to use: the navigation menu.

Using Tables for Menus

Small multi-celled tables make excellent navigation menus. The first question is, How do you create such tables? The second is, What do you put in them? And the third is, Where do you put them?

Multi-Row, One Column

Use a table with multiple rows and only one column to create a narrow column that can go to the left or right at the top of the Web page or somewhere in the text. With a narrow text column, such a menu can even go to the right or left of the text column.

Composer

Open Composer. Click on the table icon and enter *6* for Number of rows, *1* for Number of columns, and *140* for Table width. See the table in Figure 12.1.

Type the following in the requisite six rows:

1. SITE GUIDE
2. Road Map
3. Topo Map
4. Canyon Plants
5. Animals
6. Anasazi Ruins

These will become links to other Web pages.

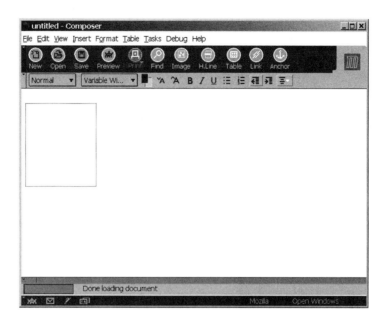

Figure 12.1   A 6-row, 1-column table 140 pixels wide (borders not shown).

Make "SITE GUIDE" bold. Place the cursor in the first cell (SITE GUIDE) go Table, Cells, Selection, Cell, Background, Color and click on the arrow. Select the sixth color from the left at the top (green) and click *OK*. The background color for the navigation menu title is now green. Highlight the remaining rows and repeat this process, selecting the color the fourth from the left at the top (yellow). Now you have a colorful navigation menu with a green heading and a yellow list. (These two colors happen to be browser-safe. Use the longer process of specifying colors if you want to use browser-safe colors. Not all colors on the Composer color chart are browser safe. See Chapter 9.)

Next highlight "Road Map" and click on the link icon. Enter the URL *roads.html* (see Chapter 6) and click *OK*. The words "Road Map" now link to the Web page *roads.html*. This navigation menu is now active (see Figure 12.2). Change the border to *0* before you test the table in your browser.

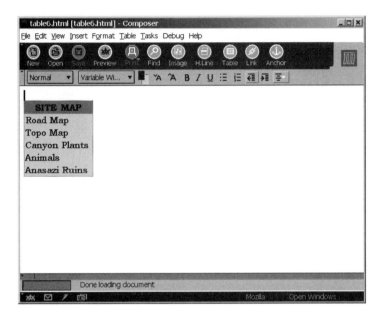

Figure 12.2   Narrow navigation menu.

Of course, only one item on the list is active. You will have to create a link (to an appropriate Web page) for each menu item to make the menu fully functional.

Double Table?

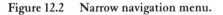

Can you use this menu inside another table? Sure. Just cut and paste the entire menu into a larger table. The menu is then called a "nested" table.

FrontPage Express

Open FrontPage Express. Go Table, Insert Table, and in the Insert Table window enter *6* for Rows and *1* for Columns. Under Width enter *140* pixels. (See the table in Figure 12.3.)

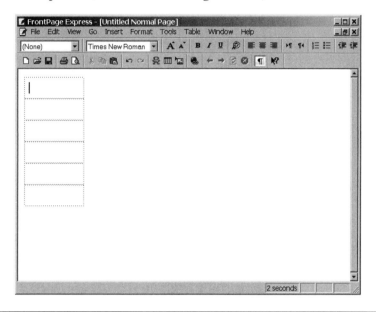

Figure 12.3   A 6-row, 1-cloumn table 140 pixels wide.

Type the following in the requisite rows:

1. SITE GUIDE

2. Road Map

3. Topo Map

4. Canyon Plants

5. Animals

6. Anasazi Ruins

Make "SITE GUIDE" bold. Place the cursor in the first cell (SITE GUIDE). Go Table, Cell Properties, Custom Background, Background Color and click on the arrow. Select *Lime* and click *OK.* The background color for the navigation menu title is now green. Highlight the remaining rows and repeat this process, selecting the color Yellow. Now you have a colorful navigation menu with a green head and a yellow list. (Keep in mind, Microsoft colors are not necessarily browser-safe. Use the longer process of specifying browser-safe colors when you work on your own website. See Chapter 9.)

Next highlight "Road Map" and click on the link icon. Enter the URL *roads.html* (see Chapter 6) and click *OK.* The words "Road Map" now link to the Web page *roads.html*. This navigation menu is now active (see Figure 12.4).

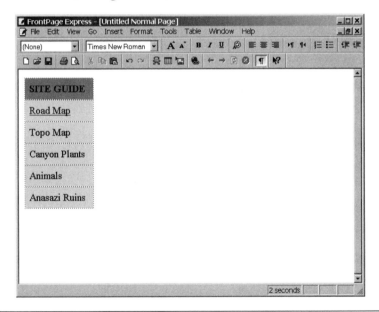

Figure 12.4   Narrow navigation menu.

Of course, only one item on the list is active. You will have to create a link (to an appropriate Web page) for each menu item to make the menu fully functional.

Double Table?

Can you use this menu inside another table? Sure. Just cut and paste the entire menu into a larger table. The menu is then called a "nested" table.

Multi-Row, Multi-Column

Use a table with multiple columns—usually two or three—to create a menu that you put at the top or bottom of the Web page. It's usually too large to gracefully integrate into the text.

Using Composer

Open Composer. Click on the table icon and enter *4* for Number of rows, *2* for Number of columns, and *300* for Table width. See the table in Figure 12.5.

Type the following in the requisite rows:

2.Road Map	Animals
3.Topo Map	Anasazi Ruins
4.Canyon Plants	

Place "SITE GUIDE" in row 1 and make it bold. Place the cursor in the first cell (SITE GUIDE) and go Table, Table Properties, Cells, Selection, Cell, Size, and enter *2* in Cell spans. Then click *OK*. Highlight "SITE GUIDE," click the alignment icon, and select *center*.

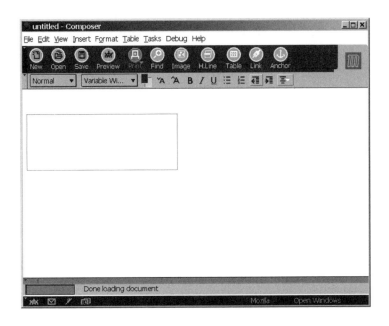

Figure 12.5   A 4-row, 2-column table 300 pixels wide.

Proceed to enter the remaining words, set the color backgrounds, and make the links the same as you did earlier. You now have a colorful menu that you can put at the top or bottom of the Web page (see Figure 12.6).

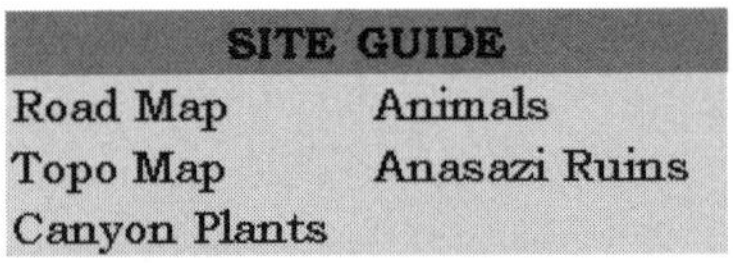

SITE GUIDE	
Road Map	Animals
Topo Map	Anasazi Ruins
Canyon Plants	

Figure 12.6   Wide navigation menu.

Using FrontPage Express

Open FrontPage Express. Go Table, Insert Table, and in the Insert Table window enter *4* for Rows and *2* for Columns. Under Width enter *300* pixels. (See the table in Figure 12.7.)

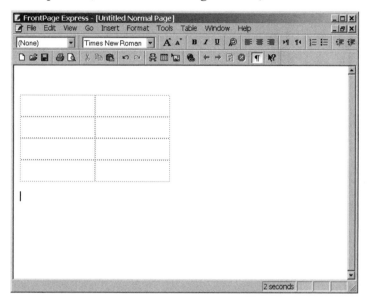

Figure 12.7   A 4-row, 2-column table 300 pixels wide.

Type the following in the requisite rows:

2.Road Map	Animals
3.Topo Map	Anasazi Ruins
4.Canyon Plants	

Place "SITE GUIDE" in row 1 and make it bold. Place the cursor in the first cell (SITE GUIDE) and go Table, Cell Properties, Cell Span, and enter *2* in Number of Columns Spanned. Then click *OK*. Highlight "SITE GUIDE" and click the center icon.

Proceed to enter the remaining words, set the color backgrounds, and make the links the same as you did earlier. You now have a colorful menu that you can put at the top or bottom of the Web page (see Figure 12.8).

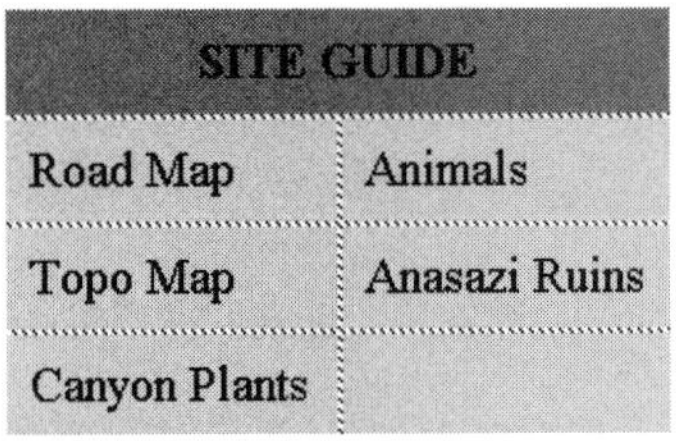

SITE GUIDE	
Road Map	Animals
Topo Map	Anasazi Ruins
Canyon Plants	

Figure 12.8   Wide navigation menu.

A Line Menu

A line menu (a text navigation bar) does not require a table. It's just a line of text with words that are links. Very simple. It's common to see the links separated by vertical lines.

Home | Site Map | Products | Contact Us | About

This is a traditional means of creating a navigation bar. However, you can also create a navigation bar with a table. This can be a more artistic approach. Make it one row with many columns.

Using Pictures in Menus

As you know, you can use images for links as well as words. Hence, you can have a navigation menu with images instead of words. Use the narrow navigation menu, and replace the words in each row with a small image (see Figure 12.9).

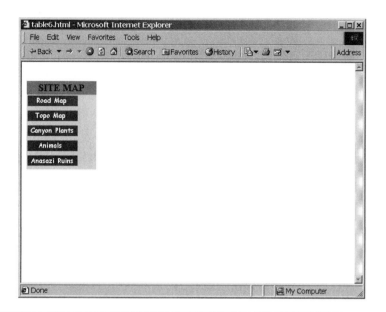

Figure 12.9   Text images instead of words in a navigation menu.

Imagemaps

An imagemap is simply an image to which have been added a series of hot spots that are links. A website visitor clicks on a hot spot, and the link activates and takes the visitor to the target. You make an imagemap with an imagemap editor.

This is a slick way of making a navigational device, particularly if you like to use an artistic approach to designing your Web pages. As you become an expert at making Web pages, you may want to start making and using imagemaps.

Summary

Navigation lists, menus, and bars can bring order and convenience to your website's navigation. Although you can use links in the text for general navigation, website visitors will find it tedious to read through the text just to find something they are looking for. Make it easy for them. Include navigation aids on every Web page.

13

Using Tables for Layout

You have undoubtedly noticed that when you use tables in Composer or FrontPage Express, the outlined table structure (as indicated by the lines) looks similar to a grid. In fact, you can do exactly that with tables: create a grid. Each cell in the grid then becomes a placement for an element of the Web page whether text, image, or another media. You can even set spacing with empty cells.

Multiple Columns with Composer

You can make multiple columns without too much additional work beyond creating a single-cell table for text. Why make multiple columns? Sometimes you can make a text Web page more usable by having one column for text and another for a navigation menu.

Text and Menu

Open *myfirst.html*. Place the cursor below the text. To create two columns, click on the Table icon. Set the Number of rows to *1*, Number of columns to *2*, the Table width to *540*, and click *OK*.

Highlight the text and cut. In the new column on the right, paste the text. In the new column on the left, you put some short text lines (one or two words) for a menu, make the text into links (see Chapter 6), and thereby create a navigation menu (see Figure 13.1). Change the border to *0*.

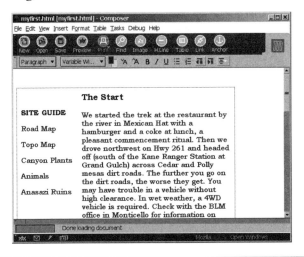

Figure 13.1   Navigation menu and text column.

In the alternative, you can cut and paste a preconstructed navigation menu (see Chapter 12) into the left column; that is, a table
within a table (see Figure 13.2).

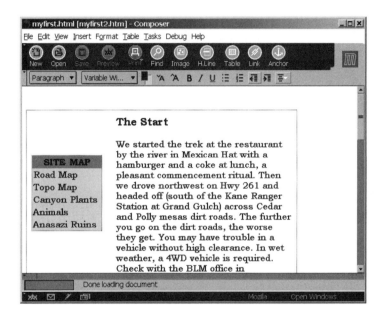

Figure 13.2   Preconstructed navigation menu and text column.

This makes an attractive and useful layout. Make the text column
on the right the proper width for reading. Make the menu column
on the left wide enough to display the menu. Place the cursor in a
table cell and go Table, Table Properties, Cells, Column, Size,
Width, and enter a pixel width (e.g., *145* for the left column and
395 for the right column).

A Table

Someday you will need to make a real table in a Web page. And
certainly you can use the table capability of HTML to create ordi-

nary tables. Click on the Table icon. The Insert Table window will appear. Set the Number of rows to *4*, Number of columns to *4*, the Table width to *480*, and click *OK*.

Place the following data in the table:

```
Animal, Nocturnal, Diurnal, Total
Mountain lion, 4, 1, 5
Ringtail cat, 18, 3, 21
Coyote 23, 14, 37
```

Change the border to *0*. As Figure 13.3 shows, the table function of HTML works well for making common tables.

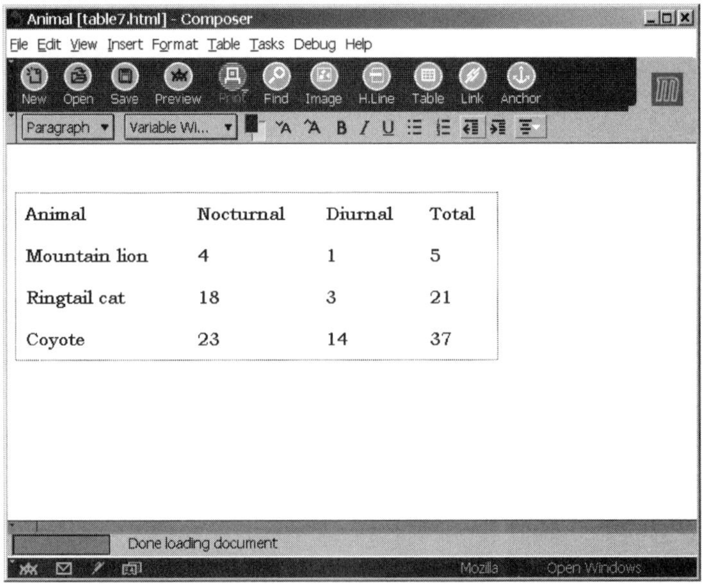

Figure 13.3   A table with data.

Make the first row bold and add a table heading (see Figure 13.4).

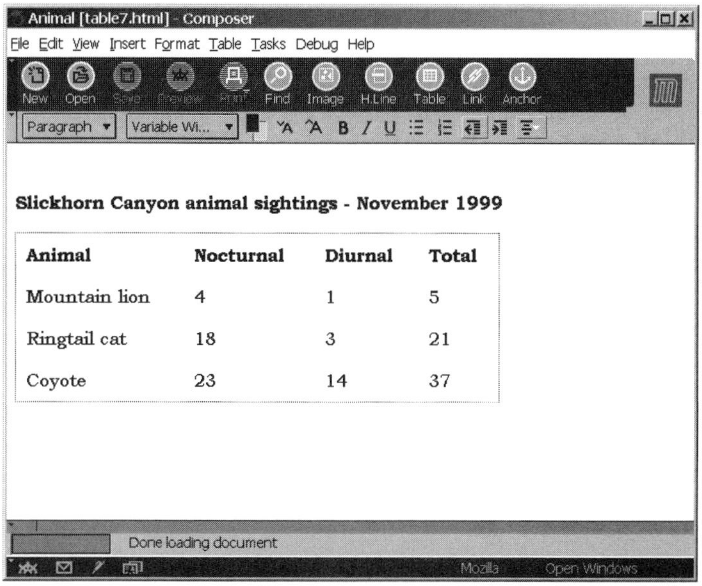

Figure 13.4   A complete table.

Multiple Columns with FrontPage Express

You can make multiple columns without too much additional work beyond creating a single-cell table for text. Why make multiple columns? Sometimes you can make a text Web page more usable by having one column for text and another for a navigation menu.

Text and Menu

Open *myfirst.html*. Place the cursor below the text. To create two columns, click on the Table icon. Set the rows to *1* and the columns to *2* by selecting the second box from the left at the top.

Place the cursor in the table and go Table, Table Properties, Minimum Width, and set the width to *540*. Click *OK*.

Highlight the text and cut. In the new column on the right, paste the text. In the new column on the left, you put some short text lines (one or two words) for a menu, make the text into links, and thereby create a navigation menu (see Figure 13.5).

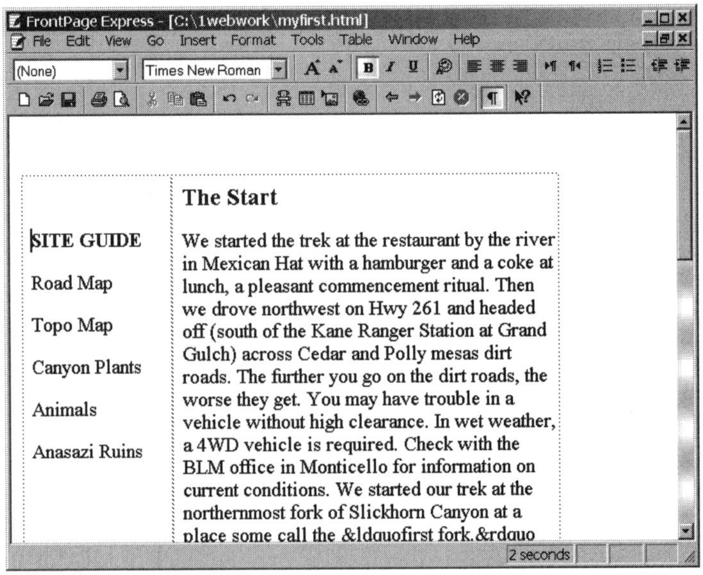

Figure 13.5   Navigation menu and text column.

In the alternative, you can cut and paste a preconstructed navigation menu (see Chapter 12) into the left column; that is, a table within a table (see Figure 13.6).

This makes an attractive and useful layout. Make the text column on the right the proper width for reading. Make the menu column on the left wide enough to display the menu. Place the cursor in a table cell and go Table, Cell Properties, Minimum Width, and enter a pixel width (e.g., *145* for the left column and *395* for the right column).

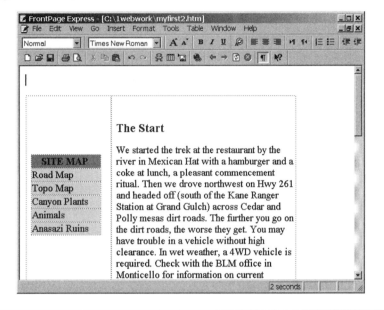

Figure 13.6   Preconstructed navigation menu and text column.

A Table

Someday you will need to make a real table in a Web page. And certainly you can use the table capability of HTML to create ordinary tables. Click on the Table icon and click on the box that's fourth from the left and fourth from the top. Place the cursor in the table and go Table, Table Properties, Minimum Width, and set the width to *480*. Click *OK* (see Figure 13.7).

Place the following data in the table:

```
Animal, Nocturnal, Diurnal, Total
Mountain lion, 4, 1, 5
Ringtail cat, 18, 3, 21
```

```
Coyote 23, 14, 37
```

As Figure 13.8 shows, the table function of HTML works well for making common tables.

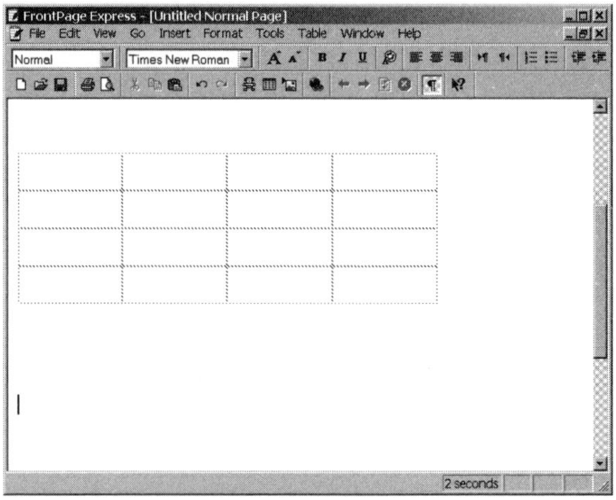

Figure 13.7   A table ready for data entry.

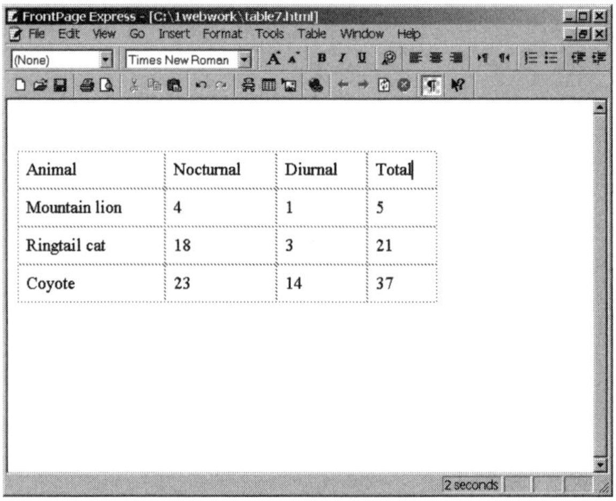

Figure 13.8   A table with data.

Make the first row bold and add a table heading (see Figure 13.9).

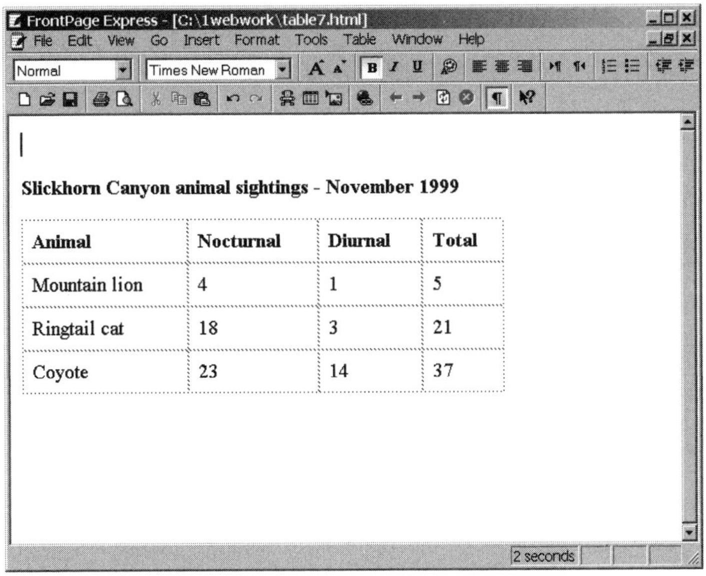

Figure 13.9   A complete table.

More Columns

Using tables for layout can be flexible and handy. You can do almost anything. Try the following simple techniques for creating a varied layout.

Text Plus Two

With three columns, you can put a text column in the middle with a navigation menu column on each side. This will make the text column more narrow, and you may have to reduce the size of the font to make easily readable text. Note that reducing the size of the font detracts from readability, so there are tradeoffs. But text with menus on each side makes an attractive layout (see Figure 13.10).

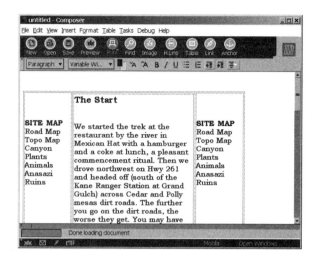

Figure 13.10   Three column layout.

What else can you do with this layout? Try a title with an image on each side (see Figure 13.11).

Figure 13.11   Title between images.

Or, use a text column between images (see Figure 13.12).

Figure 13.12   Text between images.

How about text between sidebars (see Figure 13.13)?

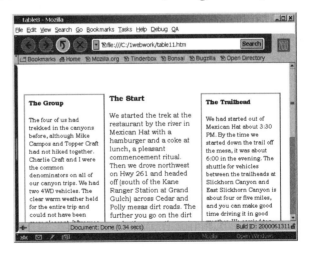

Figure 13.13   Text between sidebars.

Note that by using three columns, you run out of room quickly. Each of the sidebars in Figure 13.13 is narrow and has a small font size for better readability. Unfortunately, it's tough to get readability when you reduce the font size.

Broken Text Column

So far we've discussed columns and width. Length is important too. The length of a table (column of text) can go on seemingly forever. If the length does go on for a long way, the layout can get boring. You can break up the layout by ending the table. Below the table, create a layout that gives some relief to the lengthy column of text, perhaps some images, sidebars, or other multimedia elements. Then resume the text column in another table (see Figure 13.14).

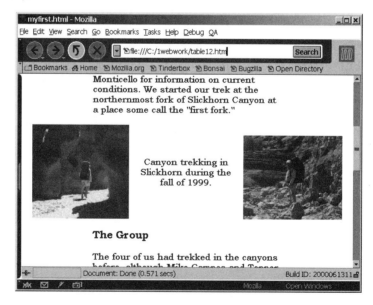

Figure 13.14   Relief for a text column.

This type of relief is even more dramatic if the table has its own background color. The text column will be one color and the general Web page background another color (see Figure 13.15).

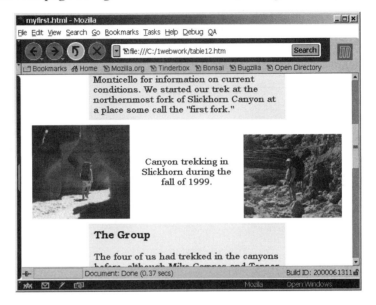

Figure 13.15   Background colors dramatize text columns.

Summary

You will find tables very handy for organizing the elements of a Web page. Create a grid. Place the multimedia elements in the grid. If this seems like a lot of labor, remember that this approach works well and you can always use these complex Web pages as templates so you don't have to keep reinventing them.

III

Posting Web Pages

14

What Is a Web Host?

You look at your Web pages just by opening the Web page files on your hard disk using a browser. When you publish your Web pages, however, presumably many people will visit your website to look at the Web pages and read them. Numerous people visiting at the same time to use your Web page files on a hard drive can cause a traffic jam. That's where a Web server comes in.

A Web server serves Web pages to numerous website visitors quickly and efficiently. It keeps the traffic from jamming. This is a necessity when more than a few website visitors attempt to use the same Web pages at the same time. Web servers, too, can get bogged down by high traffic (hundreds or thousands of people). Even so, extra-high traffic will normally just slow website response time without causing operational disintegration. In other words, a Web server is an essential part of a website.

And what is a Web host? It's the person or organization that provides the computer and Web server, connected full time to the Internet.

What Is a Server?

A server is software that runs on a computer and provides services to other computers on a network. The other computers are said to be "clients." They run client software. The server (software) and the client (software) interact over the network to do something (see Figure 14.1).

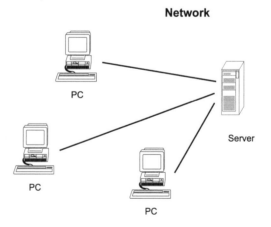

Figure 14.1   Network with server and clients.

The Web provides a typical illustration of a client-server operation. Individual computers on the network use client software (called a browser) to access Web pages on the server computer that runs the Web server (software). The Web server provides the requested Web pages to the clients (browsers).

Where Is the Web Server?

The Web server is software that runs on the network server computer. You will find it in four typical situations: Internet Service Provider (ISP), network server computer (intranet), co-location computer, and direct connection computer.

Internet Service Provider (ISP)

Many people contract with an ISP to provide Web hosting service. The ISP server computer is connected to the Internet and runs a Web server. Customers upload their Web pages to the ISP's server computer (onto its hard disk) where the Web server serves the Web pages to website visitors. This is how the World Wide Web works on the Internet.

Your ISP can be anywhere. Although I live in the San Francisco Bay Area where there are hundreds of ISPs, the ISP that I use for Web hosting is located in Florida.

Keep in mind that your ISP's Web server may handle hundreds of websites in addition to yours. One Web server can handle hundreds of lightly visited websites without overloading. It all depends on the volume of traffic. A heavily visited website may need the entire power of one Web server or even multiple Web servers.

Dial-Up Connections

When you connect to the Internet, you need a dial-up connection (assuming you connect via a modem). The number that you dial needs to be a local telephone number. Otherwise you would have to pay long distance charges needlessly making your Internet use expensive. Your dial-up ISP should be a local company or a national company that has chosen specifically to do business in your locale and provides a local dial-in telephone number. An Internet service that does not provide you with a local telephone number to use for your modem is not very desirable.

Web Hosting

What makes Web hosting somewhat confusing is that your dial-up ISP may also provide you with Web hosting service as part of your basic dial-up package of services. The ISP business is very competitive, and Web hosting service is a common component of most basic dial-up Internet service packages.

Keep in mind that such Web hosting service does not work any differently than any other Web hosting service. The point is that Web hosting does not depend on a dial-up connection. It just happens to be packaged with the dial-up Internet services. The moral of this story is that your Web host ISP does not have to be local and does not have to provide a local dial-up connection.

A Good Deal

As a practical matter, having your dial-up ISP provide you with Web hosting service at no additional cost is a good deal. You get your normal dial-up Internet service and Web hosting too, all for one low price. You may have Web hosting service already and only need to learn how to use it to take advantage of it.

Chapter 16 explains how to find your website, how to set up your website folder arrangement, and how to upload your Web pages to your website.

Network Server Computer (Intranet)

The Internet uses the TCP/IP (Transmission Control Protocol/ Internet Protocol) to operate. One interesting characteristic of TCP/IP is that it is infinitely expandable. For instance, you can have three separate TCP/IP networks. If you connect them, they act as one network. Thus, every TCP/IP network that connects to the Internet becomes part of the Internet.

The Internet has spawned a rich and robust software industry. It's now highly desirable to use Internet programs such as Web servers, Web browsers, and email programs off the Internet as well as on the Internet.

Many companies run their network on TCP/IP. If they do, it's called an *intranet* (an unfortunate choice of words because the difference in pronunciation between *intranet* and *Internet* is minimal). It works as a private Internet. It's an internal TCP/IP network. It works the same as the Internet.

Consequently, readers employed by companies may be interested in hosting their website on an intranet to serve a company purpose. Everything works the same on an intranet as it does on the Internet. You use the company Web server to host your website.

Firewalls

When a company connects its intranet to the Internet, the company intranet becomes part of the Internet. Since this raises serious security issues, a common practice is to use security protection devices generally called firewalls. Firewalls limit what outsiders can do on the company intranet.

Co-Location Computer

Sometimes when you have heavy traffic or want to do special things with your website, using an ISP's Web server is neither adequate nor practical. You need your own Web server. A relatively inexpensive way to connect your own computer to the Internet via a wide bandwidth (rather than a dial-up connection) is to physically locate your server computer in the ISP's network facility. You can control the software (e.g., the Web server) remotely via the Internet.

The ISP supplies the building, the electricity, and the wide bandwidth connection to the Internet. You supply the computer, the software, and the system management.

This service is much more expensive than normal Web hosting but less expensive than running an expensive wide bandwidth line to your office or home. It is also up to you to maintain the server computer, the Web server, and other network software, a daunting task in many cases.

Direct Connection Computer

Digital Subscriber Line (DSL) service is now available in metropolitan areas at a low cost. This is wide bandwidth service over an ordinary telephone line (twisted pair). It is not dial-up service. This is full-time Internet service around the clock. When you connect your computer to the Internet via DSL, you are connected any time your computer is turned on. You have all the security problems of a company intranet; that is, you need a firewall (e.g., a proxy server).

One benefit is that you can run your own Web server (i.e., be your own Web host). There are many easy-to-use Web servers available. One of the easiest to use is O'Reilly & Associates' Website (http:/www.ora.com), which runs on Windows. You can set it up and run it with a minimum of effort. This way you have total control over your Internet operations, just as you do with a co-location computer.

The drawback to running your own Internet operations on DSL is that the more you do, the more knowledgeable you have to be. I prefer to leave all those headaches to an ISP host.

Other Web Hosting Considerations

Some other Web hosting issues deserve your consideration:

- A simple Web hosting service by an ISP is probably all you will need for now. If you are thinking of hosting your own website via a co-location or a DSL connection, however, you need to be realistic about your level of expertise to do so.

- If you need additional Web development capability, special servers can make things easier for you; and some ISPs will provide the special servers.

The 7 x 24 Grind

Running an Internet operation is a 7-days-a-week, 24-hours-a-day grind. This is why ISP hosts are popular. They take care of running the Internet programs that you need (see Chapter 15) around the clock. Before you decide to take on this responsibility with a co-location computer or a DSL connection, you need to think through how you will provide the same level of hosting service as an ISP and do so cost-effectively.

More than Web Pages

A website can be more than Web pages. Web pages have the capability to integrate sound, video, database operations, and embedded computing. Although Web servers can handle all of these, they're not designed to do so. Specialized servers can do a better job of handling special media and applications. Keep in mind that all these specialized servers work simultaneously and in coordination with the Web server usually on the same computer.

Media Server

If you expect to use a considerable amount of streaming media, such as streaming sound or streaming video, you would do well to use a streaming media server such as RealServer (*http://www.real-networks.com*). The quality of the streaming media will be higher, and the Web server won't overload.

Database Server

For many Web-database operations you won't need a database server. However, when either the number of website visitors using the database reaches a certain critical mass or when the data stored in the database reaches a certain critical mass, using a database server such as Oracle 8 provides many benefits. You normally don't have to worry about this unless you have a large business, but some small Web business operations need powerful Web-database services.

Applications Server

An applications server enables you to create fancy Web programming using simple markups. Cold Fusion is a good example (*http://www.allaire.com*). Using Cold Fusion Markup Language (CFML) a nonprogrammer can create elaborate Web programming. CFML uses markups, which extend HTML to do things far beyond the capability of plain HTML. But the markups work only with a Cold Fusion server (runs with the Web server); and you have to learn CFML.

You can also build specialized applications such as ecommerce software. Miva (*http://www.miva.com*) sells a ready-made ecommerce software package named Merchant, written in HTML Script (a markup language similar to Cold Fusion) which is very robust and inexpensive. It requires a Miva server to run.

Summary

Most readers will choose an ISP to provide Web host services. It's a convenient and inexpensive way to establish a website. Indeed, most readers with dial-up Internet service already have Web hosting as part of their Internet services package, although some ISPs charge extra for it. You just need to activate it and get your website set up.

Chapter 15 tells you how to choose a Web host, a task that becomes more complicated if you need a lot of special services. Chapter 16 shows you how to set up your website at your Web host and upload your Web pages.

The special application servers are something you may never need, but it's worth mentioning them so you know they exist should you need special capabilities on your website.

15

Choosing a Web Host

Most people will use an ISP as their website host. How do you pick a Web host (ISP)? You have a variety of options, and which one you choose will depend on your situation. Just as for other services, convenience and price often dictate what you do, but for ISP services, there are additional considerations. This chapter alerts you to some bargains, but also gives you a dose of Web reality. Choosing an ISP for a Web host isn't always easy.

As Chapter 14 mentions, you may already have Web hosting services included in your dial-up Internet service. If so, that will give you a good start for your website. Most ISPs provide such service for no additional fee, and you don't need to go elsewhere to find it. Nonetheless, you may find your dial-up ISP lacking in the scope of Web hosting services provided, and you may need to find more robust Web hosting services from another source. This chapter will help you do so.

Criteria for Choosing

Web hosting is really not a single service but a package of services. You need to look at the entire package to determine if a Web hosting service is adequate for your website operation.

Minimum Criteria

The following are the minimum criteria for a package of Web hosting services:

Web Server A Web server is basic, of course, to Web hosting service.

Wide Bandwidth Your Web host ISP should have a wide bandwidth connection to the Internet. Wide bandwidth isn't the full story, however, because heavy traffic can slow wide bandwidth to a crawl. It's a combination of wide bandwidth and a policy of not overloading the bandwidth (and Web servers) that the ideal ISP should offer you.

CGI Access You can use CGI scripts to create embedded programming in your Web pages (see Chapter 21). To do so you must have access to the computer CGI folder. This creates a potentially grave security risk, and many ISPs do not allow it. Many ISPs, however, will set up an individual CGI folder in your hard disk space on the ISP's computer enabling you to use CGI scripts. Using CGI scripts is not difficult, and this is a capability you may eventually use. (Writing CGI scripts is a job best left to programmers.)

FTP Access   The normal means of uploading your Web pages and creating and deleting folders on the Web host computer is via File Transfer Protocol (FTP) covered in Chapter 16. This is the easiest means of maintaining a website.

Adequate Disk Space   ISPs vary in the amount of storage they offer with a basic Web hosting package. You will want to make sure that you receive adequate space. Websites tend to grow larger the more you learn about making them. Some ISPs charge a modest fee for storage overages. Others charge an unreasonable fee for overages. Make sure you check on the overage fees before you commit to a contract.

Low Cost   Basic Web hosting service is reasonably priced. It's a competitive industry. Shop around. Don't grab the first deal.

Technical Support   All ISPs expect you to learn to build your own website, and none are willing to educate you for the low cost of the typical monthly service. Nonetheless, there will be times when you need to consult with your ISP about one technical matter or another. Be sure that technical support is available.

Down Time   Down time is a matter of philosophy. My current dial-up ISP strives to maintain service all but two hours a year. In two years with this ISP, if the down time has exceeded two hours each year, it hasn't been by much. On the other hand, my prior ISP had no philosophy, and the down time in the last six months I was connected was about ten days (unacceptable). Ask your prospective Web host what its down time record was for the last two years.

Special Criteria

You may need additional Web services sooner than you think. If so, you want to make sure that you have chosen an ISP that can deliver the requisite services.

eCommerce Software If you want to sell to the public, you will need ecommerce software. The ecommerce software varies in quality so much that picking an ISP by the ecommerce software it offers has become almost standard procedure. In order to make a good choice in this regard, you will have to research ecommerce software. For each ecommerce software package, there are usually between a few dozen and a few hundred ISPs that offer it. No particular program dominates the industry.

Media Server If you use a lot of streaming media and you want high-quality streaming, you need to use an ISP that offers a streaming media server such as RealServer. Streaming via a Web server, while possible, does not work as well for a high volume of streaming.

Application Server Application servers support applications (programs) written in extended HTML languages such as Cold Fusion's CFML (see Chapter 14). If you use one of these markup languages, you will need an ISP that runs the requisite application server (e.g., Cold Fusion server).

Database Server If you run a very heavy-duty database operation, you may need a database server. You can construct Web-database applications without a database server (using an application server and a flat file database), but such applications have limitations.

Telnet Access Telnet access to your website gives you more control over security and other issues. Some ISPs provide it.

Most don't. You will have to learn some Unix to use Telnet.

Password-Protected Folders You can build parts of your website where visitors need a login and password to access the Web pages. To use passwords, your ISP must offer the means to do so. Some ISPs do. Some don't.

FrontPage Server Extensions If you use Microsoft FrontPage (not FrontPage Express) you will want your ISP to offer the FrontPage server extensions which will provide you with some website functions otherwise available only via application servers.

Pricing

Pricing for Web host service varies from $10 per month to over $1,000 per month. It depends on what you need and the pricing policies of the particular ISP.

Annual Contract?

Some ISPs offer a reduced fee for an annual contract paid in advance or paid quarterly. I advise against an annual contract the first year. You won't really know an ISP until you use its services. You may want to switch after a month. If you go a year and are still satisfied, sign an annual contract for the second year.

The Norm

The norm is not Web hosting but dial-up service that includes Web hosting. A typical price is $20 per month for a minimum package of Web hosting services together with Internet dial-up services.

For strictly Web hosting services (not including dial-up Internet services), you may be able to cut your cost a little, but generally about $20 per month is a competitive price.

For use of your own domain name, most ISPs will charge you from $5 to $20 per month extra. See Chapter 17 for more details about domain names.

The Smorgasbord

Many ISPs offer you a variety of Web hosting services a la carte. You decide what you need and add up the fees to calculate your monthly cost. Usually there's a basic package for about $20 per month. If you do a little more than the norm, you will probably pay about $25 to $50 per month. If you do a lot more than the norm, your fees can increase to a significant amount, and you may have to go to a second ISP to get all the Web hosting services you need. (See Chapter 18 regarding multiple domain websites.)

The Multiple Host Approach

Unfortunately, few ISPs offer everything you may need to run a robust website or a series of websites. For instance, I host my websites at a Florida ISP that provides a generous list of services, including a RealServer for streaming media. But I also use my dial-up ISP in California to run my ecommerce software, Miva Merchant, on a Miva application server. The Florida ISP does not run a Miva server. The California ISP does not run a RealServer. Thus, I need two ISP Web hosting services to accomplish what I need to do. Fortunately, I am able to use my California dial-up Internet service for one of the Web hosting services and do not have to pay extra for the Web hosting or the Miva server.

Multiple Host Websites

Can you use multiple hosts for one *website? Yes, you can, and it can work well. See Chapter 18 for the details.*

Traffic Charges

Today, few ISPs provide unlimited website traffic. You normally get a traffic allowance. If your website visitors exceed the allowance, you get charged extra by the megabytes downloaded. The allowances tend to be generous, and your website will have to have high traffic to exceed a typical allowance.

Allowances

The allowances are normally measured in megabytes of Web pages (and images) downloaded (viewed) each month by your website visitors.

This makes sense. No ISP can be expected to allow unlimited traffic for a low flat fee. The things to look at are the overage charges. Some ISPs charge reasonable overage fees. Others charge outrageous overage fees. Make sure you check the overage fees before you commit yourself to a contract.

Hometown Web Hosting?

It should now make sense to you that you do not need to use an ISP in your hometown for Web hosting. You need a local ISP (or a national ISP with local dial-up telephone numbers) to get connected to the Internet, but that has nothing to do with Web hosting. Your Web hosting can be done anywhere because you administer your website via the Internet. In fact, you can administer your website from any computer on the Internet.

Thus, pick your Web host ISP based on what you need, pricing, and other relevant criteria, not on whether the ISP is located physically close to you.

Host Yourself

Chapter 14 covers co-location self-hosting service and DSL self-hosting service. These two alternatives may seem attractive to you, but keep in mind that if you host yourself, you are the network administrator. You have to purchase, install, and maintain all the servers and other special software. You are probably better off leaving that to an ISP.

National Online Services

Many of the national online services such as America Online also offer Web hosting as part of their dial-up service, although the Web hosting feature is usually limited. This may be a workable hosting solution for those with modest websites.

Summary

ISPs offer a smorgasbord of Web hosting services. Decide what you need and evaluate potential ISPs based on what they offer, reliability, and price. When you start out, your best bet may be using Web hosting services provided by your dial-up ISP or your national online service.

16

Uploading Your Web Pages

Once you have chosen a Web host ISP, you deliver (upload) your Web page files for your website to the ISP's hard disk. You normally do this via File Transfer Protocol (FTP) on the Internet. This is easy to do, but you will need special software called an FTP program to do it. This chapter covers the use of the WS_FTP Lite program, a classic that many people have used over the years. It's free for many people and modestly priced for others. And it's easy to use. See Chapter 2 for details on how to download it.

FTP software enables you to do more than just transfer files. You can also add and delete files and folders on the Web host computer (in the space allocated to your website only).

Using WS_FTP Lite

Get online so that you are connected to the Internet. Open WS_FTP Lite. You will see two windows (see Figure 16.1):

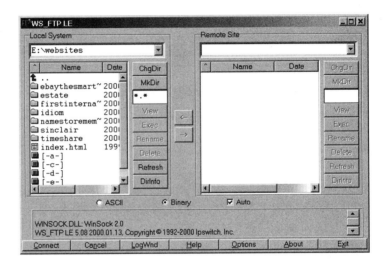

Figure 16.1   WS_FTP Lite.

The left window is a folder tree for your computer. The right window is a folder tree for your website. Remember the parallel websites? One on your computer and one on your ISP's computer? You can show your parallel websites side by side with WS_FTP LITE and transfer files between them. Clever!

Connecting

First you have to connect to the FTP site. Click on the Connect button. The Session Properties window pops up. Enter a profile name (e.g., your ISP Local Net). Then enter the domain name address of the FTP site of your Web host (e.g., *ftp.localnet.com*). Put in your User ID (login): *sinclair*. Finally, enter your password: ********. Check the box that saves your password so that you don't have to enter it again. Click *OK*, and you'll connect to your website (see Figure 16.2).

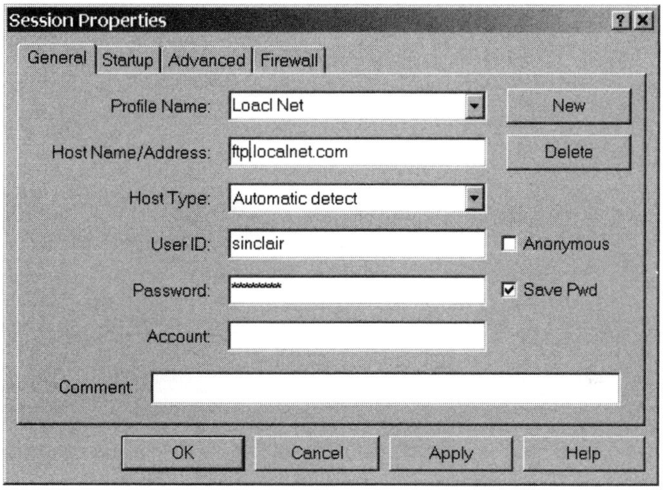

Figure 16.2   Getting set up to connect.

From Your ISP

Get the information to fill in the Session Properties window from your ISP or network administrator.

Where (on the hard disk) you connect to your website is something you'll have to discuss with your ISP or network administrator. When you connect, your website may start in the root folder to which you've connected (look at the right window). More likely, you will have to change to another folder, which will be the root folder for your website. A popular name for a root folder for a website is *public_html*. In Figure 16.3 it's *virtual_html*.

To transfer to another folder down the tree, double click on a folder name. To transfer to another folder up the tree, double click on the up arrow at the top of the list of folders and files. You do the same to navigate the tree for your own computer in the left window. The objective is to get in the same folder on the parallel websites and transfer files back and forth when necessary (see Figure 16.3). Most of the time you will be transferring the files from left to right, from your computer to the Web host computer. This is called *uploading*.

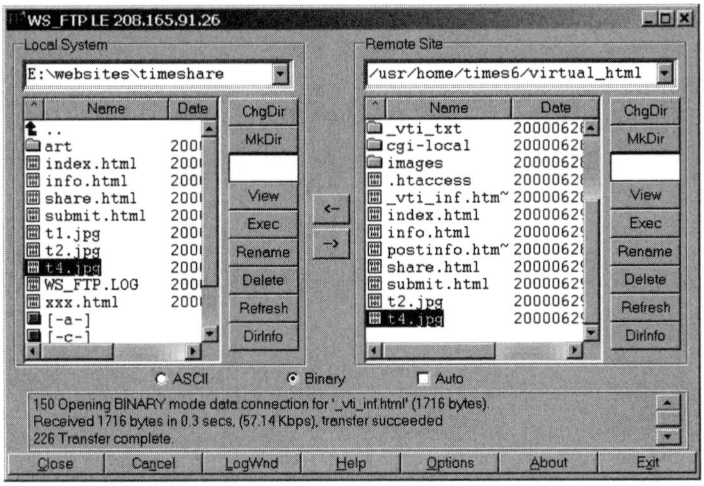

Figure 16.3   WS_FTP Lite ready for action.

Uploading

First you may need to create a folder on the Web host computer. Click on the *MkDir* button.

MkDir

Put the name of the new folder in the Input window, and click *OK* (see Figure 16.4).

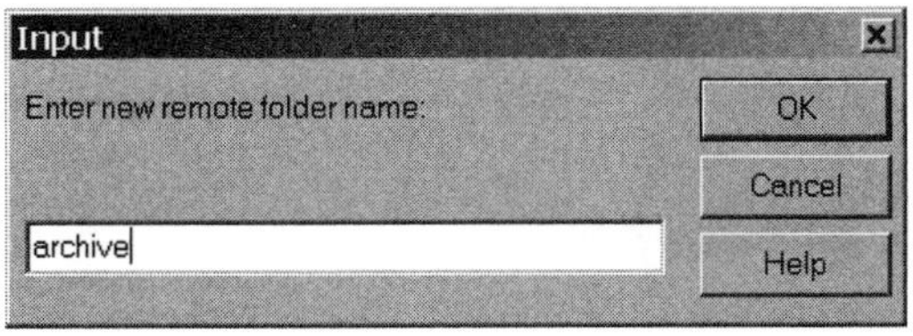

Input		☒
Enter new remote folder name:		OK
		Cancel
archive		Help

Figure 16.4   Input window.

To transfer a file from your computer to the Web host computer, check the Auto check box. Highlight the file in the tree in the left window and click on the arrow button pointing to the right. The file will be uploaded and will appear in the folder tree list on the right. See Figure 16.3 earlier.

Other Functions

To delete a file or folder, highlight it, and click on the Delete button.

WS_FTP Lite will delete it. If a folder has files in it, you will be unable to delete it until you first remove or delete all the files from it. To rename a file or folder, highlight it and click on the Rename button.

Rename

Type the new name into the Input window and click *OK*.

WS_FTP Lite offers more functions than this chapter covers. Play with it and become familiar with it, because when you operate a website, you will need to do uploads regularly. You can also purchase WS_FTP Pro (shareware) with additional functions should you feel you need a more powerful program.

Other Software

WS_FTP Lite is not the only FTP software. Many other programs are available, and you may want to try one. Interesting, the capability to upload files to a website via FTP is built into many programs, such as Web authoring programs. If you have such a program, give the FTP function a try before you buy something.

WS_FTP Lite Is Easier

My experience with FTP functions in authoring software is that they don't work well, don't have enough features, or they're difficult to learn. Using the same program all the time (e.g., WS_FTP Lite) will save you time and energy.

Some online services such as America Online have built into their proprietary software their own procedures for uploading and downloading files.

Other Chores

FTP programs are not limited to uploading files to the Web. For instance, you can use WS_FTP Lite to *download* files from anywhere on the Internet that runs an FTP server. Many people and businesses on the Internet have FTP sites where files are available to the public for downloading.

Authoring Uploads

Composer and FrontPage Express will upload your Web page files to your website. This is handy for light work on your website. It's a quick way to upload an individual file. When you work intensely on your website, however, it's hard to beat WS_FTP Lite.

Connected

You do have to be connected to the Internet when you try the Composer or FrontPage Express uploads. Sometimes the uploading mechanism will initiate the dial-up procedure, but I've found that's something you can't depend on, particularly when you regularly use multiple browsers.

Composer

To upload with Composer, go File, Send Page. In Composer 4.0 the command was Publish; it brought up a window that lead you through the FTP uploading process. In my beta version of Composer 6.0, it was not yet apparent how to do an upload, but the function will undoubtedly be in Composer by the time you try it.

FrontPage Express

To upload with FrontPage Express, go File, Save As and the Save As window will pop up (see Figure 16.5).

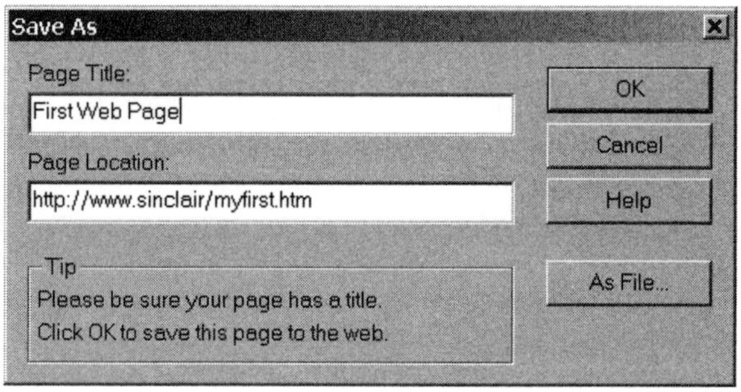

Figure 16.5   Save As window.

Fill in the title and the URL and click *OK*. This starts a series of windows that logs you into your FTP service for your website.

Download-Upload

Don't forget downloads. If you have the URL of a Web page, you can download it in either Composer or FrontPage Express. Go File, Open Web Location for Composer; or File, Open, Other Location, From Location for FrontPage Express. The Web page will download into the authoring program just as if it were in a browser (no login). You work on the Web page a little and then upload it. Slick!

Parallel Website

If you maintain parallel websites, as I recommend, the download-upload technique can cause confusion. Make sure that you save a copy of your revision (to your hard drive) to your parallel website on your own computer.

Summary

Don't try to reinvent the wheel every time you need to upload Web pages to a website. No reason to learn more than one procedure. Learn to use WS_FTP Lite, or a comparable FTP program, and forego the use of built-in FTP upload capabilities in a variety of programs.

17

Registering a Web Address

You get a Web address for your website from your ISP that provides Web hosting service, but you may not like the address. The best way to establish your unique identity on the Web is to use your own domain name for your Web address. To use a domain name, you must register it. If someone else already has it, you're out of luck; you'll have to choose and register another domain name. Chances are that you will not be able to get what you want on the first attempt and will have to make many attempts to find a suitable name that someone else has not already registered.

What You Get with Your ISP

Suppose your Web host ISP operates under the domain name localnet.com. Your account (and login) name is *selec* (short for Smith Electronics). Your purpose in setting up a website is to sell consumer electronics on the Web. Your website address (URL) is most likely to be:

> *www.localnet.com/~selec*

This URL doesn't make much sense to prospective customers. How can you improve it? You can't change the domain name. Only the ISP can do that. But you can change your account name. In this case, a change to *smithelectronics* makes sense. Your website address will then be:

> *www.localnet.com/~smithelectronics*

Although not elegant, this URL will at least make sense to prospective customers.

The best change you can make is to get your own domain name (e.g., *smithelectronics.com*). Only then will you have control of your Web address.

Can't Take It with You

If you change ISPs, you can't take the URL www.localnet.com/ ~smithelectronics *with you. You may be able to use* smithelectronics *at your next ISP, but the* localnet.com *remains the property of and stays with the original ISP.*

On Your Own

Once you have obtained your own domain name, you're on your own. Your domain name is your URL. Like choosing a name for a new business, you should not take choosing a domain name lightly. It should sound good, look good, and be relevant to your purpose for operating a website.

Choosing a Name

How do you choose a domain name? Well, you probably spent a lot of time choosing the name for your business. Why reinvent the wheel? Use your business name. Suppose, however, *smithelectronics.com* is not available. You need to choose something else.

Conforming to Your Business Name

The domain name system relies on absolute logic. One changed character is a completely different name. Consequently, you may be able to find a name that conforms to your business name. For instance, try the following:

smith-electronics.com

The hyphen creates a completely different domain name, and the new domain name may be something you can live with if it's available. If it's not available and you're incorporated, try the following:

smithelectronicsinc.com

or

smithelectronicscorp.com

or

smithelectronicsltd.com

One of these may be available and may prove to be a suitable domain name for you.

Another approach is to indicate what you're doing. For instance, try:

smithelectronicsonline.com

This indicates that you're probably involved in ecommerce. If you're not selling on the Web but are simply using the Web for customer service or to sell locally, you might use the name of the city in which your business is located:

smithelectronicscleveland.com

You get the idea. There are hundreds of variations. Brainstorm and come up with something workable.

Choosing a New Name

If you start a new business specifically intended to be on the Web, you would do well to choose a business name that is your domain name. The following are some guidelines for choosing a good business-name domain name:

Easy to Remember This may be the most important attribute of a good domain name.

The Shorter the Better Shorter names are usually easier to remember. Most of the single words in the English language have been registered as domain names, so you may find it more fruitful to look for two or three word combinations.

No Abbreviations Complete English words are easier to remember than most abbreviations or cute word substitutes, such as using "2" as a substitute for "to."

Relevant to Your Business If the name is relevant to your business, it will probably be easier for customers and prospective customers to remember.

Use Dot Com   This is the most popular suffix because it is the easiest to remember (*.com*). You can also choose *.net* or *.org*. By the time you read this, there will be other choices.

Don't Infringe   Be careful that you don't use a trademark as a domain name. Check the trademark registry at the US Patent and Trademark Office (*http://www.uspto.gov*). If you use a trademark that someone else owns, you may be liable for trademark infringement.

For more information on choosing and appraising domain names, go to *http://www.namestoremember.com*.

Nonbusiness Names

If your activities on the Web are not business activities, the guidelines for choosing a name still apply in most cases. Even nonprofit organizations need to market to their audiences, and a good domain name is good marketing.

Even if you have a family website, you will want everyone in the family to remember the URL easily. Consequently, it pays off to devote some time to picking a good domain name.

Choosing a Registrar

In the beginning, there was only one registrar, Network Solutions. Network Solutions still maintains the master database of domain names, but there are now hundreds of registrars. Go to Domain Name News (*http://www.domainnamenews.com*) for extensive information on domain names including a list of registrars. Different registrars charge different prices and have different reputations.

Before You Register

You will want to check to see if the domain name you want is available before you attempt to register. Go to Network Solutions (*http://www.networksolutions.com*) and use the Whois database. For example, if you want the name *smithelectronics.com*, don't enter *smithelectronics* in Whois. Enter *smithelectronics.com*.

Making the Registration

Registering is easily done online at a registrar. You supply the domain name, your business name (if any), your name, and the usual address and credit card information. You also have to name a technical contact, a server, and a backup server; your ISP can provide these to you.

Once registered, your domain will be inactive until you activate it. Your ISP may charge you a nominal monthly fee for an inactive domain (i.e., you can't get the domain name without the technical contact and two servers).

When your website is ready, your ISP activates your domain in the domain name system. It takes a day or two to propagate throughout the system. Soon everyone on the Internet can visit your website. Your ISP may charge you an additional monthly fee for using your own domain name for your website.

Expenses

You pay for registration on an annual basis. The fee is from $20 to $35 annually, and most registrars collect two years in advance when you register a name. If you don't pay the annual fee, you lose the name.

Purchasing a Domain Name

If you buy a name that's already registered (owned by someone else), the price will be between $100 and $10,000,000. The domain name resale market seems a bit inflated, and you will do well to negotiate aggressively for any name that you decide to purchase.

There are a generous supply of domain name brokers on the Web (e.g., *http://firstinternationaldomains.com*). Domain Name News (*http://www.domainnamenews.com*) maintains a list of brokers. Some people believe it's the new real estate!

A huge number of domain names have already been registered, many by people who aren't using them. You may be able to find the name you want for sale. Although prices seem high in most cases, it doesn't hurt to make what you think is a reasonable offer. Although it appears to be a seller's market, it's really a buyer's market. Make an offer.

What You Can Do

When you have your own domain name, you become part of the "in" crowd on the Web. You control your presence on the Web. No one can take your domain name away from you (so long as you pay your annual registration fee). You can switch ISPs and take your name with you. You can move to Pakistan or France, get an ISP there, and take your domain name with you. Your domain name is a place where everyone can find you on the Internet regardless of where your Web page files are located physically (i.e., which ISP's computer they're on).

You can use your domain name for a variety of purposes in addition to the Web. For instance, you can use it for your email address (e.g., *gloria@smithelectronics.com*).

Your domain name is your URL. It may be a lifetime asset for you, your business, your non-profit activities, or your family.

Summary

The domain name you use determines your Web address (URL). Your ISP will provide you with a Web address, but you may want to consider getting your own domain name. If so, choose carefully. Make it easy for your audience to remember.

IV

Website Skills

18

Storing and Linking Web Pages

The first rule of Web authoring is to keep parallel websites. The first website is on your hard drive. Once you have finalized each Web page or image, you upload it to your Web host hard drive (ISP or intranet). The website on the host hard drive always remains identical to the website on your hard drive (except for Web pages or images not finalized or undergoing revision).

The best practice for most small websites (under 20 Web pages and 20 images) is to store everything in one folder. When the pages and the images multiply, however, it's time to use more folders to keep well organized. Like the Web pages and images, the folders on your Web host hard drive should be identical to the ones on your own hard drive.

Disk Crash

If you have a disk crash, you can restore your website to your own hard drive from your Web host's hard drive. If your Web host has a disk crash, you can restore your website on the host's hard drive from your own hard drive. Think it won't happen? It has happened to me once on my own hard drive and once on my host's hard drive. Be cautious.

Most hosts keep daily backups, but occasionally the backups don't get made, perhaps because the network administrator is distracted by the problem that eventually causes the crash.

Keep in mind that the folder arrangement of your website is for organized and convenient *storage*. It has little to do with the structure of your website. Links define the structure of your website.

This chapter shows how to arrange your file storage via a system of folders. It also provides you with the background knowledge to use links to build websites. In addition it explains how to use relative links so that the website at your Web host can be identical to the website on your own computer and still work. Relative links (covered in Chapter 6) make possible the parallel websites mentioned earlier.

Folders

You can create folders and subfolders, as briefly outlined in Appendix III. Organize your folders in a way that makes sense to you. This section suggests some possible strategies for practical storage.

Every person and every website is different, however, and you can judge best what folder arrangement works for you.

When other people work on your website, they need to understand your storage scheme. In that case, you need to give consideration to what will make sense to others as well as yourself. Don't make your storage arrangement difficult for others to understand.

Don't' worry about putting too many files in one folder. The limit is not a technical one. The limit is how many files you can keep track of easily without splitting the collection into smaller groups. When you think storage, think folders.

Storage by Media

One useful arrangement entails storing by media. Put all the Web pages in one folder and all the images in another. If you use sound, put all the streaming sound files in yet another folder.

Storage by Sections

Your website most likely has at least a couple of sections. It makes a good strategy to place the files for different sections in different folders.

This makes sense, particularly for large websites with a half-dozen sections or more and for websites for which different people have the responsibility to maintain the various sections of the website.

Storage by Media and Sections

People commonly divide their storage by both sections and media. Consequently, you might have a folder for a section of your website and have an image subfolder just for that section. You store your Web pages in the section folder and all your images in the image subfolder. Use this approach for large websites.

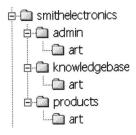

Links

Remind yourself: *Folders don't define websites, links do.* Where you store your website files is your own business. No one else cares, because it doesn't matter to website visitors. Links are a different matter. Links provide the structure for navigating your website, and they are important for your website visitors. After all, your website visitors have to use those links to navigate around your website. If you make a serious blunder with your links, your website visitors will be navigating in a fog or jumping ship.

Links establish the relationships between Web pages. And websites are merely collections of Web pages. If you display the links between Web pages graphically, you will see the structure of the website.

See Chapter 6 to learn the basic steps for adding a link to a Web page and for details on absolute and relative links.

Absolute Links

You can't go wrong with absolute links. These are the full URLs of every Web page or every image. The primary drawback is that you can't use such links to navigate your own parallel website on your own computer. URLs are unique and cannot be used for the same Web pages on two different computers.

Testing

The only way to test absolute links is to put your Web pages on the Web. You cannot test absolute links in Web pages on your own computer unless that computer also hosts your website.

Relative Links

Absolute links fit some situations, but most of the time you will want to take a different approach. You can use abbreviated links (less-than-full URLs). You express such links by how the Web page being linked relates to the Web page that includes the link (relative linking).

A relative link tells your browser where to find the next Web page with an instruction telling where the next Web page is in the folder (storage) structure. See Chapter 6 for more on relative links.

Multiple Domain Websites

We like to think of websites as being completely inside one domain name address. That's true for most websites. Nonetheless, you can use multiple domains for a website.

Two Domains

Suppose you have a website that sells consumer electronics *smith-electronics.com*. You locate all your Web pages at *smithelectronics.com* (at the ISP *localnet.com*) except for your ecommerce transaction Web pages.

Why would you do something like this? Well, Localnet may not offer ecommerce software or may offer ecommerce software you don't want to use. Because Localnet is also your dial-up ISP, your website there is free. You get your ecommerce application service from another ISP (Ecom Services) that offers you a special monthly rate since it does not host your website but provides only ecommerce services.

Your customers visit your website to browse through your catalog. When they decide to buy an item, they click on a link that takes them to the ecommerce Web pages such as the "Check Out" Web page (at another domain name).

Let's stop here. Up until this link, you can use relative links at your website. This link must be an absolute link, because it goes to another domain name.

Once this absolute link takes a website visitor to the second domain (*ecomservices.com*), you can use relative links to link the various ecommerce Web pages. They are all within one domain. Eventually, a website visitor may want to return to the catalog to browse some more. You need to provide a link back to the main Web pages at the first domain (*smithelectronics.com*). The link back must be an absolute link.

Website Visitor Confusion?

If you set up this seemingly bizarre two-domain website structure, won't it confuse website visitors? Few website visitors will ever notice. Few will look in the URL window (in the browser) to see where they are. If you do it properly, the navigation will appear seamless to website visitors.

How do you make it appear seamless? Remember, you control the Web pages (and links) for your website at both *smithelectronics.com* and *ecommservices.com*. Your actual URL at Ecom Services will be something like:

ecomservices.com/~smithelectronics

So long as you control the Web pages and the links, you can make the navigation smooth. The key here is to use relative links for navigating Web pages within each domain but absolute links when linking Web pages at different domains.

Auctions on Your Website

Online auction software cost a lot and takes a considerable amount of administration. Yet you can incorporate auctions into your website easily and inexpensively by using eBay (http://www.ebay.com).

Conveniently, eBay allows you to put links and other HTML in your auction ads. This enables you to control your auction Web page at eBay. Your auction Web page at eBay has a unique URL. Because you control both your own website and your eBay auction Web page, you can effectively integrate your eBay auction into your own website by creating and controlling the links in each direction. Since your website and eBay's website are different domains, you must use absolute links.

See my eBay the Smart Way (AMACOM, 2000) for more information on integrating eBay auctions into your website.

Website Structure

By now you can see that storage has little to do with website structure. Website structure relies on the links between Web pages. By a simple absolute link, you can even extend a website across the Internet to another domain. This chapter provides you with the information you need to create links that work.

Creating website structure with links is at once a science and an art. This chapter presents the science (the technical means). The next chapter presents the art. The next chapter is not about building a geometric structure, as for a building. Rather, it's about human navigation. The navigation (structure) you create answers the question, "How can I organize my Web pages in such a way that website visitors will be able to easily and effortlessly find what they want?"

Summary

Storing and linking Web pages (and images) are two different concepts. The first uses folders and is strictly for storing files. The second uses links and is for building a navigation structure for your website. To avoid confusion, don't get these two concepts mixed up.

19

Organizing Web Pages

How do you construct a website? It's simple. You organize two or more Web pages to make a multipage presentation. As mentioned in Chapter 18, where you store your Web pages has nothing to do with the structure of the website. It's the links. The links between Web pages provide the structure for your website. As you plan the navigation through your multipage Web presentation, you are planning your website structure. As you put in the links to facili-

tate your navigation scheme, you are building your website structure.

One-Page Website?

*Can you have a one-page website? Sure. If so, the only structure
is the page itself. Any links are to external URLs that are not part
of your website, or they are links to anchors within the Web
page itself.*

Interactivity

You can create a linear presentation through a group of Web pages,
one by one. You might call this a slide show presentation. It
doesn't give website visitors much choice (see Figure 19.1).

Figure 19.1   Linear presentation.

Most websites, however, take advantage of flexible hyperlinking—
an intregral part of the Web—to create nonlinear structures. Such
structure gives website visitors choices, even if only to go in one
direction or another (see Figure 19.2).

When website visitors have choices, a visitor becomes a participant
in the Web page presentation. The choices a visitor makes determines how he or she experiences that Web page presentation. The
presentation is said to be *interactive*, because the visitor interacts
with the Web page presentation. The visitor is not just a passive
viewer.

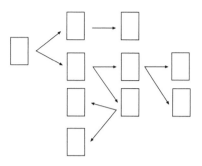

Figure 19.2   Nonlinear presentation.

The Web is an interactive medium, and website visitors interact with the multimedia elements (the content) of the Web medium.

This raises a serious question for you and all other Web page makers. How do you handle an interactive medium? How do you make links? How do you use links? And how do the links structure the content?

Interactivity Isn't New

Books enable some degree of interactivity. You can decide to read a footnote or not read it. You can look at the table of contents and decide to read Chapter 14 but not chapter 19. However, the navigation isn't convenient. The Table of Contents is at the front of the book. The Index is at the back. In many books even the footnotes are all at the back of the book (as endnotes).

The Web is different than a book because the links are part of the Web page and can take you to any other Web page in the entire world. In addition, some links provide functions such as the mailto: link which triggers your email program. Thus, the navigation is more flexible and convenient, and the Web is said to be more interactive than a book. It potentially provides more choices and more convenience for users.

A Web of Links

The first notion that all budding Web page makers have is that they can create lots of choices which enable a website visitor to go in any direction to satisfy his or her inclinations. Instead of a linear presentation, think of a branching presentation where there are at least two choices in whichever direction a website visitor goes.

A Spider's Web

The World Wide Web was not envisioned as a cable extending from the valley to the mountain top (linear). It was envisioned as a spider's web, with strands running in every direction (non-linear). You don't have to make decisions to navigate the cable. You must make a decision at every juncture to navigate the spider's web.

This is a great concept, but not a new one. Educators, game makers, and other authors have used this concept since the personal computer was invented. There is a considerable body of research and knowledge about interactivity that has inspired more than a few books on the topic. It's difficult to summarize what we know about interactivity in one section of one chapter, but a few tips about interactivity are appropriate here:

1. Don't get carried away with branching. It may make your Web page presentation too complex (see Figure 19.3).

2. Keep your branching shallow, otherwise your website visitor will get lost in your Web page presentation (see Figure 19.4).

3. If your visitor gets lost in your Web page presentation, he or she will get frustrated and angry at you and will be unlikely

to return to your website.

4. Don't create branching just to branch. Use branching for specific purposes to communicate your content.

5. Educated people are often compulsive and tend to want to eat the whole thing (years of striving to learn everything in the textbook). Don't make it impossible for them by creating excessive interactivity. Cater to their narrow linear impulses.

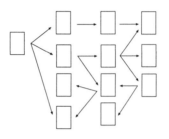

Figure 19.3   Complex branching.

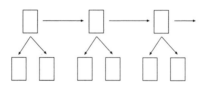

Figure 19.4   Shallow branching.

In other words, don't get carried away with interactivity just because the Web makes it easy to create. Alas, simple interactivity that moves along in an orderly manner—in a linear direction— seems to satisfy the late-twentieth-century mind.

In the future, as people grow up with interactivity and learn to use interactivity naturally, robust interactivity will play a greater role in education, information, and entertainment. For now, however, keep it simple.

Usability

Usability has to do with how your website visitors use your Web pages and how they interact with your Web pages. In other words, how usable is the navigation (linking) to get around your website and find what one is looking for? Is it self-evident? Mysterious? Is it easy? Torturous? Fortunately, the first research has been done (usability research, some free, some for a fee, at User Interface Engineering *http://www.uie.com*), and we have some answers.

The research shows that the best structure for your website is hierarchical. Remember in fifth grade when you learned to make a hierarchical outline? That's how you need to construct your website for most purposes. That's how we are used to handling information. We find such a structure natural and easy to follow and understand.

The diagram below shows how the Smith Electronics website might be organized (see Figure 19.5).

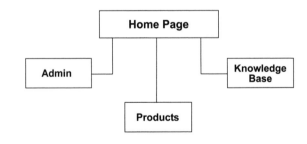

Figure 19.5   The hierarchical structure of the Smith Electronics website.

Note that the Administrative section provides Web pages about the company, listing personnel and their phone numbers and email addresses, and posting job openings. The Knowledge Base section contains informative articles on camcorders, VCRs, and televisions. The products section groups products into camcorders, VCRs, and televisions.

More detail reveals a further breakdown of the hierarchical structure (see Figure 19.6).

The camcorder section contains information on Sony, JVC, and Sharp camcorders. Finally, even more detail reveals more hierarchical structure, which yields information on individual products (see Figure 19.7).

Each individual product includes the initial Web page (promotional) with three supporting Web pages for specifications, excerpts form technical reviews, and lists of accessories.

This is a lot of branching. It looks like and upside-down tree. But because it's hierarchical, we intuitively understand it. Is anyone going to get lost in this tree? Probably not.

Keep in mind that this hierarchical structure shows the primary navigational paths. You can also use secondary navigational paths where the content requires them. For example, from each of the camcorders (from the promotional Web pages) you may want to put a link to the Camcorder section of the Knowledge Base section or even to specific articles in that Camcorder section. These links provide convenience and are not hierarchical (see Figure 19.8).

Even though the linking between Web pages sometimes seems like a complicated scheme, the navigational logic must always remain simple.

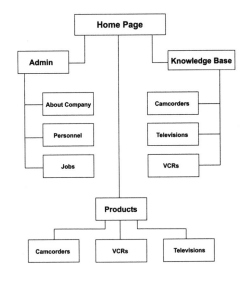

Figure 19.6   More structural detail for the Smith Electronics website.

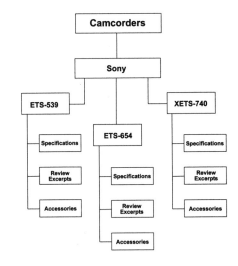

Figure 19.7   Even more structural detail for Smith Electronics.

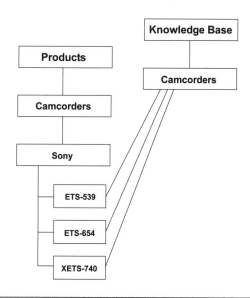

Figure 19.8   Some nonhierarchical links.

This is a simple tree for a limited retail operation. Obviously, a hierarchical structure for even a modest retail operation can be a huge upside-down blossoming tree that can strain the most logical mind. To make the navigation easier, you can publish a site map for the website. The site map looks like a hierarchical outline, because that's exactly how the website is structured. People will find the site map easy to understand.

There's more to usability than just hierarchy. You need to create groupings of Web pages in a logical manner and use words that accurately reflect the content of such Web pages. In other words, you need to use words in your outline that help visitors understand and navigate your hierarchy.

Always Hierarchy?

Most websites present information, and the hierarchical struc-

ture has proved to enable the most intuitive and convenient navigation for website visitors. Whether you publish articles in an online newsletter or sell merchandise out of an online catalog, the hierarchical structure proves its worth.

On the other hand, the hierarchical structure may not be appropriate for certain types of information. Artists will experiment with a variety of structures as they create multimedia works of art on the Web. Entertainers will deviate from the hierarchical approach, too, in their Web presentations. However, even artists and entertainers need to have their creations make sense and need to make their websites reasonably easy to use if they desire to have an audience. Consequently, deviations from the hierarchical approach should be made with great caution lest they fail to provide a usable structure.

No information in this Chapter or this book should be interpreted as suggesting that you shouldn't use the potential interactivity that the Web enables. The message here is: Use interactivity carefully and rationally.

Links

Links are the structural steel girders that hold your Web pages in a matrix. Links are the pathways one travels from Web page to Web page to navigate the subdivisions of your content. Links are the conveniences afforded to your website guests. In other words, the concept of links serves more than one purpose.

Navigational Links

Navigational links take your website visitors from one Web page to another, in an intuitive manner, through the content of your website. In most cases, you will want to organize such links so as to give your Web pages a hierarchical organization, as mentioned earlier. In some cases, a more free-form organization can work. If the organization is not intuitive for website visitors, however, they will get frustrated. Frustrated website visitors can become angry and dissatisfied.

If you have a navigational structure that requires a lot of explanation to use, has flawed logic, or is overly complex, it's not intuitive; you will lose a lot of people. Keep your organization (navigation) simple and easy to understand.

Common Links

On each page, usually at the bottom or top, provide your website visitors with a navigation bar. This can be a line of links (horizontal), an image map, or a menu (vertical). Usually it includes two or three links common for every Web page and two or three links common to the group of Web pages to which the particular Web page belongs. It might also include one or two unique links.

Examples of links common to every Web page at a website are: Home, Help, Support, Contact Us, and Site Map. An example of a link common to a group of Web pages is the name of the website section (e.g., Products).

Don't consider the common links as part of your navigational scheme. They are more like escape hatches. They usually take website visitors back to a familiar place in your website, to a new place where visitors can get help in coping with your website, or to a reference resource. Even though these common links are not necessarily navigational, they are still useful to website visitors.

Convenience Links

These links take on various configurations. Links can provide amazing convenience. For instance, suppose in an online article you refer to a work of art in the Museum of Modern Art (MOMA) in New York City, and the art happens to be on display on the MOMA website. You can create a link that goes directly to the work of art on the MOMA website.

Is this a navigational link? Not really. You have sent your website visitor off to another website. You have no control over what happens after that. This link is merely a convenience to your website visitors.

To Send or Not to Send?

Many Web developers advocate never sending a website visitor off your website. Since you have no control thereafter, the theory is the website visitor will be lost forever. This is foolishness. A website visitor who is motivated to patronize your website will find his or her way back. Links to other websites can provide legitimate convenience to your website visitors and thereby enhance your website.

A convenience link is like a footnote. The content of the footnote is subordinate to the main body of content, but it may be important to some readers. The capability to easily and instantly refer to footnotes via links is one of the essential ingredients of the Web.

Gratuitous Links

On some websites, you see link-o-mania. Dozens, if not hundreds, of links in the text go to every conceivable destination. This can be very confusing to website visitors. Keep all links relevant to the content you present on your website. If a link is not relevant, it shouldn't be there.

There is a place for lots of links. You can make lists of links. The key to doing this successfully is to organize the lists into categories that make sense. Then such lists can sometimes be a valuable resource for website visitors. Ultimately, however, even lists of links should be relevant to the content of your website. For example, a link to the website of a nuclear power plant seems out of place on a website where you sell clothing (unless the clothing is radiation proof) no matter how "cool" the power plant website is—and so what if your brother-in-law is a manager at the power plant?

The Metaphor

Many Web developers advocate that you should organize your website around a metaphor, so that website visitors will understand it better. For instance, a website selling cowboy collectibles might organize around the metaphor of a frontier town. Thus, the saloon becomes the chat room, the general store becomes the catalog, the stable becomes the auction, ad nauseam.

In my opinion, the metaphor idea is overdone. Most metaphor websites are inherently corny. If you use a metaphor, do it well or don't do it at all. The questions to ask yourself are:

- Is the metaphor fresh and tasteful? Or, is it old, tired, and trite?

- Does the metaphor intuitively add to the understanding of the navigation and the content? Or does it have to be explained?

- Does the metaphor require a huge amount of original artwork? Can you afford such art work?

Metaphor websites can be wonderful when done properly. Nonetheless, there's still a lot to be said for a simple, well-organized, hierarchical, nonmetaphoric website that provides easy navigation.

Planning

Like all endeavors, your website building will proceed much more efficiently if you plan it first. There are dozens of ways to plan, from napkins to storyboards. However, to keep things simple, you might try notebook paper or lawyers' foolscap. Rough out your individual Web page layouts. Indicate your text blocks, images, and links. Then draw your folder arrangement and list the Web page and image files in each folder. Finally, draw your website structure using boxes for Web pages and lines for links. For large websites the structure can get quite complex, and website building programs can actually display your structure for you once you have created your Web pages. For modest websites, however, a sketch will do.

Summary

Links make up the structure of your website. They primarily serve a navigational purpose. The most usable structure proves to be hierarchical for most purposes. If you understand this and your website has useful content, your website will be valuable to its website visitors.

V

Advanced Skills

20

Adding Dancing Digital Doodads

Add some action to your website. Add some movement. It wasn't long after the multimedia Web was established (1993) that programmers began to tinker with it. Their objective: breathe some life into the static Web. Their tinkering produced several technologies popular today for adding animation in the broadest sense of the word. You can use traditional animations (e.g., cartoons), educational animations (e.g., animated drawings and diagrams), presentation animations (e.g., moving text and images), photographic animations (e.g., slide shows), photographic transitions (e.g., dissolves and wipes), and even multimedia animations (e.g., moving presentations with diverse media).

These technologies are mostly for experts, but you may find it practical to use some animations that others have created by copying, pasting, and embedding them into your Web pages. This chapter briefly covers how you can get started doing this.

Animated GIFs

Animated GIFs are your best bet. They're simple and easy to use. They are the same as normal images for all practical purposes. You simply place them in a Web page as you would any image. The difference is in the viewing. They are really a series of cells creating an animation that displays cell by cell in sequence in a continuous loop.

Making animated GIFs is something you may want to try someday, but you can find plenty of them around the Web that other people have made for free distribution. You can also save them right out of any Web page on the Web just as you can any image (as explained in Appendix III). But be careful not to infringe on a copyright by publishing an animated GIF without permission.

Keep in mind that animated GIFs may have their place (I'm not sure what it is), but they also create a considerable distraction on Web pages you intend for people to read. And a reader cannot turn them off.

Templates Everywhere

If you can find JavaScript animations that you want to use, it may be possible to adapt them to your use. Although we think of templates as Web pages (intentionally made for pouring in content), other digital devices sometimes make good templates too.

Suppose you find a JavaScript (in a Web page) that provides a drop-down navigation menu. A website visitor passes the cursor across a word or image, and a navigation menu drops down. Since the JavaScripts are right in the Web page, there's no hiding them. You can look through the JavaScript——which will generally mean nothing to you—and find the place where the menu words and the link URLs are stated. You can substitute your own. Consequently, the JavaScript starts to seem like a sort of template. Because you have the actual code (source code), you can make substitutes even without being a programmer. You can alter the program for your own use.

Mouseover

When the cursor passes over a word or image and thereby initiates an action, it's called a mouseover.

JavaScripts

Don't even think about writing JavaScript unless you're a programmer. This is a programming language for programmers only. Programmers will tell you it's a scripting language that anyone can master. Don't believe them. Programming is programming. Unless you want to be a programmer, don't try your hand at writing JavaScript.

JavaScript and Java

Java is a full-fledged programming language, not a scripting language like JavaScript. Oddly enough, there is no relation between the two except in name. Sun owns Java, and Netscape

(America Online) ownes JavaScript. Both are for programmers, not for Web page makers.

You can find many sources of free JavaScripts around the Web that will provide various functions in Web pages. Find some that provide the capability that you seek and copy and paste them into an appropriate Web page. The code goes directly into the page. (For instance, Dynamic HTML depends on JavaScript to work.)

A handy JavaScript is one that initiates an action with a mouseover. In the following JavaScript, the mouseover initiates a change of the image. Both images, the original and the replacement, must have the same pixel dimensions. When a website visitor passes the cursor over the image, another image replaces it instantly. When the cursor passes away from the image, the original returns instantly.

```
<!-- TWO STEPS TO INSTALL CHANGE
IMAGE:

1. Paste the coding into the HEAD of
your HTML document

2. Add the last code into the BODY of
your HTML document -->


<!-- STEP ONE: Copy this code into the
HEAD of your HTML document -->

<HEAD>

<SCRIPT language="JavaScript">

<!-- This script and many more are
available free online at -->

<!-- The JavaScript Source!!http://
javascript.internet.com-->
```

```
<!-- Begin

function movepic(img_name,img_src) {

document[img_name].src=img_src;

}

// End -->

</SCRIPT>


<!-- STEP TWO: Put this code into the
BODY of your HTML document -->

<BODY>

<!-- Be sure to give each image a
name! (<img name="button">)

Include that name in the onmouseover/
onmouseout tags! -->

<CENTER>

<A HREF="http://
javascript.internet.com"

onmouseover="movepic('button','pic-
off.gif')"

onmouseout="movepic('button','pic-
on.gif')">

<IMG NAME="button" SRC="pic-off.gif"
ALT="Image"></A>

</CENTER>
```

After you install this (without other content) in a Web page, the HTML without the comments is as follows:

```
<html><head>
```

```
<title>Change Image</title>
<script language="JavaScript">
<!-- Begin
function movepic(img_name,img_src) {
document[img_name].src=img_src;
}
// End -->
</script>
</head>
<body>
<center>
<a href="http://
javascript.internet.com"
onmouseover="movepic('button','pic-
off.gif')"
onmouseout="movepic('button','pic-
on.gif')">
<img name="button" src="pic-off.gif"
alt="Image"></a>
</center>
</body>
</html>
```

The following images (pic-on.gif and pic-off.gif) simulate an image in a browser that changes when you do a mouseover.

First Image   Second Image

To use this JavaScript as is, you must name your GIFs *pic-on.gif* and *pic-off.gif*. If you want to name them something different, you will have to make substitutions in the code.

Link

Note that the way the image change is programmed, it's a link to http://javascript.internet.com. *If you want to link somewhere else, change the URL in the code.*

This JavaScript works better if you preload the images. Otherwise, upon the first mouseover, a website visitor will have to wait a short time for the second image to download. You can get a JavaScript that preloads the images at *http://javascript.internet.com* and include that in the same Web page.

Dynamic HTML

Dynamic HTML (DHTML) enables you to move multimedia elements, such as text paragraphs and GIFs, on the page by means of JavaScript. Theoretically you need to be a programmer to create the JavaScript that enables such movement, but you can also use a Web authoring program such as Macromedia's Dreamweaver, which doubles as a DHTML authoring program. Using such a program for creating a dynamic Web page presentation does not require you to be a programmer.

SMIL

Simultaneous Multimedia Integration Language (SMIL), pronounced *smile*, enables nonprogrammers to create presentations with movable multimedia elements. SMIL is a Web standard that is essentially an extension of HTML. It adds additional markups to HTML for you to use. This is a technology you can look forward to using someday as your Web skills grow.

SMIL requires a separate player in addition to a Web browser. The leading provider of such players is RealNetworks. They have distributed copies of their RealPlayer to over 125 million unique Web users. The RealPlayer acts as the engine behind the presentation; that is, RealPlayer plays the presentation in the Web page (i.e., in the browser). Many users never even know RealPlayer is there.

Once you learn HTML, the next step is to learn SMIL. It has a small number of markups, and as an HTML veteran, you will find SMIL easy to master.

Other Technologies

This chapter has not covered several other technologies which facilitate animation and other functions. You can do almost anything with CGI or Java, and Chapter 21 covers both CGI scripts and Java applets.

Summary

The movement of multimedia elements in a Web page makes a Web page dynamic. Such movement is a type of animation. Animated GIFs, JavaScript, and DHTML provide you with technologies that enable a variety of Web page animations. Creating animation is programmers' work. However, you can use animations by obtaining ones that others have programmed and installing them in your Web pages or by creating dynamic Web pages with a DHTML authoring program.

21

Adding Special Software

Sooner or later websites that have only text and images may seem dull. Computers can do so much. Why not have programs operate right in the Web page? The possibilities are endless. Once you add programming to a Web page, you can make the Web page do almost anything.

Although the readers of this book are not likely to start writing code (programming), there are plenty of Web page programs available free at various places on the Web. You can visit programming archive websites to see if you can find some programming code that you can use in one of your Web pages.

CGI Scripts

Common Gateway Interface (CGI) enables you to use programming with Web pages. The programming can be written in any programming language that will run on the server computer. Unless you are a programmer, you're not going to write CGI scripts yourself, but you might consider hiring a programmer to write some programming for you to satisfy a special need.

For the mundane day-to-day website building tasks, you will find CGI scripts available free at various places on the Web. Your ISP may offer a selection of free CGI scripts for you to use.

As mentioned in Chapter 20, you may be able to use a CGI program as a template by substituting your own content for that found within the CGI source code. However, read The Template Approach section later in this chapter to understand the limitations.

You must load a CGI script (file) into a special folder on your Web host hard drive (e.g., *cgi-bin*). Then you reference that URL to run the program (see the Minimum Criteria section of Chapter 15).

Security

One means of maintaining security, a problem with CGI, is for your ISP to give you a special CGI folder (e.g., cgi-local) in your own space on the hard disk. This links to the root CGI folder to provide computing power without as much security risk.

Sound interesting? When you realize that CGI unlocks the power of a computer to provide almost any type of program through a

Web page, it becomes a very attractive technology. In other words, you can do almost anything you want to do in a Web page through CGI.

What's the catch? The CGI programming runs on the Web host computer. If dozens of website visitors attempt to use the same CGI scripts simultaneously, it puts a substantial load on the server computer. Consequently, it may not be practical to use substantial CGI scripts without beefing up your server capacity or to use CGI scripts at all for host Web servers with heavy traffic.

Perl

Perl is one of the favorite programming (scripting) languages for creating CGI scripts. When you hear about Perl scripts, people are talking CGI.

JavaScript

JavaScript (covered in Chapter 20) is a scripting language you can use in a Web page to add functionality to the Web page. It's not a full-fledged programming language, but it will provide a useful range of functions. It has no relationship at all to Java. What makes JavaScript different than CGI scripting is that it resides in the Web page and is run by the client computer. Thus, it puts no load on the server computer.

The other unique characteristic of JavaScript is that the coding is not hidden. It's right in the Web page, and anyone can see it, modify it, or copy it. CGI scripts are in a file outside the Web page and inaccessible to website visitors, and Java is compiled into files after being coded and is practically impossible to access, read, or modify.

Java

Java is a full-fledged programming language that you can use for nearly anything. But it was designed to run on a network, making it unique among popular programming languages. The program files are called "classes" and use the *.class* file extension.

Not Related

Java is not related to JavaScript. Java is a full-fledged programming language. JavaScript is a limited scripting language.

Servlets

You can use Java for CGI scripts creating Java "servlets;" that is, the Java servlets run on the Web host computer. This use gives Java no advantage over other programming languages. But Java does something unusual. It can run on client computers, too, via the network.

Applets

The most interesting uses of Java on the Web are Java programs (applications, applets) that run on client computers. The browser first downloads the Java applet and then runs it. Once the browser closes or the client computer turns off, the applet evaporates. This system makes more sense than CGI scripts. A Java applet runs on a client computer and requires no computing power from the server computer except for the initial download.

Don't let the word applet fool you. Many Java applications (applets) are full-fledged programs; some are large and take a considerable time to download.

A Java applet is segregated from the normal computing in a client computer so hackers can't create deadly Java viruses. Nonetheless, running a succession of Java applets may cause your browser to crash. The remedy? Reopen your browser and start over.

Java applets are easy to embed in your Web pages. Use the *<applet>* markup to make Java programming a part of your Web page presentation. Programmers can provide controls for Web page makers in their Java applets. If controls exist, you use the *<param>* markup to include the controls in the embedding process.

Java has generated much excitement in the programming community since its introduction in 1995. It is a means for creating any kind of programming and distributing it to your website visitors via the Web.

Example Applet

The freeware Snow Applet (by David Griffiths) takes any image you have and makes snow fall in it. Fortunately, the snow does not accumulate in drifts at the bottom of your JPEG, so there's no need to shovel. The HTML embedding code follows:

```
<applet code="alcsnow" width="349"
height="169">

<param name="grph" value="image.jpg">

<param name="snows" value="500">

<param name="threadsleep" value="50">

</applet>
```

Substitute your own JPEG image file for *image.jpg*. Make sure you enter the width and height (in pixels) of your image. The *snows* value creates more or less snow (e.g., 100 = less, 900 = more). The *threadsleep* value regulates the speed of the falling snow (e.g.,

20 = faster, 80 = slower). The class file is *alcsnow.class*, and you store it in the same folder as the Web page. See Figure 21.1 for falling snow in a photograph taken in a Utah canyon in May.

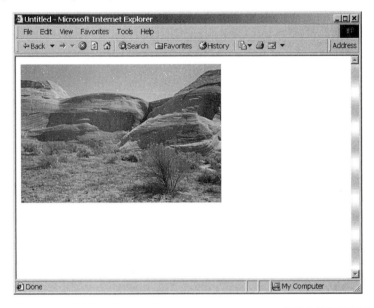

Figure 21.1   Snow falling in the canyon.

This is an example of an applet that enables some parameters to be set by the Web page maker. Note that there is only one Java class that makes up this applet. Some applets have many more classes.

Another Example

I created this simple calculator using a specialized Java authoring program (by Visual Numerics) that converts Excel spreadsheet applications into Java applets (see Figure 21.2). This a three-cell spreadsheet application.

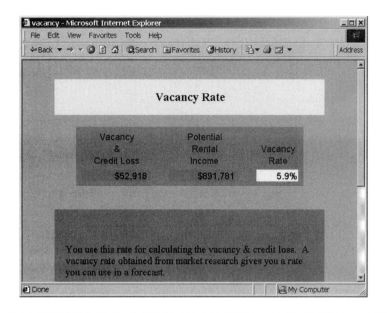

Figure 21.2 Vacancy Rate calculator Java applet.

You enter an income property's dollar loss due to vacancy and credit problems. Then you plug in a property's potential income (as if the property had been fully occupied) in dollars. The applet calculates the vacancy rate as a percentage. This *<applet>* markup is simple because it enables no user controls:

```
<applet code=vacancy width=455
height=116 codebase=classes>

</applet>
```

The setup for this applet, however, is a little complicated because it requires about three dozen Java classes in an elaborate folder-sub-folder arrangement (see Figure 21.3).

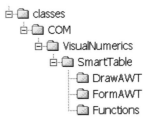

Figure 21.3   Folder arrangement to house Java classes for Vacancy Rate calculator Java applet.

Although it seems complicated, it works smoothly. The same class and folder setup supports many other Java applet calculators for Web pages at the same website.

The Template Approach

Chapter 20 explains how a JavaScript can sometimes make a useful template. Unfortunately, the source code for CGI scripts or Java is usually unavailable, so you can't make substitutions. Nonetheless, a Java programmer can provide you with some controls.

In the Snow Applet above, the programmer enables you to switch image files. Thus, you can use the Snow Applet as a template and use any image with it. In the Vacancy Rate calculator, no controls are enabled. It doesn't make a good template because you're stuck without any capability to make any changes in it.

Whenever you consider using special programming for Web pages, you should immediately check to see whether you have the capability to adapt the program to your own custom use. Because you are unlikely to create the programming yourself, you need to look for programs to use that you can customize a little, if necessary. There are plenty of free JavaScripts and Java applets available. You will find many difficult to use as templates (to customize) but others that are easy to customize.

Plug-ins

Plug-ins are programming modules that extend the capabilities of a browser. You download a plug-in and install it like any other program. When you install it, it forms a connection with your browser. When your browser needs it, the plug-in springs into action. For instance, the RealPlayer plug-in does nothing except open the RealPlayer (see Chapter 22 about streaming media). When your browser finds a Web page with a RealMedia file, the RealPlayer plug-in opens the RealPlayer (that already resides on your hard drive) and plays the streaming media in the Web page.

Installing

You download and install a plug-in ahead of its use so that your browser stands ready to do whatever the plug-in does. When the appropriate time comes, a plug-in does what it is supposed to do, usually playing a special type of presentation that a browser won't play without the plug-in.

What's the Point?

The plug-ins are of interest to Web page makers, because they can do things that browsers cannot. If you want to use a presentation that requires a plug-in, such as RealMedia, you need to analyze the market to determine whether you can reach your audience. For instance, if your audience is the general (Internet) public and you want to use RealMedia, you can take comfort in the fact that over 125 million people have downloaded the RealMedia plug-in and RealPlayer. If your audience is the general public and you want to use QuickTime streaming media technology, you might have second thoughts. Only about one-fourth as many people have downloaded the QuickTime player; thus, you will reach a much smaller fraction of the general audience.

Summary

Unleash the power of computing. Use CGI scripts or Java to provide computing right in your Web pages. The possibilities are limitless. You will see much more embedded computing as the Web matures.

22

Adding Sound and Video

You can add music, voice, or video to your Web pages easily. It's just a matter of downloading software and running a simple procedure (encoding) with your media files. The software then adds the encoded media files (streaming media) to a Web page, which you can use on your website.

Your first question might be, Why can't I just use the sound and video files I have? Well, most media files are huge. A website visitor must download them and then play them enduring, a long wait during the download. Wouldn't it be better if a website visitor could hear them immediately? In fact, several systems make it possible to stream media; that is, play the media *as* it downloads rather than *after* it downloads. These systems require that you encode the media files first.

What is encoding? It's simply a procedure that takes a normal file, compresses it, and otherwise prepares it for efficient streaming. You supply the media files, and the streaming media system, such as RealNetworks, supplies the encoding software. The steps follow:

- Encode the media file.

- Embed the media file in a Web page.

- Deliver the streaming media file.

This works well if you already have some sound or video files you want to use. Otherwise, you need to obtain media files or produce them yourself. This chapter covers acquiring media files. Appendix IV covers producing media files in the following steps:

- Production

- Digitizing

- Editing

Appendix IV is a list of tips rather than a thorough treatment of these processes. Consult books covering home studio music recording, or using a camcorder, for useful information on recording music and video.

Before jumping into these procedures, however, there's something you should know about how streaming media works. It plays through a player, a program that coordinates with a browser to make streaming media play in the browser.

Streaming Media Player

Browsers don't stream media. Without a streaming media player, you won't be able to use sound or video effectively in a Web page. Fortunately, as of spring 2000, RealNetworks claimed its RealPlayers had been downloaded by 125 million unique individuals. That's a substantial market to consume your sound and video presentations. At about the same time, Apple claimed over 20 million QuickTime players downloaded.

Consequently, you don't have to worry a lot about your website visitors using streaming media. They may already have a player. If not, they can conveniently download one for free.

Players

Both RealPlayer and the Quicktime player work on Windows, Mac, and other operating systems, so streaming media is cross-platform. Take your choice. Microsoft has its Media Player, which streams media but is not cross-platform. It is not covered in this chapter.

RealPlayer

RealPlayer seems like another type of browser when you see it as a stand-alone player. But it also acts as an engine to play streaming sound in a Web page behind the scenes (transparently). A browser plug-in opens the RealPlayer when the browser detects RealMedia present in a Web page. RealPlayer plays the embedded RealMedia. Most website visitors never see the RealPlayer. If website visitors don't have RealPlayer, you can direct them to the RealNetworks website (http://www.real.com) where they can download it and install it. Once a person has installed RealPlayer, the RealNetworks website automatically upgrades RealPlayer when the person uses it online. Thus, RealPlayer is, in theory, always the current version.

QuickTime Player

The QuickTime player (*http://www.apple.com/quicktime*), also a free download, plays streaming sound too. It works similarly to RealMedia and has similar functions. However, RealMedia files and QuickTime movie files are not compatible. They are separate streaming media systems requiring separate players.

What Plays?

Both the RealPlayer and QuickTime player will play a wide variety of media in various formats including sound and video media. Unless the media are streaming media, however, they don't work efficiently. As a practical matter, only streaming sound and video are relevant to your website operation.

Encoding

Encoding prepares a normal sound file for use as a streaming sound file. It compresses to stream (download) faster and adds programming to stream more smoothly and at higher quality. The encoding process is simple and straightforward, a routine procedure for putting media files online. This chapter uses RealMedia to illustrate the process. Although many audio and video editors have RealMedia encoding built in, you will be able to use more up-to-date encoding by using the latest RealNetworks software. This can be important because encoding software constantly improves.

For RealMedia, you use RealProducer, a free download at the RealNetworks website (*http://www.realnetworks.com/devzone*). Look for it in the Devzone (developers section).

Real Stuff

RealNetworks provides the RealPlayer and Real Producer free. It also provides upscale (Plus) versions of each for a price. The free versions are quite adequate.

After you download and install RealProducer, you're ready to encode. Open RealProducer and then open the media file you intend to encode (e.g., a WAV file or AVI file). Go File, Recording Wizards, Record from File to start the process (see Figure 22.1).

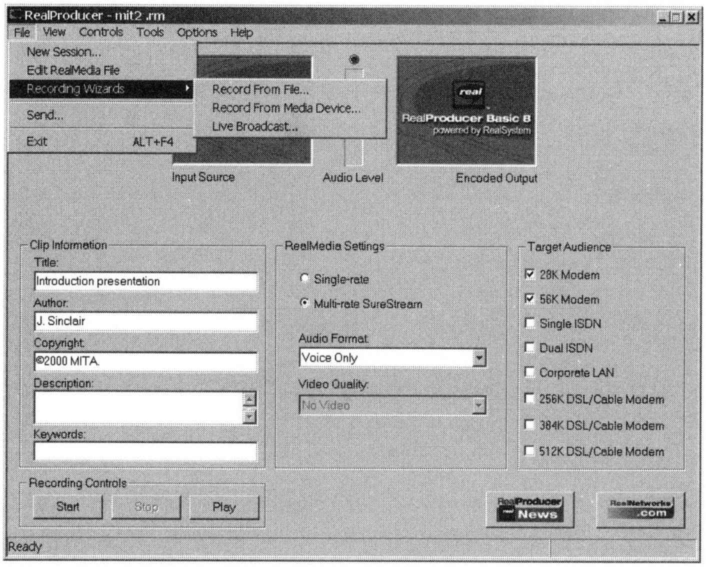

Figure 22.1   RealProducer

The program will lead you through a series of windows which help you customize the resulting RealMedia file (see Figure 22.2).

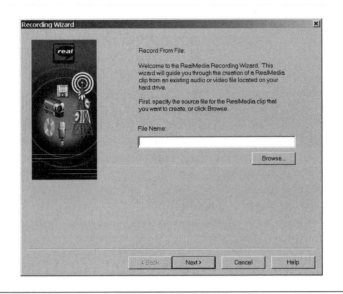

Figure 22.2   The first RealProducer encoding window.

You provide such information as the file name, the bandwidth, and the type of media. RealProducer uses different codecs (algorithms, programs) to do the encoding. For instance, one codec will encode sound for the 28.8K and 56K bandwidths, another for DSL, and yet another for video.

SureStream

You can choose to encode via SureStream, which encodes for all bandwidths automatically. It takes longer and the resulting file size is larger, but it saves you the trouble of having to encode the same file for a variety of bandwidths.

The result of the encoding is a RealMedia (*.rm*) file ready to embed in a Web page.

Embedding

Unfortunately, embedding a RealMedia file in a Web page is an arcane process, perhaps the most complex process in this book. You can find detailed information about it in the RealSystem G2 Production Guide (about 200 pages), a free download in the Devzone. It's not difficult, just a little confusing. Download and print the Production Guide if you use RealMedia a lot. Use the Guide as a reference.

Fortunately, RealProducer will automatically create a Web page for you with the proper embedding. You can copy and paste the markups from that Web page into a Web page of your own. In RealProducer, go Tools, Create Web Page, and a series of windows will lead you through the process (see Figure 22.3).

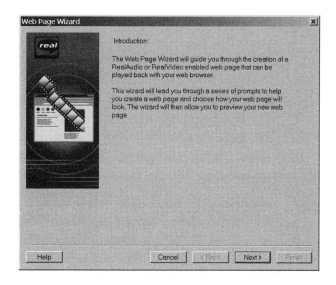

Figure 22.3   RealProducer embedding.

RealProducer will even do the FTP upload for you, although you may find it easier to do the upload yourself (see Chapter 16).

As part of the process, RealProducer creates an ASCII (plain text) file, which contains the URL of the RealMedia file. That must be uploaded to the website with the Web page and the RealMedia file. It's called an RPM (*.rpm*) file. Without the RPM file, the RealMedia file will not play. In summary, here's what you need to upload:

1. RealMedia file

2. RPM file

3. Web page containing the embedding markups

Delivery

You can deliver streaming media files two ways: via a Web server or via a streaming media server. Web servers and the Web protocol (HTTP) were not designed for streaming media. Although HTTP will handle streaming media, it does not do so with optimal performance. RealNetworks helped establish a Web standard Real Time Streaming Protocol (RTSP) to transmit streaming media via the Internet. A RealServer uses RTSP to enhance the delivery performance of RealMedia.

If you want to use RealMedia extensively, find an ISP that offers a RealServer, particularly if you have a lot of traffic to your website. QuickTime has a comparable server, the QuickTime Streaming Server, which is a part of Mac OS X Server.

HTTP

If you're not worried about substantial visitor traffic at your website, use HTTP (a plain Web server) for your streaming media. It works fine for light traffic.

RealServer

If you anticipate heavy traffic, you will need a RealServer. They come in various capacities measured in the number of concurrent website visitors they can handle, and they're expensive. You might want to choose an ISP based on the capacity of its RealServer.

Free RealServer

RealNetworks offers a free RealServer, which handles 20 concurrent users, available for download in the Devzone. It's not licensed for commercial use (e.g., ISPs can't use it), but you can use it for noncommercial use or experimentation.

Both

You use the same procedures for both streaming sound and streaming video. In fact, the resulting streaming media file is the same for both sound and video (e.g., *.rm* for RealMedia and *.mov* for QuickTime).

This book provides production, digitizing, and editing tips for both sound and video in Appendix IV. That will get you started.

Streaming sound has reached a high level of performance for use on the Web, and its use has started to blossom. Over 2,000 radio stations now broadcast on the Web.

Streaming video does not yet compare favorably to television. Nonetheless, hundreds of television stations offer some programming on the Web, usually in video archives. This is a time of experimentation for Web video, but soon streaming video will work better and will come to be commonplace on the Web.

Summary

Streaming media is exciting. Most webmasters have not tried it simply because producing sound or video is a separate and complex endeavor notwithstanding the Web procedures required to get the files online. In contrast, encoding those files and getting them online is not difficult. With a little attention to detail, you can put streaming media on your website.

Because this book is not a book on streaming media, it cannot adequately cover the topic for you. If you have a WAV or AVI file, however, use this chapter as a guide to encode your media file and get it on the Web. Doing that much will get you off to a good start on using this exciting technology.

VI

Using Your Website

23

Sharing a Website with Others

If you operate a family website or an organization's website, you will probably need to grant at least several additional people access to post Web pages and make changes to existing Web pages. The questions arise: How can numerous people operate a website and still maintain security? Do you need security? What security capabilities exist that you can use?

Security

Today you read almost weekly about a new virus or a new hacker's attack on some network. The threats are real even if they're unlikely to happen to you. Can you protect yourself? Probably not against an expert and determined hacker. Nonetheless, there are plenty of recalcitrant hackers, and only a handful of them rise to the expert level. Every measure you take to protect yourself will keep out even larger percentage of these hackers, even if it won't keep out all hackers.

The more security you can create in your Web operations, the more confidence users will have in your website and the more you'll be able to do with it. The ability to handle confidential information on a website can provide tremendous benefits, but it won't work unless people perceive the website to be secure.

Planning

First you have to plan your security. Read about it and learn about it. Explore what capabilities your ISP provides to help you maintain security on your website. Review software that promises security. Come up with a plan even if it's only a simple plan.

The most prevalent security breaches come from inside through malfeasance and carelessness. Disgruntled employees sometimes sabotage networks, and that's something to be aware of. But often network users are careless and ignorant of security practices. Only through training can you change that situation. Therefore, the cornerstone of security planning is to train network users to use secure practices and particularly train those to whom you grant access to work on your website.

If you are part of an organization, you should seriously consider making the training formal, with perhaps an examination at the end. This not only tests skills but sends the message that you're serious about security.

For a family, formal training is seldom practical, but you need to take security as seriously as possible within the dynamics of your family situation.

Limit Access

Never give everyone access to work on a website (i.e., via FTP as Chapter 16 explains). Most people in an organization or in your family don't need such access. Don't grant it. Limit work access to as few people as practical.

If possible, don't use one login and password for your website work access. Give each person his or her unique login and password. If you experience a breach of security, you may be able to trace it to the careless party by reviewing the FTP logs.

You can even limit access to *browsing* your website to those with a login and password. This is an extreme measure, but plenty of organizations and families use it.

Asset Security

Even if you're not a victim of malfeasance or carelessness, you can still have your digital assets (Web pages, images, programming) wiped out by a disk crash or another equipment failure. What can you do?

Backup Tape

Most ISPs run a daily backup tape and store a month of tapes. That provides some security. But ask your ISP specifically what it does to back up so that you can factor that into your security plan.

Whatever the interval is between backup tapes dictates the amount of work you can potentially lose. If it's two days and the crash occurs at the end of the second day, you'll lose two days of work.

Parallel Website

As mentioned in Chapters 18 and 19, keep a parallel website on your hard disk. Upload the Web pages to your Web host as you make them and retain copies on the parallel website on your hard disk.

Although you should be able to count on your ISP for backups, you can ensure that you won't lose your digital assets by maintaining a parallel website. You have to stay organized regarding your Web work and do a lot of testing on your own computer in any event. Do it with a parallel website.

When other people contribute to your website and do their posting separately, you need to work even harder to maintain your parallel website. You can do that by downloading Web pages that others post and include such Web pages in your parallel website. As an alternative, you can require that all those with work access to your website maintain a parallel website as well or send you copies of any Web pages they post.

Business Website

When you work as an employee at a business firm, you need to read and understand the rules that govern the use of your intranet. A breach of the rules can get you fired in some companies. In any event, normally you won't have to worry about the security of others; the system and the network administrator will take care of that. You just need to understand and follow the rules yourself.

When you are granted access to the firm website, or one of the firm websites, consider that a special privilege. You can be sure your network administrator will consider it a privilege. Don't be careless.

No one will be as concerned about your work as you. Therefore, follow the practice of keeping a parallel website. Even if you're responsible for only a few Web pages, keep parallel Web pages.

Always keep in mind that the network and the intranet are there to serve you. Don't be intimidated by the possibility that you may make a mistake. If the intranet doesn't serve employees, it loses its raison d'etre. But be careful to keep the security rules in mind.

Summary

Most people maintain their websites privately. But in families, businesses, or other organizations, you may need to work with others to build and update websites. If so, create a security plan, limit access, make backups, and keep a parallel website on your hard disk.

24

Family Fun

What can you put on the Web? You probably have your own ideas. Put them into action—Web action! This chapter provides some ideas to get you thinking about some of the family activities you can do on the Web. Don't take this as a definitive list. It's just a small list of some of the family things people do today on the Web.

Share Photographs

Families have been sharing photographs for well over a century. The Web provides an opportunity to share photographs with everyone in your family, not just with a few people, at no extra expense. Just put them in a Web page. Moreover, you can create an album of annotated photographs almost as easily as putting photographs into a Web page by themselves. Anyone in the family can save the Web pages, including the photographs, and keep them on their own computer or even print them.

What do you need? Only a Web authoring program, some digitized photographs, and something to say (write). You can easily make such Web pages and post them to your family website for all to enjoy.

Keep your Web pages simple, just photographs and text. If you keep the Web pages simple, you will make them more often, and your relatives will appreciate the volume more than they will extra fancy Web pages. If you have a compelling drive to make your Web pages fancy, use a template to save yourself repetitive work.

Just Photographs

You don't have to add text. To share photographs without text, just embed the photographs in a Web page. Your relatives can view them without commentary.

Share Privacy

One way to ensure that only family members can access your website, or certain parts of your website, is to protect it with a password. For access, each family member must use a login and password. Consult with your ISP on how to set this up. Most ISP's offer this capability for both entire websites and individual folders within a website.

Most people, however, will find administering passwords to be a chore. Another way that's not so secure but as a practical matter will work well is to have the entrance to the private portion of your website buried several levels of subfolders below the root folder. For instance, you might purposely create empty subfolders between the root folder and the *basket* folder.

```
www.familysite.com/brass/replay/
dingo/tap/basket
```

Your normal website starts with the file *index.html* in the root folder. The subfolders *brass*, *replay*, *dingo*, and *tap* are bogus and empty. Your private website starts in the *basket* folder with the file *index.html*.

Who's going to find this remote website? Unless one has the complete URL, one is highly unlikely to find this website even though access is not password protected.

Extra Security

If you want to be extra careful, place a file index.html *in the root folder and in each of the bogus subfolders. The* index.html *file in the root folder should be the home page for the website. The* index.html *files in the bogus subfolders can be blank Web pages.*

It is always a sound security practice to have an index.html *file in each folder (or subfolder). It prevents most website visitors from viewing your folder tree.*

What do you put on this website? Any information you want to share with the family but not with the rest of the world.

Family Forum

Most online forums (mailing lists, discussion groups, newsgroups) do not use the Web. They use other Internet protocols, such as email protocols. Nonetheless, the Web also supports forum programs. You can set up a family forum using a Web forum program. It will track all message topics (threads) and keep an archive of all messages. Although it works through a Web browser, you use it just like email.

Many ISPs make it easy to set up and use forums. If you're interested in starting a family forum, put forums on your checklist for choosing a Web host (see Chapter 15).

Many Web forum programs enable passwords, so you don't have to worry about outsiders seeing private family communications.

Plain Old Website

Perhaps *publishing* information is too strong a term for what you do on a website. If you think of website as *sharing* information, it doesn't sound as intimidating. You just post on a Web page whatever written information you want to share, and everyone in the family can read it. The information can be as simple as a letter to Grandma Louise that you want to share with other family members or as complex as a doctor's report on Uncle Harry's bypass operation complete with digitized x-rays. How about little Judy's story about dolphins for her third-grade class?

Without Retyping

As more and more of our routine information becomes digital, you will be able to share almost anything on a Web page for the family website without retyping it. See Appendix III for information on copying and pasting.

Don't make a big deal out of Web publishing. Make it plain. Make it often. Don't try to impress the world with dazzling Web work. Just share information with the family. But do make it readable, and use templates to conveniently make a readable presentation. Remember, too, you can easily include other media besides text (e.g., images).

Family Voices

Streaming media presents a great way to communicate to everyone in your family.

For those who want to learn a lot and experiment, try streaming video. It's workable today if you want to spend some time with it. Within a few years when computers are more powerful, all camcorders are digital, and readily available bandwidth is much wider, video will be much easier for everyone. Until then, it's a difficult activity but far from impossible.

On the other hand, streaming sound is usable today and makes a terrific medium for publishing on the Web. Many people, even well-educated people, have trouble with writing and find it a difficult, time-consuming endeavor. Talking is easier and takes less time. Appendix IV provides tips on what you need to do to produce streaming sound and video.

Getting set up is the hardest part. Once you've set up to record and encode, doing it routinely for family messages can be easy and convenient. Be thoughtful and don't overdo it. Your relatives have busy lives just like you do. It takes more time to listen to sound recordings than to read comparable information. Nonetheless, streaming sound can be a great means of sharing information with the family. And it can save a lot of long-distance telephone calls too.

Alternative

Many families send cassette tapes to share family information. These are more trouble, more inconvenient, and more expensive than sharing talk via streaming sound.

Remember, you can also include other media (e.g., images) in addition to sound.

Your Project

If your Aunt Bessie visits Denver as a tourist and publishes details of her trip on the family website, it may interest you, but it's probably not something that will keep you and other family members glued to your monitors.

Some activities and projects are sufficiently interesting (to the family), however, as to merit special treatment. For instance, suppose Aunt Bessie visits Colorado and climbs Mt. Sneffles (14,150), a modest climb (a "walk-up") but one that requires preparation and considerable energy. If your family is from Kansas, no family member has ever climbed a mountain, and Aunt Bessie is 67 years old, this activity should be of great interest to the entire family. It's probably something your family will want to hear about in greater detail than a tourist trip to Denver.

If Aunt Bessie chronicles her climbing adventure in great detail with accompanying photographs, chances are she will have the attention of the entire family. She should definitely go to the trouble of doing a good job of reporting this activity (travel project) on the family website.

Suppose Cousin Jackie just completed her college degree after 11 years. During that time, she was married, raising two children, and working full time writing advertising scripts for the local radio station. Her prospects for moving up to a job in management in the broadcasting industry seem excellent. If she wrote a report reviewing her entire 11-year effort to pursue her degree, it might be something of keen interest to members of the family. She should do it and post it on the family website. It would be an inspiration to younger family members, and perhaps to older ones as well.

Don't be modest about important projects you are working on or have completed. Keep family members informed.

Family History

Millions of people have pieced together their genealogy and family history. When you do this, it's not only something you want to share with your family but something for which you want family assistance. Family histories are inevitably collaborative efforts, even when one person does most of the work. After all, most members of the family have some relevant information unknown to (or perhaps forgotten by) the other members. What better way to get help from other family members than to post your research on the family website?

Important elements of a family's history are family artifacts. Many of these (e.g., personal journals, old photographs) can be digitized and shared with other family members. This can make your family history richer than what it would be if it included only the family artifacts in your possession.

The inexpensive and convenient resources to research genealogy and family history are much greater today than they were just a few years ago. Many such resources are already available on the Web. The resources will grow in the future as the Internet continues to make family history a growth industry. Family history can be a fun project, an ongoing project, an inspirational project, and one which you will definitely want to post on your family website.

Vacation Communication

In Costa Rica, almost every shop has an Internet connection. For a small fee, you can use that connection. The Web is almost everywhere now. Use the family website as a family bulletin board when on vacation. Post communications on Web pages.

Now the family can split up without worrying about getting back together. While in Nova Scotia, Aunt Courtney can go to Halifax to see the museums, and Dad and Johnny can go hiking in Cape Breton Highlands National Park hundreds of miles away. If you don't all meet as scheduled to resume your family Nova Scotia trip, each member of the family can use the family website as a bulletin board to keep in touch with all other members of the family on vacation. You can even keep the folks at home up to date on what you're doing.

Family Warehouse

You gave away that VCR to Fred, a neighbor down the street. Then you heard that Cousin Lois needs one to take to college. Darn, if only you had known.

What about creating a family warehouse on the Web? A family member who has an asset they want to get rid of can put it on the warehouse Web page for other family members to claim before they give it away to Fred down the street. The warehouse list (on a Web page) can even include photographs.

For valuable items such as cars, there might be an exclusive offer made to family members before selling the car on eBay, to a dealer, or through a classified ad.

Family Investments

In some families, members share investments usually under the management of one family member. The Web is a good way to keep everyone informed about the investments and even to reach consensus on investment decisions.

Information fuels investment decisions, and you can post information (from reliable sources) on the family website. In many cases, particularly in regard to the stock market, just posting URLs where relevant useful information is located will accomplish the same thing.

Family Résumés

Your daughter has a marginal chance of getting into the University of Wisconsin. Anything you can add to her college application will help. Did she know that her late grandfather was an alumnus? Although he got his undergraduate degree at Purdue and was always a fervent Purdue alumnus, he also received a master's degree at the University of Wisconsin. This is a fact that might help make your daughter's application less marginal, but only if she is aware of it.

Have family members post their life resumes on the family website and keep them updated. Who knows when one family member can help another get a job, provide an important contact, or even provide specialized services.

Family Portal

Avoid having your family website deteriorate into an incomprehensible hodgepodge. Run it like a Web portal (e.g., Yahoo!). Create different sections for the activities covered in this chapter and for others that you invent. Create special sections for traditional family activities. For instance, if you have a family tradition of bowling, water skiing, or fly fishing, create a special section for it. You can even study portals to get ideas for what you can include on your family website. In other words, keep the family website well organized.

Summary

The Web presents a great opportunity to bring family members together in a central place where information can be posted and exchanged. This works well even for family members in the same locale, but it works especially well for family members spread across the country. Think of it as the family bulletin board.

25

Group Activities

This Chapter provides some ideas for things you can do to support the activities of the groups to which you belong. This includes nonprofit, professional, recreational, educational, and charitable groups. Business entities are purposely left out because Chapters 27-29 cover business.

Schedule

Few things are more convenient for a group than a schedule of events. Every organization should publish one, and most do. What's the biggest problem with most schedules? They're not up to date because they were printed three weeks ago (or three months ago). The Web presents an opportunity to make schedules more useful by publishing them in a timely manner and keeping them up to date.

Many organizations now have websites, and most of those publish schedules. Unfortunately, the potential has not been realized by most organizations. Schedules, even on the Web, are more often out of date than up to date.

Consequently, you need to keep the publication of schedules simple. A simple list is best. Why? Because it will be easy to change quickly and post when it needs to be updated. Complex schedules are more difficult to update and, therefore, less likely to be updated regularly. Keep it simple and keep it updated. Your organization's members will appreciate an up-to-date schedule.

A simple list in chronological order of events makes a useful schedule. People can read lists rapidly and pick out what they look for. Complex lists (e.g., categorized) often cause more confusion than convenience. They are slower and more difficult to read. Keep it simple; it's more likely to be useful.

Sales

Many organizations have something to sell. It might be publications, seminars, T-shirts, or professional equipment. Whatever it is, sell it at the website.

Website sales should be considered as ecommerce, which is briefly covered in Chapter 28. If you're going to sell, do it right. Hire a knowledgeable Web developer or take the time to beef up your own Web development skills.

eCommerce

Sales mean ecommerce. It's ecommerce even if the sales effort is for a nonprofit organization. You need the normal website devices that you do for ecommerce such as a catalog, a shopping cart, a checkout, transactional services, and shipping (see Chapter 28). It may be worth it. Your website may be the best place to sell your organization's products or services.

Sales should always be backed by a capable fulfillment process that delivers the goods in a timely manner. People's expectations are high, and the best Web businesses provide fast delivery. Anything less will be an irritant to customers.

Fund-Raising

What about fund-raisers for a nonprofit? Temporary sales on the Web for raising funds such as candy sales may not work well without accompanying promotional efforts. Temporary sales don't have time to generate a following. They may require expensive Web promotions to be successful. The expense of the promotional effort may erode any profits from the sales. You may be better off selling candy and the like in the traditional way offline.

Permanent Sales

Permanent sales on the Web have the ongoing opportunity to build a following of customers over the years. Sales should increase steadily. Website sales often present a convenience to organization members that they grow to appreciate over the years. Permanent sales to members are likely to thrive without expensive promotion.

Many fund-raisers do not sell anything. They just raise money. The Web may be more effective in priming members to donate funds than in actually raising dollars. It often takes the hands-on human touch to elicit the funds. Nonetheless, the Web presents an opportunity to tell your fund-raising story in as much detail as you think will interest members and others.

Memberships

At your website, the very least you should do is accept applications to the organization and provide a way to pay dues by credit card or other online means (i.e., sell memberships).

Newsletter

Almost every organization has a newsletter for members or wants to have one. Publishing a newsletter on a website is easy. It's a money-saver too. You don't have the cost of printing and postage, which are major line items in many organizations' budgets.

It's worth stating the obvious that *newsletters are to be read*. When you put the text on a Web page, make sure your members can read it easily. Newsletters don't have to be fancy, but they do have to be readable. Use a template so you don't have to reinvent the newsletter for every issue.

One particular advantage of printed newsletters is that when you receive one in the mail, you know the new issue is out. You've got it in hand. When the new issue comes out on the website, you won't know it until you happen to visit the website.

For that reason, many newsletters on websites go unread. You have to notify members that the new newsletter is out. The best way to do that is by email. Include a short digest of articles in the email announcement, with a URL for each article. In most email clients, the URL will act as a live link, and readers can go directly to the article (website) from within the email with one click of the mouse.

There may be other, better ways to induce members to read the newsletter on the website. Search for ideas and invent some of your own. Getting members to read the newsletter is not an easy problem to solve, and the problem is not going to go away. As they say, be *proactive*. It's essential for most organizations that members read the monthly newsletter to keep informed.

Web-Based Training

Web-Based Training (WBT) spans the whole gamut of Web devices, from simple Web pages to complex website creations that give instruction and exams and then grade the exams for the instructors. WBT can cost a fortune or can cost less than comparable printed materials.

Creating comprehensive WBT is an ambitious undertaking. But you can create simple Web pages that provide a seminar or a course and thereby can provide simple but useful WBT. This takes training knowledge as well as what you learn in this book, but it doesn't have to be difficult. Today, if you add streaming sound, people will think you're a WBT pro, and you can add the sound easily as covered briefly in Chapter 22 and Appendix IV.

One of the primary purposes of many organizations is to provide training for members. WBT can deliver certain types of training cost-effectively. WBT is an area in which no one is an expert yet. Don't despair if you don't have $250,000 in the budget to create a showpiece. You may be able to do something straightforward that's more effective for $2,500. If you're an instructor, you can create a good WBT presentation for peanuts.

Will WBT replace a good instructor in a classroom with motivated students? Not likely. But WBT has its place. For instance, use WBT as a primer to bring students up to speed for a difficult course, *before the course starts*. That way the instructor won't have to spend a lot of his or her time bringing undertrained students up to a level where they can manage the coursework. Find a place for WBT in your organization, and save money and provide convenience to members.

Think Small

Create small WBT tutorials on minor topics that don't justify class time. Post dozens of them. Keep them short and to the point. People will find them very useful when they need to know something specific. These tutorials are available all day and all week (7 x 24).

Archives

Many organizations have archives. Make the archives useful to the members and even the general public. Publish the archives on the website. Past newsletters, special reports, articles of incorporation and bylaws, lists, statistics, and the like can be made permanently available.

Many organizations deal with the government or other bureaucracies. The rules, regulations, and guidelines of such bureaucracies (or statutes and court rulings) can be published for reference. Often the documents are public domain (as are most government documents), and you can obtain them free in digital form.

For access to such documents, the alternative is to provide links on your website to other places on the Web where members can review the documents. In many cases, convenient links are just as useful as having the documents actually on your website.

Providing access to research and reference materials can be of considerable benefit to your members. And for most efforts, it requires only the skills covered in this book.

Directory

Although needed by members, membership directories seem to be the bane of many organizations. Why? Because members and others misuse the directories, resulting in breaches of privacy. Boards agonize over creating membership directories because they're afraid the membership list is going to fall into the wrong hands (e.g., a junk mailing enterprise). Nonetheless, the need for members to keep in contact with other members is real, and the Web provides a perfect means of providing up-to-date directories of members, for members. If privacy is an issue, use password access or a remote subfolder as outlined in the Share Privacy section of Chapter 24.

Some organizations publish directories to promote members' businesses. Again, the Web is the perfect place to do this. In this case, you will want to enable members to have some space in the directory entries for member advertising.

Huge organizations normally use a Web-database system to publish directories, a technique beyond the skills covered in this book. Nonetheless, for small organizations, directories are lists easily created by simple Web authoring techniques.

Forums

Online forums are appropriate for almost every organization and particularly for professional organizations in which a high value is placed on communication among colleagues. See the Family Forum section in Chapter 24 for a few more details about Web forums.

Special Information

Organizations invariably specialize in certain activities. Publish the special information that supports such activities. The special information doesn't have to be limited to text. It can include images, sound, or video too.

One of the most useful devices you can put on the Web is an embedded calculator. You can provide such Web-page calculators to your members to help them make calculations according to organizational or industrial guidelines. Such calculators are very popular with website visitors, and they don't have to be fancy or complex. See Chapter 21 for an example of a simple real estate industry calculator (Java applet).

Probably Not Your Thing

Programming calculators is probably not your thing if you're reading this book. Nonetheless, you can find calculators (CGI scripts, JavaScripts, and Java applets) at various places on the Web that you can use for free. If you can't find what you need, consider hiring a programmer to create a calculator for you. It might be less expensive than you think. Programming math is perhaps the least expensive type of custom programming.

Publicity

Some organizations have annual awards; some make occasional awards. Whenever a member (or outsider) receives an award, it's nice to get publicity. Posting award winners on your website for an extended period is a source of ongoing publicity that costs little. You can include as much or as little information on the recipient as is appropriate.

Vendors

A list of competing vendors that provide supplies, services, and training to members of your organization can be an essential convenience to your members. On the Web you can not only keep the list up to date but provide live links to vendors' websites too.

Naturally, vendors may also be a source of advertising revenue to help support your website. Banner ads are easy to set up and maintain if you can sell the advertising.

Self-Promotion

Don't overlook self-advertising on your website. Ads to recruit membership, to urge attendance at the annual conference or other events, to sell organizational merchandise or training, or to promote other organizational objectives, are almost free. Take advantage of the opportunity.

Summary

The Web is quickly becoming essential for groups from professional organizations to recreational organizations. Groups can achieve cost-savings in publishing and otherwise find plenty of benefits to having an up-to-date website for members.

26

Publishing

Many people want to write a book or a newsletter. A thousand different reasons keep most people from doing it. Probably the leading reason is lack of a publisher. You can write it, but what publisher will publish it? If it doesn't get published, what's the point of writing it in the first place? Or, if not a book or newsletter, how about a short story, a documentary report, a travel report, a "how to" article, or a commentary? You might publish many things that others will find valuable, but in the print world, it's not easy to get published.

The Web changes publishing. Now, if you have a website, you can publish anything. In fact, you can probably find others with websites to publish your writings for the benefit of their website visitors. (Remember, content draws website visitors.) Indeed, the desire to get something published motivates many people to create Web pages and operate websites.

Opportunity

Part of the thrill of getting published is the expectation that others will read what you have created. Another part of the thrill is getting paid. The Web offers you the opportunity for both.

With over 200 million people on the Web, what you publish is likely to be of interest to someone. Even a tiny percentage of the market yields a large number of people. If you publish something worthwhile, you have an audience. Not only can you publish a newsletter, but you can also run your own radio station via Real-Media. For those who want a voice, the biggest problem now is not the publishing but the marketing; that is, How do you get people to read or listen to your publishing efforts?

Today, many authors who publish on the Web charge for their works. A large grassroots publishing industry sells books and other products.

Dryer Repair

Our clothes dryer broke. I had the choice of having someone come to my house to fix it (about $120-150) or buying a new one (about $250). I went to the search engines and found six books on fixing dryers. Six, can you believe it? Five of the

authors wanted to send me a printed version after I paid my
$8.95 via check (at least a two-week wait). One author also
offered a Web-page version for $20 (over twice the price of the
printed version) via credit card online. How do you tell your
spouse that there will be a two-week wait? I bought the Web-
page version. I learned to go to Radio Shack and buy an $18
voltmeter. With the voltmeter I probed around in the back of
the dryer for about three minutes and found the problem. I
went to the appliance supply store and bought a $32 part
which I installed in five minutes. The dryer worked again more
quickly than having a repairman make a house call.

If you want to know something, try the search engines. Chances are that someone has written a book on it.

Some authors publish their works with advertising or other financial sponsorship and offer it free to the public. Most websites need content to publish. Even ecommerce websites need content to attract customers. For instance, I wrote a short ten-chapter book (for a fee) for an ecommerce website to act as an attractor. I published it in a Web-page version at the website. It brought in a lot of sales leads.

Publishing is now a wide-open playing field. The traditional rules of print publishers do not necessarily apply.

Guidelines

What will you publish? You certainly have a lot of choices. If you look at the spectrum of Web publishing possibilities, you'll find a plain book (text only) at one end and a multimedia Web-based training (WBT) course at the other. Somewhere in between will be a multimedia enhanced book. In other words, you can start with plain text and garnish the text by adding other media. Pretty soon your publication is a multimedia-enhanced book. Add some programming to accommodate an instructor and you have a WBT product. With a spectrum so broad, it's difficult to give any practical advice on publishing. There are so many new possibilities. Most publications, however, will be text based. So, focusing on text makes sense.

Usability

Always make sure your publishing products feature easy navigating. Books with tables of contents and indexes are easy to use. Newsletters are easy to browse. Your Web publishing products must offer similar usability features. Usability means easy navigation.

Readability

People don't like to read on the screen. Nonetheless, many people have to read on the screen every day as part of their jobs. So, contrary to popular belief, it's not unheard of for people to read on the screen. Anything you can do to make it easier to read on the screen is worth it. This includes the following:

- Careful typesetting
- Careful layout
- Instruction for setting monitors and colors
- Advanced typesetting

The last technique is something you need to look into if you aspire to be a publisher. With advanced Web typography techniques, you can make screen reading much more comfortable for your website visitors. Consult my *Typography on the Web* (AP Professional, 1999).

Print on Demand

Advanced Web typography techniques now provide the capability to enable Web print-on-demand. You can enable website visitors to print a perfectly typeset, perfectly paginated document with one click on the printer button on their Web browser. This is a significant breakthrough in print publishing. It transfers the act of printing from the publisher to the consumer. Web print-on-demand is an alternative to reading on the screen of a monitor.

PDFs Have Paved the Way

Portable Document Files (PDF) have enabled print on demand for several years. However, PDFs require a couple of steps and an Acrobat reader to work their printing magic. Experts use them. Novices have trouble with them. PDFs have paved the way for Web print on demand, but website visitors will find Web print-on-demand much easier to use.

Editing

Never let anything go out the door unedited. Professional publishers edit even expert authors. The hallmark of a good publisher is picking good writers and editing their works well.

Templates

Templates make publishing efficient. You can obtain templates from numerous sources or you can create your own. If you publish only once, use someone else's template; there's no need to invent your own. If you intend to publish often, develop templates that serve your special purposes and use them over and over again.

The Other Half of the Story

If you publish to make money, when you've finally finished your well-tuned Web publishing product, you're half done. The other half of the story is marketing. And marketing is important whether you sell your publishing product or give it away.

You need to develop your marketing plan first before you create the publishing product for the following reasons:

1. You may find that the marketing doesn't look very promising, and it's prudent to kill the publishing project before the project kills you.

2. It may be wise to take advantage of some early marketing opportunities that may be gone by the time the publishing product is finished.

3. As soon as the publishing product is finished, significant sales will not begin until the marketing campaign starts to generate consumer interest. Marketing campaigns tend to have a long lead time.

4. Marketing on the Web takes a variety of techniques to be successful. There is no one technique that does it all.

5. Marketing for print publishers has always been a matter of wheeling and dealing with distributors and bookstores rather than advertising, and the Web has not changed that. Wheeling and dealing with other websites helps sell publishing products. (You sell a few newsletters here and a few newsletters there, and pretty soon it all adds up.) Wheeling and dealing takes time.

Even if you do not sell your publishing product, you still want people to use it. You will have to have an effective marketing plan just to get significant numbers of people to use it for free. A publishing product without a marketing plan may get some attention, but it will probably not attract an audience large enough to justify the effort of creating it.

See Chapter 28 for some Web marketing ideas that you can use to sell anything including publishing products.

Summary

Because the Web is a publishing medium, it makes sense to consider using publishing to draw attention to websites, to make money, or to distribute information. In particular, the Web presents a great opportunity for self-publishing. You can publish on the Web using what you learn in this book.

VII

Using Your Website for Business

27

Determining a Business Purpose

Because many readers learn to make Web pages for the purpose of doing business on the Web, this book ends with two short chapters that outline some things you need to know as you proceed to engage in ecommerce and one short chapter on using your company's internal network (intranet).

Almost everyone puts their existing or new business on the Web with the hope of expanding sales. Your sales won't expand, however, until you decide exactly what it is you need to do. This may be as simple as providing useful information to customers or as complex as conducting financial transactions. Establishing a presence for your business on the Web is meaningless without considering the specifics that will determine your success.

One way of looking analytically at the use of the Web for your business is planning. Carefully plan exactly what you will do on the Web. The planning process will lead you to consider what your business purpose is for going on the Web. Once you determine your business purpose, you can plan more effectively. Without a business purpose, planning won't make much sense.

Note that most businesses can benefit from being on the Web, but some can't. For some businesses, the cost-benefit ratio for a Web presence is so low as to make the Web an unprofitable endeavor. If this is the case for your business, this is something you will likely find out by a careful analysis of your business purpose for getting on the Web.

Getting your business on the Web will cost time, effort, and money. Before you devote the resources to building a website, determine whether you have a business purpose that justifies the cost.

General Purposes

Companies use the Web for a variety of business purposes, and the list that follows gives you some ideas for your own business website. Don't let these limit your imagination, however, because many of the Web business techniques that people will use ten years from now have yet to be invented.

Product Information Although a printed catalog typically provides customers with product information, you can do more than that on the Web. For instance, for each product you can provide full specifications and technical information that customers do not usually find in a printed catalog. Space limitations are almost nonexistent on the Web.

Product Instructions Instructions teach customers how to set up and use your products. This is information not usually provided before a customer makes a purchase. However, when provided prior to a sale, it can help a potential customer make a purchase—additional useful information always helps—or avoid a purchase that would likely result in a return.

Product Use Printed instructions that inform your customers how to use a product are often inadequate. Additional information on getting the most efficient or the most flexible use go beyond traditional instruction manuals and provide some practical coaching to your customers. The unlimited space available on the Web enables the dissemination of this additional information.

Current Information Printed information is usually outdated by the time it reaches a customer. Information published on your website can be more easily and more inexpensively kept up to date.

Convenience Can your customers do something more easily, quickly, or inexpensively via the Web than they can otherwise do it in regard to your business practices or products? If so, you need to make it possible for them to do so at your website.

Background Information There are few limits on the volume and type of information you can provide on your company and its services. This information may help potential customers decide whether they want to do business with you. If they decide not to, it may save you from wasting your time with potential customers who will not be appropriate for your business. In many cases, however, it will help sell customers on doing business with you.

Common Purposes

This chapter features more detail on three common business purposes for establishing a business website: an online brochure, a customer service operation, and a sales operation.

Brochure

Many ecommerce gurus will tell you that putting a brochure for your business on the Web is amateurish and a waste of time. They are dead wrong.

It's really a matter of expectations. If you expect to increase sales considerably just by posting a business brochure on the Web, you will undoubtedly be disappointed. On the other hand, you can use a Web brochure effectively in your business by understanding the role it can play in benefiting your customers.

Suppose you decide to post a business brochure to benefit your existing and potential customers rather than to increase sales. What information should you provide?

Basics The basics like address, telephone number, fax number, hours open, and the like are handy for customers to be able to reference 7 x 24. Make sure you keep these up to date, or your Web effort will hurt your business instead of help it.

Map Don't forget to include a map to help customers find your location. They can print it on their printers and take the map with them in their cars.

Volume Take advantage of the unlimited volume possible on the Web for little additional expense. In a print ad, you have very little space to tell your story. Consequently, you have to use *hype* to catch people's attention. People resist hype but find honest information useful. A website enables you to provide 800 or 8,000 words instead of just the few words in a typical printed ad. The Web is an informational medium. Use it to promote your products or services in a complete way.

Photographs A typical business brochure contains few, if any, photographs. A Web brochure can display many color photographs inexpensively. If photographs can help explain your business to your customers, a website can be a real asset for you.

How do you use a Web brochure? You simply refer to it in all your other advertising and promotion materials. You put your website URL on your business cards, advertisements, packaging, stationery, invoices, and the like.

Your brochure website is not going to pull in a lot of website visitors as new customers, but it will provide a convenience to existing customers and also to potential customers that you generate via conventional advertising. In providing such conveniences, you provide low-level customer service, which will tend to increase your sales with current customers (but will not likely acquire new customers from the Web).

Customer Service

If a brochure is low-level customer service, what is standard customer service? Customer services can take on any configuration you can copy or invent. It can be simple (e.g., a brochure) or complex. For instance, Federal Express enables anyone to track a parcel by its airbill number. As the parcel moves through the Federal Express transportation system, the tracking device at the Federal Express website (*http://www.fedex.com*) will tell you exactly where the parcel is. A Web service such as this requires complex programming.

Customer service is any information or device that helps customers. Software companies have found it convenient to customers to publish software documentation on the company website. Customers can read it online or download it and print it. It saves the software company a lot of money compared to print publishing, and it makes keeping the documentation up to date easier for everyone. Machine manufacturers put maintenance manuals and parts lists on the company website for customer convenience and for cost savings compared to print publishing.

Garden.com (*http://www.garden.com*), a Web gardening supply company, features an interactive visual garden planner which enables you to plan your garden on a grid (on your screen) using plant and flower icons. When you finish, you can automatically order all the plants and flowers you have planned. That's pretty slick customer service!

Sales

For many businesses that go on the Web (or start on the Web), sales are the most important purpose of the website. To generate sales, you need a catalog of products. To complete sales, you need a transaction mechanism. Software for ecommerce covers these two requirements. Chapter 28 covers the concept of ecommerce software and gives you a good idea of exactly what you need.

Summary

Like almost any endeavor, establishing a website for your business takes planning. The planning will likely lead you to the business purpose for establishing the website if you haven't figured that out already. With a business purpose to focus your efforts, your success is more assured than if you rely on a vague concept such as "a Web presence."

28

Understanding eCommerce

Want to sell something on the Web? Today ecommerce is a serious business and one in which you can engage. This chapter covers two important aspects of ecommerce: transaction procedures and online marketing.

For most readers, ecommerce means retail sales on the Web. Therefore, this chapter covers retail transactions at a website. They are essentially consumer transactions with a standard procedure. Business-to-business transactions (not covered) take on many different configurations and require different procedures and transaction schemes.

If you want to start a business on the Web, undoubtedly you know much about operating the particular business or at least are learning how to operate the business. For most businesses, however, operating is only half the story. The other half is marketing. Hence, this chapter covers Web marketing too.

Covering only these two topics in this chapter will answer a significant percentage of readers' questions about ecommerce. However, this book doesn't pretend to be an ecommerce manual. Chapters 27 and 28 serve merely as an introduction to ecommerce, a topic you may want to read more about in a book that specifically covers the conduct of business on the Web.

Retail Transaction Procedures

Online retail transactions strive to replicate typical offline retail credit card transactions. Sounds easy, but it seems a little tricky when you survey all the procedures necessary to do transactions on the Web (see Figure 28.1).

Software

A shop has shelves with merchandise. An ecommerce website has a catalog. A shop might have a shopping basket to accommodate customers. An ecommerce website has a digital shopping basket. A shop has a checkout counter where one pays. An ecommerce website has a digital checkout mechanism that accommodates conventional payment methods. A shop is bricks and mortar. An ecommerce website is software.

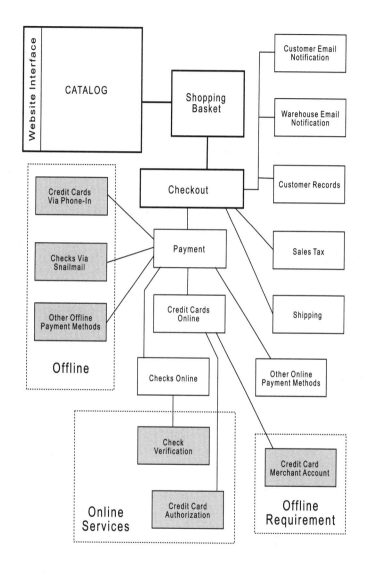

Figure 28.1   Web commerce software relationships.

Catalog

When you purchase (or rent) ecommerce software, it invariably includes a mechanism for setting up a catalog. You will find using ready-made software for a catalog much easier and less expensive than inventing a catalog yourself.

Some catalogs make you conform to their Web page design. Others allow you a lot of flexibility in your Web page designs. All catalogs use a database to store the information that goes into the catalog.

Shopping Cart

A digital shopping cart enables a website visitor to accumulate purchases as he or she goes through your Web catalog. This is an essential feature of ecommerce software. You want your website visitors to buy more than one thing at a time and need to make it convenient for them to do so.

Checkout

At the end of the shopper's visit, it's time to order the merchandise and pay for it. You need to make it convenient for website visitors to complete an order form (address, telephone number, etc.) and remit payment.

Shipping

eCommerce is like its cousin the mail order business. You have to ship the merchandise to the customer. You must provide a mechanism for offering shipping choices.

Shippers such as Untied Parcel Service (UPS) have websites which automatically calculate shipping charges. Your ecommerce software must be able to connect to such websites and obtain specific shipping charges automatically.

Sales Tax

As in the mail order business, you must collect sales tax on sales made in your state. The ecommerce software should be able to calculate this tax automatically.

You must have a sales tax license from your state and submit the sales tax you collect to the state according to its specific regulations.

Payment Input

In your checkout processing, you need to have an input for people to provide their payment information (e.g., credit card number). The best practice is to offer a variety of payment methods. Most people pay by credit card, but that may change. Since 1996, customers have been able to write checks by telephone or email. The best ecommerce software enables check writing for payment.

You don't necessarily have to do everything electronically. For instance, you can give a customer the choice of sending a money order via snailmail (US Postal Service). You hold shipping on the order until you receive the payment.

Notification

Good ecommerce software provides two notifications in regard to every transaction. First, it notifies the customer via email that merchandise has been ordered. This is a sound security practice that helps prevent fraud. Second, it notifies your warehouse of the merchandise to be shipped. This particular email message states only the merchandise to be shipped but not credit card numbers or other sensitive information.

Order Processing

Good ecommerce software also keeps track of the orders that each customer places. It does this either by sending you an email message with the information or by putting the data into a database where you can access it at any time.

Merchant Account

In order to collect payment by credit card, you must have a merchant account with the credit card company. If you don't, you have no right to collect payment by credit card. This is true whether you have a shop where you take credit cards physically or a website where customers simply submit their credit card numbers. You obtain a merchant account through a bank (that has a relationship with the credit card company). As your customers make credit card purchases, the money is deposited directly into your bank account.

Note that a merchant account is an arrangement with a bank and not part of ecommerce software.

Authorization Processing

No doubt you have noticed that merchants often get authorization for credit card transactions (usually via a phone system) before carrying out a transaction. This provides greater security to merchants against stolen cards or delinquent accounts.

You have three choices on the Web. You can subscribe to an online credit card authorization service which works automatically. You can collect credit card numbers and get the authorizations manually offline via the normal authorization system (i.e., a box connected to a telephone). Or, you can choose to go the risky route of accepting credit cards without authorization.

Note that the credit card authorization service and software is separate from the ecommerce software and costs additional money.

You can also use a verification service for checks. It doesn't tell you if there's enough money in the account to cover the purchase, but it does verify that the customer has an account and has no adverse history with regard to using checks.

What Does It Cost?

If this is all still a little confusing to you, perhaps breaking down the costs will help put it in perspective (see Table 28.1).

Table 28.1   Typical ecommerce costs.

Service	Cost
ISP Web hosting service for ecommerce	$30/month
eCommerce software rental	$35/month
Credit card merchant account charges	2% of sales
Credit authorization processing transaction fee	$25/month + per-transaction fee
Check verification processing	$35/month

In reality, these costs vary greatly. As you can see, they can add up quickly to an expensive monthly overhead if you're not careful. Many Web retailers get these services from five different providers. It makes sense to look for the lowest-cost provider in each category. Don't overlook packages of services, however, as they sometimes offer a cost savings.

ISP Hosting

Chapters 14 and 15 cover the hosting of your website. When you choose an ISP, you may want to ask what ecommerce services the ISP offers and what the extra costs are, if any.

eCommerce Software

Many ISPs offer ecommerce software today at no extra cost as part of their normal service. Other ISPs offer ecommerce software at a modest additional monthly rental. Before you decide this is a worthwhile benefit, you need to carefully analyze how well such ecommerce software works and what it includes.

All ecommerce software needs an application server to run. That is, the software won't work until an ISP runs the proper server that enables the software to work in your customers' browsers. There are hundreds of ecommerce programs. Most ISPs operate only one ecommerce program. In other words, you can't choose ecommerce software and expect to run it at any Web host (ISP). The Web host must run the specific server that makes the ecommerce software work.

The ecommerce software offered free by ISPs may be limited in the functions it performs, and before long you'll be looking for new software. Evaluate every offering carefully before committing to a service.

Generic Application Servers

Some ecommerce software runs on generic Web application servers such as Cold Fusion or Miva. These servers support any programs written in the scripting language for the application server, not just the ecommerce program. For instance, you can write a Web application in Miva and run it on any Miva server.

You can also purchase ecommerce software instead of renting it. Miva sells Miva Merchant for $500. It's a robust ecommerce package that's a bargain at that price. You can run it at any ISP that runs a Miva application server. In addition, third-party software developers sell inexpensive plug-in modules for Merchant that increase its capabilities considerably. For under $1,500 you can have the equivalent of corporate ecommerce software costing tens of thousands of dollars with valuable additional customer service and marketing features not discussed in this book.

A few ISPs actually feature Miva Merchant and third-party plug-in modules as part of their normal host service at a reasonable price. That's a combination that's hard to beat. But Merchant has no lack of competitors, and you'll do well to carefully analyze all the offerings.

Credit Card Merchant Account

Every online or offline retailer that wants to take credit cards needs a merchant credit card account with Visa/Mastercard, American Express, or Discover. You arrange this through your bank or another agency. Generally, you have to have good credit to get a merchant account, but many providers on the Web advertise that they will give you one even if you have deficient credit.

You pay a percentage of your sales for the privilege of accepting credit cards. The percentage varies. It pays to shop around for the lowest-cost provider.

Credit Card Authorization Processing

Online credit card authorization processing is separate from a credit card merchant account, and many online providers would like to have your business. Offline this service is represented by the box that many offline retailers have at the cash register and which they use to obtain authorizations. The bank usually provides the box for a monthly fee.

Online it works a little differently. You must have the capability in your ecommerce software to use a particular authorization processing service. For example, Miva Merchant allows plug-ins, and many authorization services have developed plug-ins for Merchant, enabling Merchant to seamlessly handle their automatic authorization services. Without such plug-ins, Merchant would offer only a couple of choices. Consequently, you have to be careful to match your credit card authorization service to the capabilities of your ecommerce software.

Authorization processing is usually a flat monthly fee with a nominal per-transaction charge. It's your guarantee that a credit card is valid, not over its credit limit, and not stolen.

Check Verification Processing

If you take checks via the Web, you may want to use check verification processing. This is separate from credit card authorization processing. If you receive only a few checks, it may not be worth it. If you receive a lot of checks, it's probably a wise investment. Just like credit card authorization processing, your ecommerce software must be able to accommodate the particular check verification service that you want to use. This service is usually provided for a flat monthly fee.

Package Deals

Some Web retailers get a package of these services from the same provider. If you consider one provider for multiple services, make sure you do some comparative shopping first. A package deal may look good until you discover what's been left out or what the extra charges are.

Marketing on the Web

The Web is just like real life. Marketing takes a lot of money or effort, or both. The advantage of the Web is that you can substitute your time for money.

Suppose you want to place an ad in *Time* magazine for your business. You go into the *Time* Dallas Bureau to place the ad, but instead of money, you offer to clean the Bureau office every night for three months. That offer will most likely be refused. You can't easily substitute your time for money.

On the Web, however, you can do more for your business yourself than you can by advertising on the *Time* magazine website. You can effectively substitute your time for money. The mistake many Web entrepreneurs make, though, is forming a business plan based on the fact that one can substitute time for money but then not spending the time to do what needs to be done.

Every business is different, and different owners have different business styles. There is no right way to market on the Web. You have a variety of techniques from which to choose, and you will choose a different combination than someone else with a similar business. With that in mind, some of the most effective Web marketing techniques follow.

Create Some Content

Content draws people to websites; that is, information or entertainment in which they have an interest draws visitors to websites. For instance, a Web pet shop might feature a free encyclopedia of animals. People can read the encyclopedia to learn about their favorite animals or use it for school research. The encyclopedia draws visitors to the website where they can also purchase pets and pet supplies.

Content might be text, sound, video, or even embedded calculators. The more robust it is, the bigger draw it will be. Word will get around if you put some valuable content on your website.

Court the Search Engines

Many people would like you to believe that you can register one place and enter your business into 500 Web search engines. It probably works to some extent, but it's not worthwhile. The eight largest Web search engines have almost all the search business. If you can appeal to them, you've done as much as you can do without wasting your time.

The problem is that appealing to the top eight is a big job. Books have been written on the subject. It takes a lot of initial work and a lot of routine follow-up work to keep your business name near the top of the search results lists. Don't underestimate the time it requires to put forth an ongoing effort to get found by the leading search engines.

Trade Links

Trading links with other websites is potentially an infinite job. There are plenty of potential websites that might feature a link to your website. Each trade takes time and effort to arrange. Then you must put a link to the other website somewhere on your website. The other website puts in a link to your website.

This works best where the websites are relevant to each other. For instance, would you pay attention to a link to a model-plane-building website if you were visiting a Web cheese shop? Not likely. To a website for a book with cheese recipes? Much more likely. Thus, the name of this game is *relevancy*.

Links to relevant websites are valuable to your website visitors. Because they're a convenience, such links will bring visitors back to your website. Consequently, you can establish a substantial attraction by creating a large collection of relevant links. In the meanwhile, all those links at other websites (to your website) will bring in new visitors.

No money changes hands with this practice (i.e., no referral fees). You simply exchange links.

Create Affiliates

An affiliate is a website that offers your products for sale with a link to your website. You handle the transaction and pay a referral fee to the affiliate. Use this well-proven device for generating business. You don't pay the fee until you make the sale.

Like trading links, it takes time and effort to make each affiliate arrangement; and like trading links, this arrangement works best when the affiliate website is relevant to what you sell.

Hang Out

Many people participate in online forums (mailing lists, user groups, news groups, discussion groups, etc). Forums specialize in particular topics from stock car racing to forensic medicine. Your ecommerce is relevant to dozens—perhaps hundreds—of forums. You can participate in these forums to promote sales.

People who openly solicit business in forums make a poor impression. Nonetheless, as a participant you can assist other forums members with problems they face, problems for which you have the expertise to solve based on your ecommerce line of business. For instance, suppose you sell camcorders online. If so, you undoubtedly have knowledge about camcorders that you can share. If you participate in a forum on family videos, you will have opportunities to provide other forum members with help for their problems regarding the use of camcorders. Such friendly help will promote your online camcorder business.

You transmit forum communications via email or by using an email-like software mechanism. Add a signature to your email. A signature contains information on who you are and what you do:

```
-----------------------------------

John T. Goutwise, Vice President

jtg@camcordersforall.com

Camcorders for All, Ltd.

http://www.camcordersforall.com

Your source of low cost camcorders

and video equipment.

-----------------------------------
```

In other words, the signature acts as an ad. However, don't make it too long, or a forum manager may complain.

The big disadvantage of this marketing technique is that it takes a lot of time. If your ecommerce operation deals in very specialized products, it may make sense to hang out on a few forums. If your ecommerce features a broader range of products, hanging out in the many relevant forums may be an unpractical time-consuming burden.

Run eBay Auctions

You can, of course, sell your products on eBay (the online auction) for additional income. This will be profitable as soon as you build some volume by systematically running simultaneous auctions. Some retail entrepreneurs run a few hundred auctions each week.

As an alternative, you can run one auction a week for the advertising effect. In your auction ad, you can put a link to your website. This is an effective yet inexpensive advertising strategy, which requires little time and effort. Read my *eBay the Smart Way* (AMACOM, 2000).

Other Techniques

This is not a complete list. You can use thousands of Web marketing techniques. People invent more every day. Find out what your competitors do to market their products. Find out what other relevant businesses do. Pick and choose your techniques. Invent some of your own.

Avoid Cybermalls

The idea of a cybermall seems like a great one. Get a bunch of online businesses together in one place on the Web, and people will flock there to go shopping. Unfortunately, few cybermalls—and there are thousands—are successful for small businesses. If you can find one that puts you and all your competitors together (e.g., all the scuba diving shops in one place), it will probably work well because it will become the place to go on the Web for a certain genre of customers (e.g., scuba divers). Otherwise stick to the proven portals such as Amazon.com (zShops). But don't expect too much, not even from the successful portals.

Summary

Handling transactions digitally is essential to selling online. Web ecommerce software provides you the capability to complete sales and get paid. It also provides you with an easy means of building your website catalog.

Once you're ready to roll with your ecommerce software, Web marketing becomes the priority. Marketing on the Web allows a wide range of flexibility, but it requires a considerable amount of time and effort. It's an ongoing chore necessary to your success.

29

Intranet

Conducting business on the Web (e.g., selling merchandise) makes sense, but what about conducting business in the office? Why not? The Internet runs on the TCP/IP network protocol. The TCP/IP network protocol also works well to run a network for your company, whether a small business or a corporation. It's called an *intranet*. An intranet works much the same as the Internet; in effect, it's an internal Internet. You use the same software.

The only difference is that the only website visitors on your intranet website are employees in your company.

What can you do with an intranet? Well, if you review Chapters 24 and 25, you'll get some ideas. This chapter adds a few more ideas. After all, an intranet can have a website (or multiple websites) just like the Internet.

Website

The first question is, what is a website on an intranet? Is it one large website for the whole company, or is it a series of websites for individual departments or functions? If you use your company's intranet, you need to know the answer to this question. It will help you understand better how to use your intranet Web for your department's use or for your own use.

Enlightened Executives?

The intranet was the result of enlightened executives deciding that Internet technology was good for the company and imposing it from the top down, right? Not really. In many companies, the intranet arose from the grass roots. Individual departments started using Web servers and email servers to enable their own employees to work more efficiently. Pretty soon other departments caught on and started using TCP/IP networks too. Eventually, the whole company was running on an intranet. The executives may have been the last to know.

Once you find out how your intranet works (ask your network administrator), you will know where you can post the Web pages that you want to publish to company employees.

Personnel Publications

At a medium or large company, think of all those company publications that benefit employees. You have everything from personnel manuals to newsletters. They require tons of paper and lots of printing. They're expensive to update. Some are required by law. Why not publish them on the Web and save a lot of money? In fact, many companies are doing this. If your responsibility is distributing your company's personnel publications, this book will get you off to a good start toward understanding online publishing and developing some Web publication strategies. Hint: Use Web page templates as much as possible.

Special Web Publishing Software

Special software that handles huge volumes of Web publishing systematically can make your job easier. It's expensive, but it saves a lot of employee hours.

Maintenance Manuals

Think of all those company publications relating to a company's machines and equipment: maintenance manuals. If your responsibility is publishing maintenance manuals, start writing your next one in Netscape Composer, and publish it on your intranet. Copy and paste existing maintenance manuals into Web page templates and publish them on your intranet.

Policies and Procedures

Think of all those company publications that provide direction to employee efforts. Like the personnel publications and maintenance manuals mentioned earlier, policies and procedures can be published inexpensively on your intranet.

Data Access

Many companies store their data in data systems they acquired long ago ("legacy" systems). Consequently, many employees don't have access to such data for lack of appropriate software (i.e., legacy software). The Web provides the common denominator for all such data systems. With Web-database technology, any employee can access all the data in the company (for which he or she has access authorization).

Records

Although most company records will be in a company database, many documents don't exactly fit conventional database treatment. Even though the personal and business information on clients or customers typically resides in a database, a 200-page report for the sales department on the demographics of a new potential market is usually found in a document archive. By putting such archives on the Web, employees have quick and easy access to them. This is similar to publishing company publications

Inspiration for the Troops

When the CEO wants to give a talk to the employees, he or she can do so via a Web page with streaming voice or streaming video. The same goes for other executives. This can extend a personal touch that's more difficult to achieve in a printed publication.

Ordering

Why submit paper to the purchasing department to order supplies? An electronic ordering form is quicker and less expensive. The order can be submitted via a Web form.

Directory

Once a company has more than a few employees, a company directory becomes very valuable to employees. This is a perfect application for the Web. You can update the directory as often as needed. You can even create a directory using the skills you learn in this book.

WBT

Web-based training is a natural for companies. Like any training, it can be expensive. But it doesn't have to be. If you can write a course (tutorial) outline, fill it in with some content, and put it on a Web page, you've got a good start on making a WBT product. And you can do it with what you learn in this book.

Employees must do hundreds of different tasks. Printing instructions for each task seems like an overwhelming project, particularly when you consider distribution. Yet posting instructions on the Web for each task is inexpensive and efficient. In other words, a WBT product doesn't have to be long. It can be a short tutorial on a specific task available to every computer in the company around the clock.

Recoginition

Recognizing employee achievement is very important for top companies. Certificates, plaques, awards, and gifts all help. The Web provides another dimension for recognition, like hanging a certificate on the wall. You can give an employee recognition formally or informally for a day, a year, or however long it makes sense to keep it posted.

Forums

Forums, covered in Chapter 24, prove useful to groups within a company. It gives people a chance to communicate with each other via the forum at their convenience. Web forum software enables employees to keep track of each other, assist each other, and act as a team even when out of physical contact with one another for long periods.

The forum doesn't necessarily have to be dedicated to a certain topic or set up for a particular department. It can be set up for a specific project (and a specific team) and include employees from diverse departments.

Collaboration

Forums together with Web pages also enable employees to collaborate. The Web pages contain the work product. The forum provides the ongoing communication. Special Web software is available that provides convenient features that enhance this type of collaboration. That works well for a lot of people, but a forum plus Web pages used to foster team efforts can be effective without any special Web software. Thus, with what you learn from this book, you can effectively collaborate with fellow employees on complex projects even from remote locations.

Scheduling

Scheduling is the bane of employees. Collaborative scheduling relieves much of the hassle. Web software that facilitates collaborative scheduling via a browser is easy to use and it automatically schedules events, such as meetings, based on the availability of the participants. Although you can't do this without the requisite software, this is a Web-based application that can forestall a lot of frustration.

Summary

Business organizations use their intranets for various types of Web publishing. This is a natural development resulting from the robust capabilities of the Web, which work just as well internally as they do outside on the Internet. Internet software (including Web servers) used internally enhances teamwork and enables cost-effective publishing. So practical are such uses that they are often implemented from the grassroots rather than from the boardroom. The skills you learn in this book will enable you to carry through many useful projects via your intranet website.

Appendix I 7 Steps

It's easier than you think. This is a list of 7 steps to create your first Web page. The references to each chapter in which you can find the details follow the items on the list.

Obtain and Install Authoring Software

You may have one of the required Web page authoring programs already. If you don't, you will have to download and install either Netscape Composer (free) or Microsoft FrontPage Express (free).

See Chapter 2 in regard to downloading this free but highly capable software.

Open Composer or FrontPage Express

Simply open Composer or FrontPage Express like you do any other program. Now you're ready to go with the blank Web page that automatically opens with the program. See Chapter 1 to get started.

Type a Few Paragraphs

Start typing your content (text). It's identical to using a word processor. It's hard to imagine it being any easier. See Chapter 1 for more details.

Put Headings before the Paragraphs

Once you've added your text, add some headings to organize your text presentation and help people read through it. In other words, do what you normally do with a word processor. Chapter 1 illustrates this.

Typeset the Headings

Although you will probably want to leave the text with the default typesetting, you will want to make your headings stand out. Make your headings a larger type size with bold type. See Chapter 8 for typesetting guidelines, or see Chapter 4 for instruction on using standard Web headings.

Add an Image

Images are the spice of the Web. Add an image or two to make your Web page attractive. It's best to start with digitized photographs because they can be inexpensive and convenient to use. Chapter 5 provides an introduction to adding images.

Test Your Work

When you're done with a section of your Web page, test it by viewing it with your browser. When you see it through a browser, you see it as a website visitor will see it. Chapter 3 explains testing in greater detail.

Appendix II HTML Tutorial

You can learn Hypertext Markup Language (HTML) easily. It's not programming, although many Web developers now call it *coding*. This tutorial does not attempt to give you a comprehensive grasp of HTML. It does give you a good start on using HTML to do the basics.

Sometimes using a Web authoring program you just can't get things quite the way you want them. If you know HTML, you can tune up your Web pages more precisely. Sometimes you see a Web page you really like on the Web. You can copy it to your hard disk. If you can read HTML, you can look at the markups to see how the Web page is constructed. Although copying the content of someone else's Web pages may be a copyright infringement, copying layout and typesetting is not.

For a more thorough introduction to HTML, you might try Create *Your First Web Page in a Weekend*, Callihan (Prima, 2000), or any one of a number of similar books readily available in many bookstores.

The angle bracket characters (< >) indicate markups. The markups instruct the browser how to display the content (text, graphics, etc.). The markups also enable some interactive functions such as links. Markups are not case-sensitive; that is, you can use either upper- or lowercase characters inside the angle brackets. As you can see, I prefer lowercase markups; I can read them faster.

Terms

Some people call the markups tags. *Some people call using the markups* coding *just as they would call writing a program with a programming language coding. Tags and coding are misleading terms, but we're stuck with them.*

Some markups stand by themselves.

```
<br>
```

Most require a closing markup.

```
<b>content</b>
```

The forward slant indicates the closing markup.

Spaces

HTML doesn't like spaces unless you specify them. Therefore, it will change two or more consecutive character spaces into one space. It will change redundant line spaces into one line space. See the   markup later in this appendix for a way to increase spaces.

Defining a Web Page

You use markups right from the beginning to define a Web page. This is just perfunctory work. The real job is marking up your content which falls between the *<body>* markups.

<html></html>

The entire Web page falls between these markups. This markup tells the browser that this plain text document (ASCII file) is an HTML page.

<head></head>

This markup designates the head of the document. The head of a Web page can contain all sorts of information that is well beyond the scope of this book, but the head need not contain anything. The browser does not display the information in the head.

<title></title>

Whatever you put between these markups will show at the very top of the browser.

<body></body>

The browser displays the content between these markups. This markup sets the specifications for the entire body of the Web page such as background color and text color. To set the specifications, you can use attributes which fall inside the markup itself.

```
<body bgcolor="#ffff00">
```

Attributes are beyond the scope of this tutorial, but you can learn about them in any basic HTML book.

Typical Web Page Setup

You can use the typical Web page setup that follows, without anything additional. You put your content between the *<body>* markups.

```
<html><head><title>Name of Page</
title></head><body>

content

</body></html>
```

Use the above as a template for doing basic Web pages. For instance, the following Web page is simple. All you need to do is provide the content.

```
<html><head><title>The Slickhorn
Trek</title></head><body>

Don't underestimate the ruggedness and
remoteness of this area. Inexperienced
canyon hikers will find the terrain
demanding, and you won't see many
people, if any. This is not as rugged
as many off-trail places in the Grand
Canyon, but some portions are nearly
as strenuous. Plan your water
```

```
carefully. If you find yourself about
to depart on your trek during a
drought year or during a dry spell,
you should first undergo a psychiatric
evaluation! Follow the advisory
published by the Monticello BLM
office.

</body></html>
```

The browser shows the one-paragraph Web page as indicated in Figure A2.1.

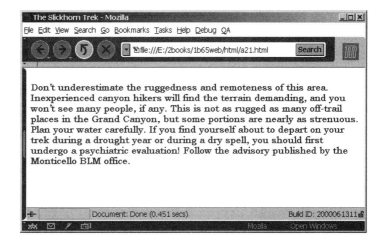

Figure A2.1   The browser displaying a simple Web page.

Markups Alphabetically

This section presents the remainder of the basic HTML markups in alphabetical order.

<b> </b>

This is the markup which creates bold type. The browser will render the text inside the markups as bold. Consult Chapter 8 for the proper use of bold in typesetting.

<blockquote> </blockquote>

This handy markup enables you to put a margin on both sides of a block of text (see Figure A2.2). If you want to use it to do a real block quote (a long quotation), you may want to reduce the size of the type one increment. But otherwise it makes a good layout tool.

```
<p>We had started out of Mexican Hat
about 3:30 PM. By the time we started
down the trail off the mesa, it was
about 6:00 in the evening. The shuttle
of vehicles between the trailheads at
Slickhorn Canyon and East Slickhorn
Canyon is about four or five miles,
and you can make good time driving it
in good weather. We carried ten
gallons of water in each vehicle (five
in each of two containers) as
recommended in my pamphlet Desert
Hiking Essentials.</p>

<blockquote> It is essential to have
extra water in your vehicle both for
off road and back road travel and as a
replenishing source at the end of the
hike.  Two five gallon containers per
vehicle (four people) is adequate for
many situations.</blockquote>

<p>We took one five-gallon container
out of the vehicle at each trailhead
and stowed it in the bushes. This is
```

```
an arid area. If your car is stolen at
the trailhead, you don't want to come
out of the canyon to find no water.

</p>
```

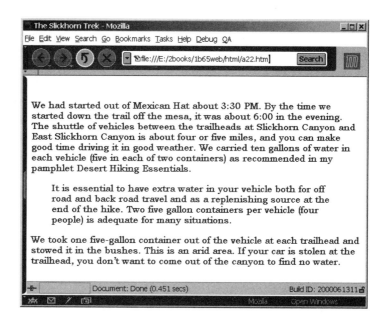

Figure A2.2   A quote in the text.

Double *<blockquote>* will double the size of the margin on each side of the content.

```
<blockquote><blockquote>content

</blockquote></blockquote>
```

This is a case where knowing some HTML will enable you to author more effectively. For instance, if you use *<blockquote>* with the Web page illustrated earlier, you will create margins on both sides of the text block (see Figure A2.3).

```
<html><head><title>The Slickhorn
Trek</title></head><body>
```

```
<blockquote><blockquote>Don't
underestimate the ruggedness and
remoteness of this area. Inexperienced
canyon hikers will find the terrain
demanding, and you won't see many
people, if any. This is not as rugged
as many off-trail places in the Grand
Canyon, but some portions are nearly
as strenuous. Plan your water
carefully. If you find yourself about
to depart on your trek during a
drought year or during a dry spell,
you should first undergo a psychiatric
evaluation! Follow the advisory
published by the Monticello BLM
office.</blockquote></blockquote>
```

```
</body></html>
```

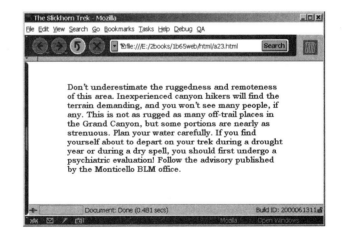

Figure A2.3   The *<blockquote>* markup creates left and right margins.

*
*

Use this markup to create a line break. This differs from the <p> markup in that a blank line does not follow the line break.

```
Charlie Craft<br>

Wilderness experience: 21 years<br>

Canyon experience: 10 years<br>

779-341-8533 Ext. 409<br>
```

See Figure A2.4 to see how this looks in a browser.

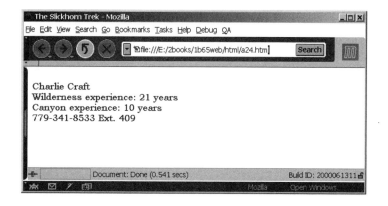

Figure A2.4   Use *
* for line breaks not followed by a blank line.

<dl> </dl>

This markup makes a list of terms and definitions like a dictionary with words and definitions. The <dl> markup creates the list. The <dt> markup marks the term. And the <dd> markup marks the definition of the term.

```
<dl>

<dt>term
```

```
<dd>definition
<dt>term
<dd>definition
</dl>
```

The term is displayed flush left. The definition is displayed indented (see Figure A2.5).

```
<dl>
<dt>Petroglyph
<dd>A design made on rock by pecking,
scratching, or carving.
<dt>Pictograph
<dd>A design painted or drawn on rock.
</dl>
```

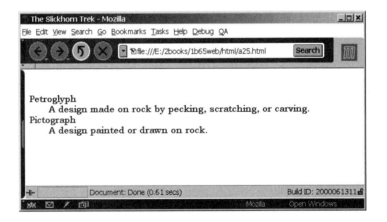

Figure A2.5   A list of terms and definitions.

This makes a good markup to use for general layout purposes too. For instance, suppose you want to make an unnumbered and unbulleted list. You can use the <dl> and <dd> markups (see Figure A2.6).

```
You will need the following 7.5 minute
topographical maps for the Slickhorn
trek.

<dl>

<dd>Slickhorn Canyon East

<dd>Slickhorn Canyon West

<dd>Pollys Pasture

</dl>

You can obtain these maps at your
nearest US Geological Survey office.
```

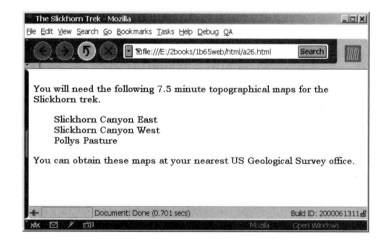

Figure A2.6 An unnumbered unbulleted list.

Note that the indent is on the left side only, not on the right side.

<dt>

This markup creates a term in a *<dl>* list. It is flush left. It must be used with the *<dl>* markup.

<dd>

This markup creates a definition in a *<dl>* list. It is indented. It must be used with the *<dl>* markup.

<div> </div>

This division markup by itself is not much use. Its attributes make it useful. Use this markup (with attributes) to lay out a section of text. The section can be a heading, a paragraph, or multiple headings and paragraphs. For instance, one attribute is *align*. You can use this to center a heading or other text (see Figure A2.7).

```
<div align="center">Slickhorn - East
Slickhorn Loop, Utah</div>
```

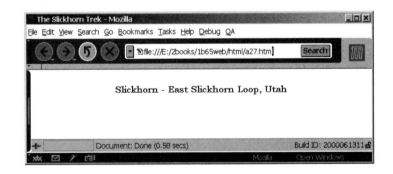

Figure A2.7   A heading centered with the *<div>* markup.

For other attributes of the *<div>* markup, consult an HTML book. Note that for the above example, you can also use the *<center>* markup. But the HTML standards committee wants to discontinue the *<center>* markup, so use the *<div>* markup instead with the *align* attribute.

<font> </font>

Like the *<center>* markup, this markup is on the way out. But in the meanwhile, you may find it handy to use because there is no substitute except Cascading Style Sheets (CSS), another markup language for advanced Web typesetting. Use the *<font>* markup to change a typeface or a type size. Chapter 8 indicates the limitations of simple Web page typesetting. You can use the *<font>* markup to create a heading (see Figure A2.8).

```
<font face="Arial,Helvetica"
size="+1">Slickhorn - East Slickhorn
Loop, Utah</font>
```

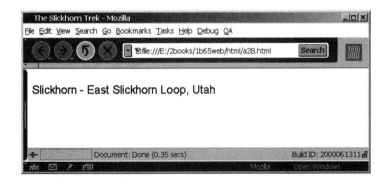

Figure A2.8   Use the <font> markup to change the typeface and type size.

Note that the attributes such as *face* (typeface) and *size* make the *<font>* markup useful.

<h1></h1>

Use this markup for headings. It comes in six sizes: 1-6. For most uses, only sizes 1-3 prove useful (see Figure A2.9). Sizes 4-6 are too small for normal use.

```
<h1>Slickhorn - East Slickhorn Loop,
Utah</h1>
```

```
<h2>Slickhorn - East Slickhorn Loop,
Utah</h2>
```

```
<h3>Slickhorn - East Slickhorn Loop,
Utah</h3>
```

```
<h4>Slickhorn - East Slickhorn Loop,
Utah</h4>
```

```
<h5>Slickhorn - East Slickhorn Loop,
Utah</h5>
```

```
<h6>Slickhorn - East Slickhorn Loop,
Utah</h6>
```

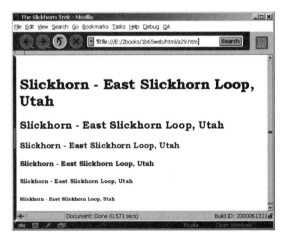

Figure A2.9   Six different headings.

The headings display in bold with a blank line before and a blank line after. The *<h1>* markup is convenient to use, but you can also use the *<font>* markup to make a line of text (heading) larger and the *<b>* markup to make it bold.

<hr>

Use this markup to make a line (a rule) across the page. The attributes control how the rule looks (see Figure A2.10).

```
<hr align="center" size="2"
width="300">
```

We took one five-gallon container out of the vehicle at each trailhead and stowed it in the bushes. This is an arid area. If your car is stolen at the trailhead, you don't want to come out of the canyon to find no water.

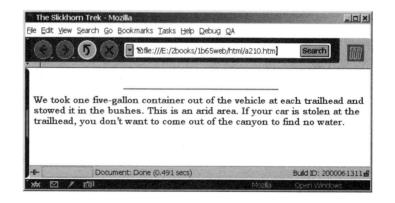

Figure A2.10 Use the *<hr>* markup to create a rule.

The rule shown in Figure A2.10 is 300 pixels wide and 2 pixels thick.

<i> </i>

This is the markup which creates italic type. The browser will render the text inside the markups as italics. Consult Chapter 8 for the proper use of italics in typesetting.

<img scr=" ">

To include an image in a Web page, use this markup. Place the URL of the image file in the *scr* attribute. The URL can be local or somewhere else on the Web. The image displays at the location of the markup.

```
<img scr="slickhorn23.jpg">
```

The *src* refers to an image file, which must be a GIF or JPEG. (The relatively new PNG graphics file format is also acceptable.) Use the attributes of the *<img>* markup to control how the image displays in a browser (see Chapter 5). Note that the URL for the image file can be anywhere on the Web. It doesn't have to be at the same URL as the Web page.

<ol> </ol>

This markup makes a list of numbered items. You do not specify the numbers. The items are numbered in order. You must use the *<li>* markup to designate the list items.

```
<ol>
<li>item
<li>item
<li>item
</ol>
```

The list is indented. For example, the earlier unnumbered list displays with numbers when you use the *<ol>* markup (see Figure A2.11).

```
You will need the following three 7.5
minute topographical maps for the
Slickhorn trek.

<ol>

<li>Slickhorn Canyon East

<li>Slickhorn Canyon West

<li>Pollys Pasture

</ol>

You can obtain these maps at your
nearest US Geological Survey office.
```

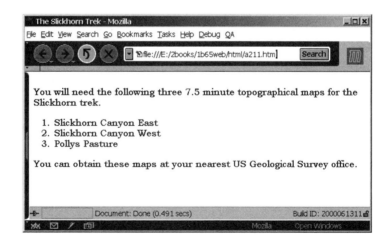

Figure A2.11 A numbered list.

<li>

This markup creates a list item in a numbered or bulleted list. It must be used with the *<ol>* or *<ul>* markups.

<p></p>

Use this markup for all your paragraphs. The difference between this and the <br> markup is that the <p> markup adds a blank line of space before and after (see Figure A2.12).

```
<p>To find the ruins, you have to
speculate. (It helps to know they are
there.) Look for a place where there
might be ruins (under an overhang).
Then climb up and look. In most cases,
you will not be able to spot the ruins
from the canyon floor.</p>

<p>We traveled about three and a half
miles for the day, not exactly a
death-defying pace. The wet potholes,
although still small, appeared more
often. It's evident that without
recent rain, and particularly in a
drought year, there would be no water
in the canyon. Even with water
present, we topped off at almost every
wet pothole not knowing whether it
would be our last.</p>

<p>We camped at another wide place in
the streambed with flat rock and small
potholes with fresh water. Ravens and
lizards seemed to be the only wildlife
in the canyon.</p>
```

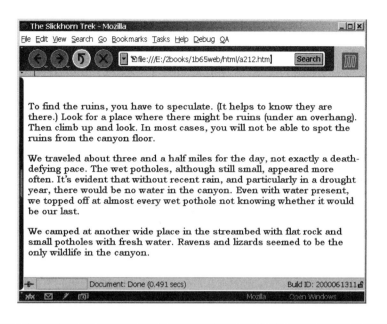

Figure A2.12 Use the <p> markup for all your paragraphs.

Note that today just the beginning markup <p> is enough, and you don't need the end markup </p>. But soon the browsers may require the end markup, too, and you don't want to have to go back and add the end markups.

This markup makes a subscript, such as in scientific notation (see Figure A2.13).

```
<p>The handiest solvent is H<sub>2</
sub>O (water).</p>
```


This markup makes a superscript, such as in mathematical notations (see Figure A2.13).

```
<p>The equivalent of 4<sup>5</sup> is
1,024.<p>
```

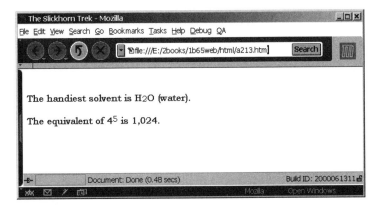

Figure A2.13   Use HTML to create subscripts and superscripts.

<table></table>

Use the *<table>* markup to create a table. The *<tr>* markup (table row) indicates a row (record), and the *<td>* markup (table data) indicates a column (field). The following is a two-column table with three rows.

```
<table>

<tr>

<td>data</td>

<td>data</td>

</tr>

<tr>

<td>data</td>

<td>data</td>

</tr>
```

```
<tr>

<td>data</td>

<td>data</td>

</tr>

</table>
```

For example, the following table shows three products (topographical maps) and their current prices (see Figure A2.14).

```
<table cellpadding="10">

<tr>

<td>Slickhorn Canyon East</td>

<td>$4.00</td>

</tr>

<tr>

<td>Slickhorn Canyon West</td>

<td>$4.00</td>

</tr>

<tr>

<td>Pollys Pasture</td>

<td>$4.00</td>

</tr>

</table>
```

Note that to create some space between the data of this table, you need to use the attribute *cellpadding* to add 10 pixels of padding within each cell. The default use of *<table>* uses no border as Figure A2.14 shows. To add the border, add the *border* attribute set to *1* (see Figure A2.15).

```
<table cellpadding="10" border="1">
```

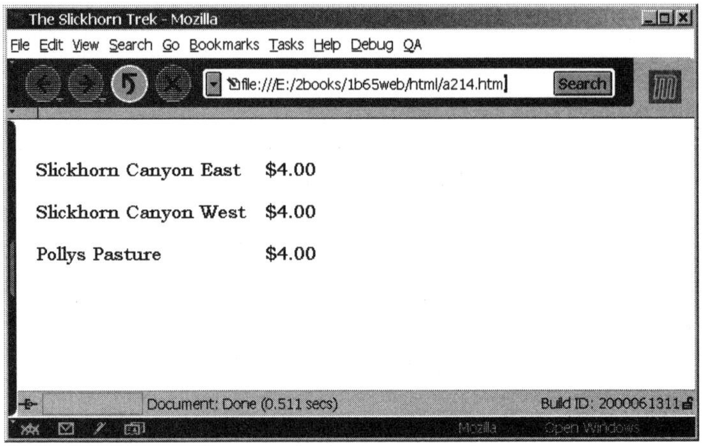

Figure A2.14 The <table> markup makes attractive tables. 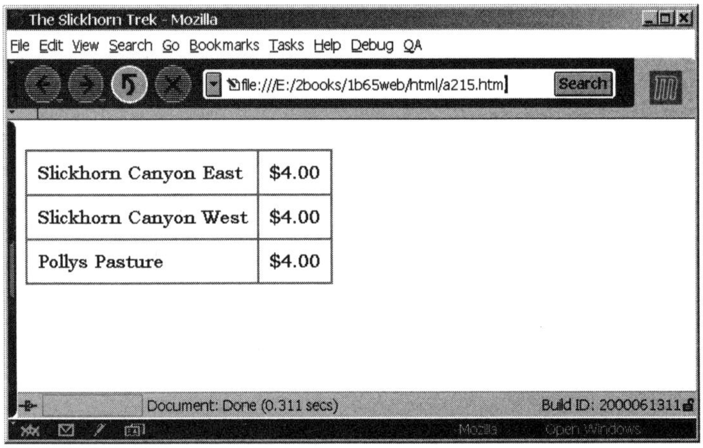

Figure A2.15 A table with borders.

As you can see, the <table> markup is handy for tables, but most of us don't use tables very often. However, tables provide another tool in creating attractive layouts. Although CSS does a better job of layout than tables, until you learn CSS, you can use tables for layout purposes.

As Chapter 4 explains, you can use tables to lay out a readable text column. The following one-cell table 480 pixels wide creates a convenient reading environment (see Figure A2.16).

```
<table width="480"
align="center"><tr><td>

<p>To find the ruins, you have to
speculate. (It helps to know they are
there.) Look for a place where there
might be ruins (under an overhang).
Then climb up and look. In most cases,
you will not be able to spot the ruins
from the canyon floor.</p>

<p>We traveled about three and a half
miles for the day, not exactly a
death-defying pace. The wet potholes,
although still small, appeared more
often. It's evident that without
recent rain, and particularly in a
drought year, there would be no water
in the canyon. Even with water
present, we topped off at almost every
wet pothole not knowing whether it
would be our last.</p>

<p>We camped at another wide place in
the streambed with flat rock and small
potholes with fresh water. Ravens and
lizards seemed to be the only wildlife
in the canyon.</p>

</td></tr></table>
```

Figure A2.16 Use the *<table>* markup for special layouts such as a text column.

This is a good example of how with a little imagination you can use the *<table>* markup creatively to concoct a variety of layouts.

<tr></tr>

This markup creates a row (record) in a table. It must be used with the *<table>* markup.

<td></td>

This markup creates a column (field) within a table. You might also say that it holds the data (content) for one table cell. It must be used with the *<table>* markup.

<ul></ul>

This markup makes a list of bulleted items. You must use the *<li>* markup to designate the list items. Figure A2.17 shows how the browser displays this list.

You will need the following 7.5 minute topographical maps for the Slickhorn trek.

<ul>

<li>**Slickhorn Canyon East**

<li>**Slickhorn Canyon West**

<li>**Pollys Pasture**

</ul>

You can obtain these maps at your nearest US Geological Survey office.

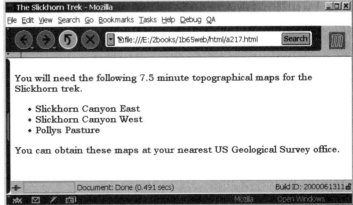

Figure A2.17 A bulleted list.

A browser eliminates redundant spaces between characters or between text blocks. In other words, a browser allows only one space between characters and only one blank line between text blocks. This particular markup establishes a space that will not be eliminated by a browser (see Figure A2.18).

```
Charlie Craft<br>

Occupation:    Wilderness
Trekker
```

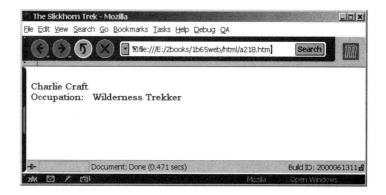

Figure A2.18 Use   to extend spaces.

To use this markup effectively for blank lines, use it with the `<br>` markup (see Figure A2.19).

```
Charlie Craft<br>

Occupation: Wilderness Trekker

<br> <br>

Topper Craft<br>

Occupation: Wilderness Trekker
```

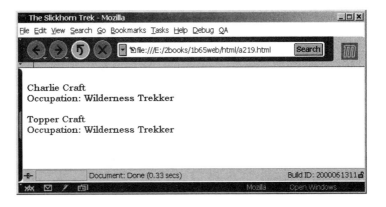

Figure A2.19 Use the * * and *
* markups to create extra blank lines.

<!-- -->

You can put this markup to good use. It marks text that does not display.

```
<!-- Change the color of this page to
offwhite when using it to display
photos. -->
```

You can leave instructions (reminders) to yourself or to others who will be working on the authoring of your Web pages.

```
<!-- This article is not part of the
series of articles by the same author
that appear in the 4/97 archive. This
article belongs in the 2/99 archive. -
->
```

You can use the comment markup for almost anything, but it's not a good idea to use any other markups inside this markup.

Anchors & Hyperlinks

Anchors and hyperlinks (links) have the same markup but different attributes. This is sometimes a little confusing, but knowing that will help you to keep these uses straight.

<a name=" "></a>

This is an anchor. The anchor is a destination. You must give each anchor in a Web page a unique name. You might put the following anchor at the top of a Web page.

```
<a name="top">Slickhorn - East
Slickhorn Loop, Utah</a>
```

This anchor makes the title of the article the anchor. With a link, you can go to this anchor. For example, a link placed anywhere in the Slickhorn trek article will take the reader to the *top* of the Web page where the title line is located.

Keep in mind that it is the attribute *name* that makes this anchor a destination.

<a href=" "></a>

This is another anchor, but it's not a destination. It takes you to a destination. The attribute *href* makes it different than an anchor that has the attribute *name*. This anchor is commonly called a link. For instance, to go to the anchor named *top*, you use the *href* anchor as follows.

```
<a href="#top">Go to top of page</a>
```

Notice that the name of an internal anchor is preceded by the character *#* in a link. In this case, the markup turns the words "Go to top of page" into a link. The words will change to the link color and will be underlined to indicate that they comprise a link. When you click on this link, it will take you to the top of the page (to the title line).

You use links to go to other Web pages anywhere on the Web. For instance, supposed you want to go to the *Hike-Utah* website to support something mentioned in the Slickhorn trek article. You might use the following link.

```
<a href="http://www.hike-
utah.com">canyon trail maps</a>
```

This link will take you directly to the Hike-Utah website which features information on hiking and backpacking in Utah. Notice that in this case the destination is not an anchor *name*; it's a normal *URL*.

You can use both a URL and an anchor destination in the same link. The following link will take you to the *1959* anchor in the *Models* Web page at the *Cars USA* website.

```
<a href="http://www.carsusa.com/
models.html#1959">1959 Models</a>
```

As you see, anchors can be destinations or they can be links depending on which attribute you use with them.

Example Web Page

The following is an example Web page which includes many of the markups this Appendix covers (see Figure A2.20).

```
<html><head><title>The Slickhorn
Trek</title></head><body
bgcolor="#00ffff">

 <br>

<div align="center"><h3>In Slickhorn
Canyon</h3></div>
```

```
<table width="400" cellpadding="10"
bgcolor="#ffffcc"
align="center"><tr><td>
```

```
<p>Don't underestimate the ruggedness
and remoteness of this area.
Inexperienced canyon hikers will find
the terrain demanding, and you won't
see many people, if any. This is not
as rugged as many off-trail places in
the Grand Canyon, but some portions
are nearly as strenuous. Plan your
water carefully. If you find yourself
about to depart on your trek during a
drought year or during a dry spell,
you should first undergo a psychiatric
evaluation! Follow the advisory
published by the Monticello BLM
office.</p>
```

```
</table></tr></td>
```

```
</body></html>
```

Viewing the Web Page Source

Want to see the HTML in a Web page? You can do so with any Web page. In your browser go View, Page Source. You will be able to see the HTML markups together with the page text.

Viewing the HTML in Web pages that you find attractive is a great learning technique. The next step is to use these Web pages to help create your own templates for your own Web pages. One can copyright content but generally not typesetting and layout.

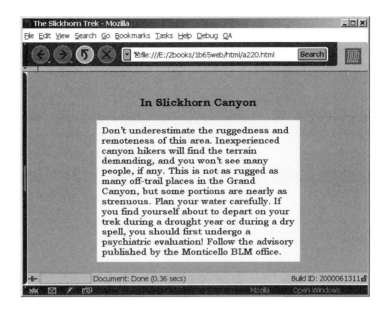

Figure A2.20   An example of a readable Web page.

Summary

This basic tutorial is designed to whet your appetite for under-standing and using HTML. It doesn't include much information on attributes for the markups covered, and it doesn't include all the HTML markups. But it will get you off to a good start.

Appendix III Useful Skills

This book requires that you know how to perform certain tasks with your computer that are not necessarily the usual techniques covered in a basic Web page making book. Thus, this supplementary appendix covers the digital skills that will help you more effectively use your computer.

Using the File Directory

Use Windows Explorer, the file directory for Windows, to view files (see Figure A3.1).

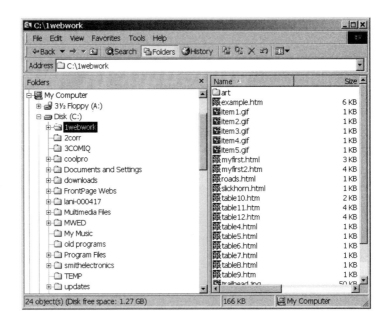

Figure A3.1   Windows Explorer (Details).

Windows Explorer shows files four different ways. Figure A3.1 shows the Details (detailed list) view. Figure A3.2 shows the Large Icons from the large icon view.

Figure A3.2   Windows Explorer (Large Icons).

To open Windows Explorer, go Start, Programs, Accessories and click on the Windows Explorer icon.

For convenience, it's best to create a shortcut icon on your desktop for Windows Explorer. To do so, right click on the Windows Explorer icon and drag it to your desktop while pressing the right mouse button. Release the button and select Create Shortcut Here. A shortcut icon will appear on the desktop. Click on the icon, and Windows Explorer will open.

To set the view go View and make your choice between Large Icons, Small Icons, List, Details, and Thumbnails. I find Details or Large Icons to be the most useful.

Navigating the Folder Tree

The folder tree (directory) is a hierarchical arrangement of folders on the left side of Windows Explorer. Each folder contains a list of files. You can expand the tree by clicking on the plus (+) in the box.

⊞ ☐ 1webwork

You can contract the tree by clicking on the minus (-) in the box.

⊟ ☐ smithelectronics
　⊞ ☐ admin
　⊞ ☐ knowledgebase
　⊞ ☐ products

When you highlight a folder, the list of files shows on the right side of Windows Explorer.

Transferring Files

You move files in Windows Explorer with *drag and drop*. Highlight a file. Right click on it. While still pressing the right button on your mouse, drag the file to the folder to which you want to move it. Release the right button. The popup menu will give you the option of Move Here or Copy Here.

Creating New Folders

To start new tasks it's often useful to create new folders to house the resulting files. For instance, Chapter 2 recommends you establish a *download* folder. Whenever you download a file from the Web, put it in the *download* folder. That way you always know where it is.

Thus, you need to create the folder *download* on the *C:* drive. To create the *download* folder, open Windows Explorer.

Windows Explorer shows with the directory (folder tree) on the left side. Find the *C:* drive and expand it (by clicking on the + in the box) so that all the folders show. Select *C:* (see Figure A3.3) and go File, New, Folder. Windows Explorer will open a new folder labeled *New Folder* for you. The new folder name will be highlighted. Simply type the name of your new folder *download* and press the *Enter* key.

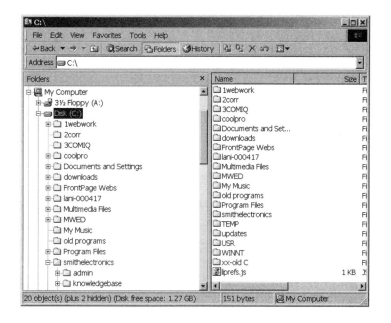

Figure A3.3   Select drive C: in the Windows directory.

The new folder shows in the folder tree.

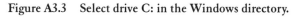

You have established the folder for your downloads, and you're ready to download files from the Web. Make sure that everything you download is saved to that folder. That way, you won't "lose" something you download.

Saving to Folders

Whenever you save a file you're working on, it automatically saves to its current location (folder). If you want to save it somewhere else (to another folder), you use Save As on the File menu. This enables you to choose the folder to which you want to save the file.

Likewise, when you download something from the Web, it's the same as using the Save As command. It enables you to choose the folder to which you want to save the file (see Figure A3.4).

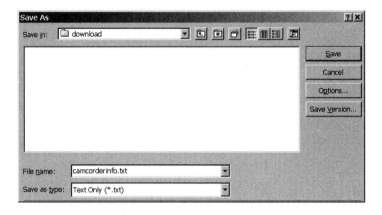

Figure A3.4   Saving to a designated folder.

To select a folder, click on the up-tree icon to go up the folder tree.

Click on a folder to open it and save a file to it.

Click on the new folder icon to create a new folder and name it.

After you create the new folder, you must click on it to open it and save a file to it.

Copy & Paste

Do you have to type text into a Web page? Not necessarily. If you already have the text in a file somewhere, simply open the file and use *copy & paste*. Figure A3.5 shows a word processor file with text.

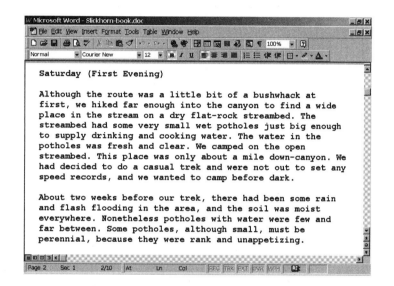

Figure A3.5   Word processor file with text.

Highlight what you want to copy (see Figure A3.6).

Copy it to the clipboard either under the Edit menu or via the copy icon.

Then paste it into Composer. You do this by moving the cursor to where you want to paste the copied text. Then paste it into the Web page either under the Edit menu or via the paste icon.

The text you copied will appear in your Web authoring program (see Figure A3.7).

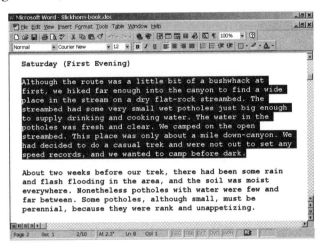

Figure A3.6   Highlight what you want to copy.

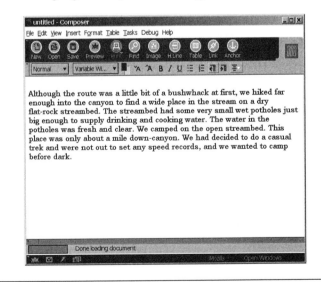

Figure A3.7   Paste the copied text into your Web authoring program.

You can copy & paste one sentence, one paragraph, or several pages of text. You can even copy & paste an entire document. It's quick and easy and saves a lot of typing. It enables you to convert your existing content into Web pages with an easy process that requires additional work only for formatting.

Cut & Paste

Use *cut & paste* the same as copy & paste. Instead of copying the highlighted text, it *moves* the text to where you place the cursor.

Saving Browsed Web Pages

Your browser actually caches Web pages on your computer. So, every Web page you view resides someplace in your computer until you erase your cache or until the browser erases the cache (after a certain period).

If you want a Web page saved to a place where you can find it, go File, Save As and save it to a folder you will remember.

Saving Images

If you want to save the images that go with a Web page, put the cursor on an image and right click. From the menu select Save Image As, and save the image to a folder you won't forget.

Zip Files and Automatic Installation

Some downloading procedures may put a large file on your hard disk, usually a Zip file. You click on the Zip file in Windows Explorer, and the archive unzips. Then you install the software.

This procedure requires that you have a Zip program installed on your computer. If you don't, go to any freeware or shareware archive on the Web and download a Zip program. Follow the instructions to install the Zip program. Once installed, the unzip function of the Zip program should unzip any Zip file (*.zip*) you click on.

Today, many software downloading procedures include automatic installation at the time of the download. You don't need to worry about Zip files.

Summary

These skills have been included in the book because there will be some readers who don't have all of them. For other readers, this stuff is old hat. For those who don't have all these skills, you will find that they come in handy and will make the tasks covered in this book easier.

Appendix IV Media Tips

Use this as a guide to produce, capture, and edit (digitally) your media. If you don't know much about these processes, use this as a guide to seeking more information.

Production

Production seems difficult. Nonetheless, it can be easy. It consists of a long series of little tasks (details), each easy to master. If you can handle the details, you will find producing sound or video not only possible but also great fun.

Sound

- Use a high-quality recorder. But keep in mind that $250 buys a lot of audio quality today.

- Consider recording directly to a PC (onto a hard disk) with a high-quality sound card and a high quality sound editor (software).

- Use high-quality microphones preferably with balanced cables.

- Use a mixer for more than one microphone.

- Learn to properly mike for a recording session.

- Use high-quality shielded cables with proper connectors from a supplier such as Markertek (*http://www.markertek.com*).

- When making a recording for digital use, lower the headroom from *0 to 10 dB* to *-10 to 0 dB*.

- Turn off all electrical appliances in the room during a recording session.

- Read *Home Recording for Musicians*, Anderton, (Amsco Publications, 1996).

Video

- Minimize movement inside the frame as much as possible. Reduce movement to a small area of the frame if possible.

- Don't pan or zoom. If you do, do it very slowly.

- Use a tripod.

- For indoor shots, learn to use proper lighting.

- Video requires double duty. Pay attention to your sound recording too. Don't use the camcorder's built-in microphone.

- Use S-Video cables. For digital video, use DV cables.

- Read *Videomaker Handbook* (Focal Press, 1996).

Creativity

Getting through the production process successfully is one thing. Almost anyone can learn to do so and even become something of an expert. Producing a presentation that appeals to an audience is another thing. That is an art, and this book doesn't even pretend to touch upon that realm of knowledge.

Digitizing

Believe it or not, the most important consideration in using a sound card or video capture card is to use one that has the proper connectors for your equipment. Otherwise, your system may be inoperable or noisy.

Sound

- Use a high-quality sound card such as Sound Blaster Live!

- Use a high-quality sound editor, such as CoolEdit (*http://www.syntrillium.com*) or Sound Forge XP (*http://www.sonic-foundry.com*).

- Use high-quality shielded cables with proper connectors.

- Open the Windows Volume Control, set it to Recording mode, and keep it open during recording sessions. If something goes wrong, check the settings on the Volume Control first (see Figure A4.1).

- Record (capture) sound with the headroom set from *-10 to 0 dB*, unless the performance was originally recorded with such a setting for headroom.

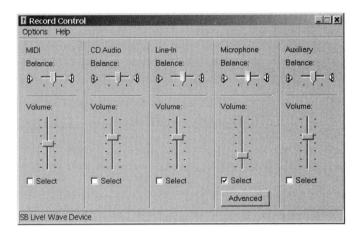

Figure A4.1   Windows Volume Control (Record Control mode).

Video

- Use a video capture card that provides the proper connectors for your equipment.

- Use high-quality shielded cables (S-video or DV) with proper connectors.

- Watch the Windows Volume Control for the sound in your video recording.

Editing

Editing digitally gives you the power of a million-dollar studio for the modest price of the software.

Sound

- Use cut & paste or copy & paste.

- Use filters such as noise reduction, hiss reduction, noise gate, and de-essing.

- Always check the DC offset.

- Always use audio compression and normalization.

- Equalize the recording to suit specific listening environments.

- Use double the size of your recording to determine the space needed on your hard drive (i.e., a 20 MB recording requires 20 MB to store and an additional 20 MB for editing for a total of 40+ MB).

Video

- Use the editing software that comes with your video capture card or be prepared to spend a lot for additional software.

- Use cut and paste or copy & paste.

- Use double the size of your recording to determine the space needed on your hard drive (i.e., a 120MB recording requires 120MB to store and an additional 120MB for editing for a total of 240+ MB).

Appendix V Top 14 Reasons

The top 14 reasons to establish your own personal website follow, not necessarily in order of priority:

1. Resume. There's nothing like an opportunity for the extended promotion of your education and employment accomplishments. Use a one-page paper resume but include your Web address where one can view a more robust and complete resume. In your Web resume include photographs and even scanned images of important documents such as college diplomas or certificates that authenticate your completion of proprietary training programs. Don't make your Web resume too long, or no one will read it, but take advantage of the opportunity to promote yourself in color with plenty of up-to-date information for those who become interested in you through your one-page paper resume.

Even if you don't need a job, keep your resume up to date and routinely let people know it's on the Web. Someone within your own organization may take a look and offer you a more desirable job than you have. Don't assume that even your boss is completely familiar with your background. Explain to your boss that you feel the perpetual publication and updating of your resume is important to your career: ask him or her to look at it.

2. Hobbies. Many people love to share their interest in their hobbies with others. You can use the Web to post information on your collections or other hobby activities for fellow hobbyists. For hobbies that routinely involve trades, or even sales, the Web presents a good opportunity to initiate such transactions.

3. Recreation. Like hobbies, many people love to include others in their recreational activities. Sometimes teams and clubs are not available locally, and you need to share information with others who pursue the same activities, or even include them in your activities. The Web is an easy way to share information and even propose events.

Peak Bagging and Canyoneering

I like to climb mountain peaks (walk-ups) and explore canyons in Colorado and Utah. At my age, the biggest obstacle to pursuing such activities is finding others to join me (i.e., it's not safe to go alone). Consequently, I post trek reports on the Web. If someone shows interest in joining me on a future trek, I can direct them to the trek reports to get an idea of what my peak bagging and canyoneering treks are like. Then they can make an informed decision as to whether they want to go.

4. Publishing. The Web is a great way to publish your creative writings or even works of art that would otherwise be too expensive to publish and distribute. See Chapter 26 for more details.

5. For Friends. Keep your friends informed of what you're doing by posting information on your website. You're more likely to keep in touch and include them in your activities. Put up your schedule and post information on your current projects. If you have a close group of friends geographically dispersed, you might even try setting up a forum for them.

6. Have-Want. We all routinely have things we want to sell (or exchange) and things we want to buy. A have-want list on your website tells your website visitors what's on your mind.

7. Projects. Working on a project? Post information about it on the Web. Perhaps you'll get some help from friends or colleagues. For instance, suppose you're planning a trip to Bayreuth, Germany. Some of your friends may have been there, may have relatives living nearby, may have information on the Wagner festival, or may know a charter flight operator that can provide you a low-price flight to Europe. When they see your plans on your website, perhaps they'll volunteer to help.

8. Announcements. There are milestone events that you want everyone you know to be aware of: graduation, marriage, job promotion, change of address, etc. Post these announcements on your website where everyone interested in keeping up with you can find them.

9. Event Planning. An easy way to plan an event with others is to manage it on your website. Suppose you want to get your friends together for a weekend boating party. You can post the schedule and a list of things to bring to the party on your website with specific assignments. Sam sees that he is supposed to bring the beer. Sylvia sees that she is expected to bring her boat. Brian sees that he is supposed to bring the steaks. All the participants can see the organization of the whole event.

10. Sideline Business. Many people have a sideline business that provides a portion of their income. It may not be worth building an ecommerce website to accommodate such a limited business activity. Nonetheless, if it's profitable, it may be possible to expand sales or other activities via a personal website.

11. Medical. When you have a major illness, few activities beat comparing notes with others who have the same affliction. This sort of information exchange has saved a lot of lives and enabled a lot of people to cope better through trying times. Your website presents you with an opportunity to better accommodate such an information exchange with others.

12. For Colleagues. Your best source of career security is to develop a network of colleagues in your industry. Having a website to keep them apprised of what you are doing can lead to transactions and other business benefits. Industry news is also important to everyone. Although you don't have to play the role of a newspaper reporter, you can pass along unpublished facts of interest (or important articles of interest) that you run across as you do business.

One important service that you will always want to provide is publishing job openings that you find out about. At any given time, probably at least ten percent of your colleagues are looking for jobs. Your website can help them. When your turn comes to look for a job, hopefully they will be enthusiastic about helping you.

13. Cool Lists. Everyone has their lists of cool websites regarding one topic or another. The Web is a good place to share them. In your lists you can provide live links directly to the websites you recommend so that your website visitors can go to a website on the list with just a click of the mouse.

14. Spiritual. One of the compelling pursuits many people have is a religion or other spiritual endeavor. The churches and other spiritual organizations have often been leaders in communicating with their congregations via the latest technologies. You can do the same. For instance, you may want to post important scriptures that you have found in your Bible readings on your website for friends, relatives, and fellow parishioners.

––––––––

This Top 14 list is not all-inclusive, but it will get you thinking. You might consider keeping your Web business activities and your Web personal activities on separate websites. If you are applying for a job with the Animal Protection Society of Chicago, you may not want them to know that you trap, skin, and tan river otters as a hobby.

Keep security in mind when operating a personal website. You may want to limit access to your website to friends, relatives, or colleagues. This will enable you to be more candid with less risk of offending people outside the immediate circle of people you know. Unfortunately, assigning passwords probably won't work. People forget passwords. Try the remote subfolder explained in the Share Privacy section of Chapter 24.

Don't assume that people you know and loved ones will check your website regularly. Remind them with an email when you post something new, and include a live link directly to your website in the email.

In the old days way back in the twentieth century, people kept track of one another via letters and the telephone. The problem was that with the advent of the telephone not many people wrote letters, and most people couldn't afford to use the telephone (long distance) very often. But the people who did write letters or used the telephone regularly managed to keep in touch with their friends, relatives, and colleagues. In the twenty-first century you now have new tools for keeping in touch. These tools, the Web and email, have many advantages over letters and the telephone. Those who use these new tools will enjoy the benefits of more effectively and efficiently keeping in touch with people they care about.

And if keeping in touch doesn't interest you, keep in mind that some of the highest-flying businesses on the Web started as websites for personal activities (e.g., eBay).

Appendix VI Top 12 Reasons

The top 12 reasons to establish a website at your K-12 school follow, not necessarily in order of their priority:

1. School Schedule. The annual school schedule affects a lot of families and many other people, but it's easy to lose your xeroxed copy. By posting the schedule on the school website, everyone can see the schedule (and any updates) easily at any time. You can create a schedule easily with the skills learned in this book.

2. Homework Assignments. By giving teachers access to the school website to post Web pages, they can publish homework assignments regularly. They can also post class assignments for students who miss class. Other class information including announcements are also helpful to students and parents.

3. Cafeteria Menu. Many students plan their lunch by what's on the cafeteria menu. When it's something they don't like, they bring their own lunches. Otherwise, they buy their lunches at the cafeteria. Some students eat at the cafeteria everyday and appreciate knowing ahead what's on the menu.

4. Student Honors. Honoring students for scholastic and other achievements is a healthy tradition. Usually, however, such honors go unrecognized publicly except for minor coverage by the newsmedia. Publishing such honors on the school website for an extended period increases the recognition in a cost-effective way.

5. Announcements. Schools always have announcements, most of them important. When the announcements get sent home with students, they tend to get lost or discarded. Mailing is expensive. By posting announcements on the school website, everyone can see them any time they choose to visit.

Impoverished Families

One argument against school Web publishing is that it discriminates against students and parents in improvished families who do not have Web access outside the school. Clearly it does, and schools should be sensitive to this fact. For those families without Web access, printed material should be sent home. Nonetheless, even a dual system will save paper, xeroxing costs, and postage.

PCs with monitors are now under $500, and Internet service is as low as $10 per month. Some Web companies even distribute

PCs and Internet service free for the privilige of presenting Web advertising to customers. The day is coming when even impoverished familes will have access in their homes to the Web.

6. PTA. The parents are an essential part of the school community. By enabling the PTA to make postings on the school website (special PTA section), the PTA can, in effect, operate it's own website. See Chapter 25 for ideas for organizations.

7. Information about School. Information and statistics about the school are important for parents and students choosing a school or planning to attend the school. By making such data available on the school website, people can access it any time.

8. Student Projects. Worthwhile student projects take a lot of time and work. Publishing them all, or even a select few, provides well deserved recognition. Naturally they must have been done in digital form or converted to digital form. The thrill of being published heretofore has been reserved primarily to a small group of authors whose works are published by print publishers. Now publishing (on the Web) can distinguish authors who are elementary, middle, and high school students.

9. Parent Work Projects. Many schools now require parents to donate time (work) as a condition of enrollment. This is particularly true of charter schools and private schools. Parents working on school projects, such as building maintenance and repair, can get organized by posting work assignments and schedules as well as other useful information on the school website.

10. School Intranet. Don't forget that a school with its own network (intranet) can also host internal websites. This opens unlimited opportunities for students, teachers, and staff to use Web technologies for a variety of activities internally.

What about Colleges?

Why doesn't this book cover college Web activities? Colleges have been among the leaders in developing intranets and using the Web. College students and professors don't need ideas from me. Nonetheless, a college student or professor with a need to learn Web-page authoring can use the hands-on instructional portion of this book.

11. Web Books. There is now a lot of talk in the press about the ebooks available to read on special ebook readers. Indeed, several companies now market ebook readers and provide a well-stocked inventory of ebooks. Although this seems to be interesting technology for schools with the thought that it may eventually bring some cost savings, the fact remains that the Web itself is a far more interesting publishing technology. Anyone capable of writing a book is also capable of converting their book into readable Web pages and publishing it on a website.

Consider that most nonfiction books provide far more information than most readers need. Readers more often than not read only the parts of nonfiction books that they need. This fact indicates that there is a potentially large unsatisfied market for shorter books on more narrowly defined topics. And what does a short book bring to mind? Certainly, a short book is a project a teacher can not only handle but might carry through enthusiastically. In the print publishing world, there's no reason to write such a book, as publishers are unlikely to publish them. Short print books are not normally economically feasible. Now with the Web, however, any teacher who writes such a book can at least publish it on the school website at no expense and will undoubtedly have many more opportunities to publish it at other educationally oriented websites. Moreover, today there is a huge new grassroots Web-book publishing industry—Web books for money—that can make it financially worthwhile for interested teachers to self-publish education books that they write.

Beyond short books, it is certain that in the future schools will have plenty of full-length books in Web form from which to choose at lower prices than printed books. Such books can be posted on the intranet for all students to read. This can lead to a significant savings in the cost of text books and library books.

12. Web Based Training (WBT). One step up from Web books is WBT. For WBT, there is no traditional length. Teachers can easily create short or long WBT modules and make them available on the school intranet. See Chapter 25 for more on WBT.

———

This Top 12 list does not include everything, but it will give you a start on developing ideas. The great thing about learning the basics of Web authoring is that you can do all the things covered in this Appendix.

This book provides you with most of the skills you need to publish readable books on the Web. The only skill left out that you may want to acquire is advanced Web typography; but with careful typesetting you don't even need advanced typography to publish readable and attractive books. With the skills you learn in this book, you can even create simple WBT. And if you can create projects of such magnitude, which you can, you can certainly publish schedules, announcements, and the like.

Web authoring presents a huge opportunity for K-12 education, for students and teachers alike.

Index

<!-- --> markup (HTML), 381

absolute links, 235
absolute references, 84–85
Adobe, 23
affiliates, website, 339
Allaire, 23
"all caps," 111
America Online, 216
anchors, 88–90
  in FrontPage Express, 89–90
  in Netscape Composer, 88–89
animation(s), 255–262
  with Dynamic HTML, 261
  with GIFs, 256

  with JavaScript, 256–261
  with SMIL, 261–262
announcements
  personal, 405
  school, 410–411
applets, 266–270
application servers, 206
applications servers, 200–201
archives, 306–307
authoring, 16
authoring software, 16–25, 351–352
  downloading, 20–22
  limitations of, 22–23
  Microsoft FrontPage Express as, 18–20
  Netscape Composer as, 17–18

authoring software (continued)
   and page breaks, 24
   word processor approach to, 23–24
authorization processing, 332–333, 335–336
automatic installation, 21–22, 396

background color, 131–132, 136–137
backup tapes, 287–288
bandwidth, Web, 204
<b></b> markup (HTML), 360
<blockquote></blockquote> markup
(HTML), 360–362
<body></body> markup (HTML), 358
bold italic type, 111
bold type, 111, 115–116, 121
books
   interactivity in, 241
   Web, 412–413
borders, 112

</br> markup (HTML), 363
brightness, image, 153–154
brochures, 324–325
browsers, 31, 33
bullets, 111, 117, 122–123
business websites
   determining purpose of, 321–326
   and intranets, 343–349
   shared, 288–289
   for sideline businesses, 406
   see also ecommerce

cafeteria menus, 410
camcorders, 143
Cascading Style Sheets (CSS), 45, 113
catalogs, online, 330
centering, 117, 122
CFML (Cold Fusion Markup Language), 200
CGI (Common Gateway Interface), 264
CGI scripts, 204–205, 264–265

clip art, 62
Cold Fusion Markup Language (CFML), 200
collaboration, online, 348
colleagues, 406
co-location computers, 198
color designations, 134–135
color(s), 129–138
   in background, 136–137
   of background, 131–132
   combinations of, 130–132
   in Composer, 135
   designing with, 137–138
   digital, 132
   in FrontPage Express, 136
   and Hex number system, 133–134
   within images, 160
   and RGB system, 132–133
columns, creating multiple
   with Composer, 178–181
   with FrontPage Express, 181–185
Common Gateway Interface (CGI), 264
common links, 249
company records, online, 346
Composer, see Netscape Composer 6.0
contrast, image, 152–153
convenience links, 249–250
"cool" websites, lists of, 406–407
copy & paste, 12, 393–395
cost(s)
   of ecommerce, 333
   of Web address registration, 226
   of Web hosting, 207–209
cropping, 154–155
CSS, see Cascading Style Sheets
customer service, 325–326
cut & paste, 395
cybermalls, 341

database servers, 200, 206

<dd></dd> markup (HTML), 366
DHTML (Dynamic HTML), 261
dial-up connections, 195–196
digital cameras, 141–143
digital color, 132
digital photographs, 62, 139–145
    creating, from analog photographs, 140–141
    creating, with digital camera, 141–143
    file formats for, 143
    quality of, 144–145
    shared, on family website, 292
    from stock photos, 143–144
Digital Subscriber Line (DSL), 198–199
digitization, 399–400
directories, membership, 307
disk crashes, 232
 markup (HTML), 366–367
<dl></dl> markup (HTML), 363–365
domain name(s), 223–228
    checking availability of, 226
    choosing, 223–225
    fee for, 226
    multiple, for single website, 235–237
    purchasing existing, 227
    registering, 226
    registrars for, 225
    uses of, 227–228
downloading
    of authoring software, 20–22
    of Web pages, 38
Dreamweaver, 23
DSL, see Digital Subscriber Line
<dt></dt> markup (HTML), 366
Dynamic HTML (DHTML), 261

eBay, 340
ecommerce, 327–342
    and authorization processing, 332–333, 335–336

    costs of, 333
    and cybermalls, 341
    as group activity, 303
    and ISP hosting, 334
    and marketing, 337–341
    merchant accounts for, 332, 335
    software for, 206, 328–332, 334–335
editing, 315, 400–401
email links, 90
embedding
    of pictures, 63–67, 67–73, 71–72
    of streaming media, 279–280
employee directories, online, 347
event planning, 405–406
Extensible Markup Language (XML), 24–25

family activity(-ies), 291–300
    and access control, 292–293
    forums as, 294
    genealogy as, 297–298
    investments as, 299
    media as, 295–296
    portals as, 299–300
    project posting as, 296–297
    resumes as, 299
    sharing photographs as, 292
    vacation reports as, 298
    warehouse as, 298
    Web publishing as, 294–295
File Transfer Protocol (FTP), 26, 205, 211–217
fill-in-the-blank web page(s), 93–102
    and HTML, 101–102
    PageBuilder as, 96–99
    PageWizard as, 95–97
    and templates, 99–100
    as templates, 99–100
film scanners, 140
folder(s), 232–234
    creating, 4

folder(s) (continued)
  download, 21
  in Windows Explorer, 389–392
  working, 4
<font></font> markup (HTML), 367
font size, changing, 49–51, 55–57, 112, 116, 122
forums, 339–340
  family, 294
  as group activity, 307
  on intranets, 348
friends, 405
FrontPage Express, see Microsoft FrontPage Express 2.0
FTP, see File Transfer Protocol
fund-raising, online, 304–305
Fusion, 23

gamma, 154
genealogy, 297–298
GeoCities, 96
GIF files, 61–63, 148, 161, 256
GoLive, 23
gratuitous links, 250–251
group activity(-ies), 301–309
  archives as, 306–307
  directories as, 307
  forums as, 307
  newsletters as, 304–305
  publicity as, 308
  sales as, 302–304
  schedules as, 302
  self-advertising as, 309
  specialized information as, 308
  vendor lists as, 309
  Web-based training as, 305–306

<h1></h1> markup (HTML), 368–369
have-want lists, 405

<head></head> markup (HTML), 357
headings
  for tables, 49, 50, 55, 56
  text in, 116–117, 122
Hex number system, 133–134
hierarchical structure, 244–248
hobbies, 404
Homesite, 23
homework assignments, 410
host computer, 37–38
Hot Dog, 23
Hot Metal Pro, 23
<hr></hr> markup (HTML), 369
HTML, see Hypertext Markup Language
HTML editors, 23, 34
<html></html> markup (HTML), 357
HTTP, see Hypertext Transfer Protocol
Hypertext Markup Language (HTML), 15, 355–385
  anchors/hyperlinks in, 382–383
  color designations in, 134–135
  defining Web page with, 357–359
  example of Composer version of, 57–59
  exotic markups in, 33
  markups in (list), 359–381
  in sample Web page, 383–385
  templates in, 101–102
Hypertext Transfer Protocol (HTTP), 84, 85, 280

<i></i> markup (HTML), 370
image editors, 25–26, 157
  choosing, 149–150
  using, 151–160
image links, 83
imagemaps, 175
images
  adding, to text, 113
  brightness of, 153–154

images (continued)
  changing colors within, 160
  contrast in, 152–153
  cropping, 154–155
  file formats for, 143
  GIF, 161
  planning, 162–163
  resizing, 155–156
  saving, 152, 395
  sharpening, 156–157
  text, 157–160
  see also pictures
<img scr=" "> markup (HTML), 370
installation, automatic, 21–22, 396
interactivity, 240–248
  in books, 241
  with links, 242–244
  and usability, 244–248
Internet Explorer, 3
Internet Service Providers (ISPs), 35, 195–196, 199
  choosing, 203–210
  co-location computers at, 198
  and Web addresses, 222
intranets, 343–349
  access to data on, 346
  collaboration via, 348
  company directory on, 347
  company records on, 346
  forums on, 348
  maintenance manuals on, 345
  ordering via, 346
  policies and procedures on, 345
  publishing on, 345
  recognition of achievement on, 347
  scheduling via, 348
  school, 411
  streaming media on, 346
  Web-based training via, 347

websites on, 344
investments, family, 299
IrfanView, 25–26, 150, 153–157
ISPs, see Internet Service Providers
italic type, 110

Java, 266–270
JavaScript, 256–261, 265, 270
JPEG files, 61–63, 148–149

Kodak Picture CD, 140–141

layout
  of text, 107–109
  using tables for, 177–189
<li></li> markup (HTML), 372
line menus, 174
linked images, 83
links, 77–91, 234–235, 242–244, 248–251
  absolute, 235
  common, 249
  convenience, 249–250
  creating, with Composer, 79–80
  creating, with FrontPage Express, 81–82
  email, 90
  gratuitous, 250–251
  image tricks with, 82–83
  navigational, 248–249
  relative, 235
  trading, 338–339
  and URLs, 84–90

Macromedia, 23
maintenance manuals, online, 345
marketing, 316–317, 337–341
media, 397–401
  digitizing, 399–400
  editing of, 400–401
  production, 397–399

media (continued)
    storage by, 233, 234
    streaming, *see* streaming media
media servers, 200, 206
medical websites, 406
membership directories, 307
menu(s), 165–176
    creating, in Composer, 166–168, 171–172
    creating, in FrontPage Express, 169–171, 173–174
    line, 174
    pictures in, 174–175
    using tables for, 166–174
merchant accounts, 332, 335
metaphors, website, 251
Microsoft FrontPage, 23
Microsoft FrontPage Express 2.0, 3–4
    anchors in, 89–90
    as authoring software, 18–20
    color in, 136
    creating links in, 81–82
    creating menus in, 169–171, 173–174
    embedding pictures with, 67–73
    entering text in, 9–12
    multiple columns in, 181–185
    opening, 9
    tables in, 51–57, 181–185
    template Web pages in, 100
    text in, 9–12, 121–126
    tutorial for, 5–6, 9–12
    uploading with, 218
Miva, 201

national online services, 210
navigational links, 248–249
navigation menus, see menus
  markup (HTML), 380–381
NetObject, 23
Netscape Communicator, 3

Netscape Composer 6.0, 3–4
    anchors in, 88–89
    as authoring software, 17–18
    beta version of, 18
    color in, 135
    columns in, 178–181
    creating links with, 79–80
    creating menus in, 166–168, 171–172
    embedding pictures in, 63–67, 71–72
    entering text in, 6–8
    and HTML, 57–59
    opening, 6
    tables in, 45–51, 178–181
    template Web pages in, 100
    text in, 6–8, 115–120
    tutorial for, 5–8
    uploading with, 217
newsletters, online, 304–305
numbered lists, 111, 118–119, 123–124

<ol></ol> markup (HTML), 370–371
organization, Web page, 239–252
    and interactivity, 240–248
    with links, 242–244, 248–251
    metaphor concept for, 251
    and planning, 252

PageBuilder, 96–99
PageWizard, 95–97
parallel websites, 288
parent work projects, 411
passwords, 207
PDF files, 315
personal websites, 403–408
photographs, digital, see digital photographs
pictures
    adding, 61–75
    correct pixel dimensions for, 73–75
    embedding, with Composer, 63–67, 71–72

pictures (continued)
  embedding, with FrontPage Express, 67–73
  file formats for, 148–149
  in menus, 174–175
  preparing, 147–163
  see also digital photographs
pixel dimensions, setting, 73–75
planning
  event, 405–406
  for images, 162–163
  for security, 286–287
  website, 252
plug-ins, 271
PNG files, 149
policies and procedures, online, 345
portals, family, 299–300
<p> </p> markup (HTML), 372–373
preloaded software, 22
printing, 24
programming, adding, 263–272
  with CGI scripts, 264–265
  with Java, 266–270
  with JavaScript, 265, 270
  with plug-ins, 271
  template approach to, 270
  see also animation(s)
projects
  family, 296–297
  personal, 405
  school, 411
PTA websites, 411
publicity, 308
publishing, 311–317
  to family websites, 294–295
  guidelines for, 313–315
  and marketing, 316–317
  personal, 345, 405
  and readability, 314
  and usability, 314

Web as opportunity for, 312–313

QuickTime player, 276

readability, 314
RealMedia, 275, 276, 278–280
RealNetworks, 277
RealPlayer, 275–276
RealProducer, 277, 278
RealServer, 206, 281
Real Time Streaming Protocol (RTSP), 280
recreation, 404–405
refreshing (Web pages), 32
registration, Web address, 221–228
relative links, 235
relative references, 85–87
requests, 38
resizing
  of fonts, 49–51, 55–57, 112, 116, 122
  of images, 155–156
resolutions, 32, 43–45, 144
resumes, online, 299, 403–404
RGB system, 132–133
RTSP (Real Time Streaming Protocol), 280
rules, 112, 117, 123

sales
  as group activity, 302–304
  as purpose of business website, 326
sales tax, 331
Sausage Software, 23
saving
  of images, 152, 395
  of Web pages, 31, 395
  with Windows Explorer, 391–392
scanners, 140
schedules
  group, 302
  on intranets, 348

schedules (continued)
    school, 409
school websites, 409–413
search engines, registering with, 338
security
    on family websites, 292–293
    with shared websites, 286–289
self-advertising, 309
servers, 194–195
servlets, 266
sharing websites, 285–289
sharpening, 156–167
shopping carts, 330
sidebars, 120
sideline businesses, 406
Simultaneous Multimedia Integration Language (SMIL), 261–262
Soft Quad, 23
sound, adding, see streaming media
spiritual websites, 407
stock photos, 143–144
streaming media, 273–282
    delivery of, 280–281
    embedding of, 279–280
    encoding for, 276–278
    in family websites, 295–296
    on intranets, 346
    with QuickTime player, 276
    with RealPlayer, 275–276
    servers for, 200
structure, Web site, 238
student honors, 410
subscripts, 111
 markup (HTML), 373
superscripts, 111
 markup (HTML), 373–374
SureStream, 278

tables, 177–189
    adjusting, 47, 53
    changing font size in, 49–51, 55–57
    creating, 45–46, 51–53
    creating varied layouts with, 185–189
    in FrontPage Express, 51–57, 181–185
    for menus, 166–174
    multi-row, multi-column, 171–174
    multi-row, one column, 166–171
    in Netscape Composer, 45–51, 178–181
    placing text in, 47–49, 53–55
    typesetting headings in, 49, 50, 55, 56
<table></table> markup (HTML), 374–378
TCP/IP, see Transmission Control Protocol/Internet Protocol
<td></td> markup (HTML), 378
Telnet, 206
template Web pages, 99–100, 109, 315
testing, 29–34
    advanced procedures for, 32–34
    procedure for, 30–32
text, 41–60, 105–126
    adding images to, 113
    bold/italic, 115–116, 121
    bulleted lists, 117, 122–123
    centering, 117, 122
    changing typeface of, 116, 122
    changing type size of, 116, 121
    communicating with, 106
    with Composer, 6–8, 115–120
    entering, with copy and paste, 12
    future of, 126–127
    with FrontPage Express, 9–12, 121–126
    in headings, 116–117, 122
    layout of, 107–109
    in numbered lists, 118–119, 123–124
    resolution of, 43–45
    rules in, 117, 123
    in tables, 47–49

text (continued)
  for tutorials, 114–115
  typesetting, 110–113
  unnumbered, 119–120, 124–126
  using templates with, 109
  and visitors to websites, 106–107
  wrapping of, 41–43
text images, 157–160
tiling, 136, 137
\<title>\</title> markup (HTML), 357
Transmission Control Protocol/Internet Protocol (TCP/IP), 197, 343
\<tr>\</tr> markup (HTML), 378
TruDoc, 113
typesetting, 110–113

\<ul>\</ul> markup (HTML), 379
underlines, 112
universal resource locators (URLs), 38, 84–90
  as absolute references, 84–85
  and anchors, 88–90
  and file names, 87
  as relative references, 85–87
unnumbered lists, 119–120, 124–126, 125
uploads, Web page, 37, 211–219
  authoring, 217–218
  with national online services, 216
  with WS_FTP Lite, 212–216
URLs, see universal resource locators

vacation websites, 298
vendor lists, 309
video, adding, see streaming media
visitors, Web site, 106–107, 236–237

warehouse, family, 298
WBT, see Web-Based Training
Web addresses, registering, 221–228

Web-Based Training (WBT), 305–306, 313–314, 347, 413
Web books, 412–413
Web hosting, 196–201
  and applications servers, 200–201
  charges for, 207–209
  choosing ISP for, 203–210
  and co-location computers, 198
  and database servers, 200
  and DSL, 198–199
  and ecommerce, 334
  hometown, 209–210
  and media servers, 200
  by national online services, 210
  and self-hosting, 210
  and TCP/IP, 197
Web page(s), 231–234
  adding programming to, 263–272
  defining, with HTML, 357–359
  definition of, 34
  fill-in-the-blank, 93–102
  linking, 234–235
  links in, 242–244, 248–251
  location of, 35–36
  organizing, 239–252
  refreshing, 32
  saving, 31
  saving browsed, 395
  steps to creating first, 351–353
  template, 99–100, 109
  uploading, 37, 211–219
  working on, 30
Web servers, 193–195, 204
website(s)
  definition of, 36
  on intranets, 344
  links in, 234–235
  metaphor concept for organizing, 251
  multiple-domain, 235–237

website(s) (continued)
  parallel, 288
  personal, 403–408
  planning, 252
  school, 409–413
  sharing, 285–289
  storing, 231–234
  structure of, 238
  visitors to, 106–107
  see also business websites
WebTV, 43
Windows Explorer, 388–392
  creating new folders with, 390–391

  moving files in, 390
  navigating folder tree in, 389–390
  saving to folders with, 391–392
word processor, Web software as, 23–24
working folder, creating a, 4
wrapping, test, 41–43
WS_FTP Lite, 26, 212–217
WYSIWYG programs, 8

XML, see Extensible Markup Language

Zip files, 21, 395–396

Colophon

The typographical design of this book and its implementation were done by Joseph T. Sinclair based on a similar design published in *SQL Clearly Explained* (AP Professional, 1998). The text was prepared in FrameMaker 5.5 and the typefaces (all from Bitstream) employed were: Courier, Elegant Garamond (similar to Granjon), Swiss 721 (similar to Helvetica), Swiss 721 Condensed, and Zapf Humanist (similar to Optima).